A Mensch

Among Men

Explorations in Jewish Masculinity

Edited By Harry Brod

Foreword by Letty Cottin Pogrebin

The Crossing Press/Freedom, CA 95019

ACKNOWLEDGMENTS

This project would never have seen the light of day without the support of the staff of *Changing Men*, and in particular Managing Editors Rick Cote and Michael Biernbaum, who initially responded enthusiastically to my proposal to edit an issue of the magazine on Jewishness and masculinity, and then helped nurture it along to publication. I wish to thank them not only for their help on this project, but for their work over the years in sustaining a magazine which has immeasurably enhanced the men's movement, to which I also wish here to acknowledge a debt of great support and comradeship. The support of John Gill of The Crossing Press made expansion and publication in this present book form possible.

Individuals too numerous to name have contributed to the development of the ideas I express in this book. Some of their names I do not know, as they were members of the audience who made helpful comments as I tried out some of these ideas in presentations at conferences of the National Women's Studies Association, New Jewish Agenda, and the National Organization for Changing Men, as well as numerous other universities, synagogues, conferences, and various assorted meeting places. I also wish to thank the members of the Commission on Spirituality of the Jewish Federation of Greater Los Angeles Council on Jewish Life for giving me the opportunity to work out many of these ideas as I prepared for a keynote speech they invited me to give at the September, 1986 conference "Wrestling With the Messenger: A Conference on Jewish Men's Spirituality."

In one mood, and in reference to some family members, I would say my family has made this book possible. In another mood, and with others in mind, I would say they have made it necessary. Both are true, and I thank them for both.

I would like to thank Rachel Adler, Phyllis Frank, Richard Levy, Bill Mack, Tom Mosmiller, Jonathan Omer-Man, Maria Papacostaki, David Schulman, Ricky Sherover-Marcuse, Michael Shiffman, and Mark Stevens for helpful comments.

Finally, I wish to express a debt to all those, some of whom I would have agreed with and others not, who over the generations have established a tradition of questioning and dissent in the Jewish community which is accepted as dissent *within* rather than *against* the community. Their courage has been the precondition for my chutzpah.

LIBRARY OF CONGRESS
Library of Congress Cataloging-in-Publication Data

A Mensch among men : explorations in Jewish masculinity / edited and
  with an introduction by Harry Brod.
    p.   cm.
  ISBN 0-89594-266-6   ISBN 0-89594-265-8 (pbk.)
    1. Jewish men—United States—Psychology.   2. Jewish men—United States—Attitudes.
3. Masculinity (Psychology)   4. Sex role—United States.   I. Brod, Harry, 1951-
HQ1090.3.M47 1988   87-33083
305.3'862—dc19   CIP

Dedicated to the memories of
Wilhelm Schüfftan, George Chapsky, and Herbert Marcuse
My biological, familial, and intellectual Jewish grandfathers

CONTENTS

FOREWORD: MEDITATIONS ON A JEWISH FATHER

(Inspired by Reading This Book)

Letty Cottin Pogrebin

I never write about my father.

During my twenty years as a writer, I've poured out thousands of words about my mother who's been dead since 1955, but my father who died only five years ago has earned barely a sentence. I've written extensively about my husband, my children, my colleagues and closest friends, but I never write about my father.

I'm afraid to read what I have to say.

I would have to start with the good things: He looked like Clark Gable—and dressed like a movie star too.

He wore cream-colored trousers and cashmere coats; breast-pocket handkerchiefs, white-on-white shirts, gold cuff-links and a pinky ring with an onyx eye. He carried his bills in a gold money clip shaped like a dollar sign. "Real snappy," he'd say, smoothing the brim of his fedora hat. "Real snappy."

As a child, even more than watching my mother dress, I loved to watch my father perform his toilette. I remember the way he tapped a little mound of Pepsodent tooth *powder* on his palm, dipped his toothbrush into his hand and then brushed methodically, uppers, lowers, left and right. But the main event was his shaving ritual: I loved watching him slap the straight razor, thwack-thwack, back and forth over the razor strap until the blade glistened, then swirl his bone-handled shaving brush against a cake of soap in a wooden bowl where it foamed like whipped cream. Sometimes he let me lather my face as well. Then both of us "shaved" together in front of the mirror, he with the straight razor making trailblazing paths down his cheeks, and I zigzagging through my soapy beard with an empty safety razor.

"Great job, Bunny," he'd say approvingly, his praise showering me with self-respect as we drizzled ourselves with Mennen aftershave lotion and a light dusting of talc. He had nicknamed me Bunny at birth, but when I was especially adorable, he called me "Sugar Pie," or "Pussy Cat," or "*Kepele.*"

To be told I had a good *kepele*, a smart head, was the ultimate compliment; brains were all that mattered and if my father said you had a good head, you might as well be Einstein.

My father knew everything. First of all, he was American-born, in Connecticut to be exact, which made him a regular Yankee, while my mother and her family were immigrants. Second, he went to Townsend Harris, a high school for gifted boys, then paid his way through City College and NYU Law School by teaching Hebrew school, and was now a lawyer while all the other fathers were cloak-and-suiters or businessmen; so you can just imagine how he could talk. Third, since he really knew his history, politics, classics, Talmud, Hebrew, Yiddish, French, carpentry, plumbing, electricity, sailing, fishing, and more—he didn't just talk, he pronounced, like a sage. And he was a brilliant teacher.

I loved it when he taught me things no one else in the family had mastered, like chess, ping-pong, or Torah-reading. Preparing me for my Bat Mitzvah was perhaps his finest hour. He did it as if he was a rabbi and cantor combined, which he could have been, having studied the sources and daavened himself into the grooves of the liturgy until he knew it all by heart. And I did it as if I was a boy, which he wanted me to be though he never said it; he only showed it by taking me seriously.

He drilled and polished me into the kind of Bat Mitzvah that legends were made of back in 1952 when girls, as a rule, did not do that sort of thing. But I did whatever my father valued. More than anything, I wanted his approval, not because I was a Daddy's Girl but because he was my mentor and I was his intellectual heir. There was no son to make that claim, only two other daughters, both much older and long out of the house. Clearly, the legacy was mine if I proved myself worthy of it.

Even when I was very young—maybe nine or ten—he made me feel worthy just by talking to me. He spoke didactically, as always, but never condescendingly the way he sometimes addressed my mother and aunts. He talked to me as if I could be trusted to "get it" on first hearing. He was an intelligent man but not a patient one.

For me, heaven was when he talked law or Judaism, explaining the convolutions of an ongoing case, the outcome of a lawsuit, the rationale for a particular Jewish ritual. I asked him a million questions and he answered them; for smart questions, he was patient. I knew that if I could get him started explicating a Biblical text, he'd smoke one Lucky Strike after another, meandering from midrash to midrash long after I was supposed to go to bed. I became adept at engaging him in conversations that fueled his interest while feeding me the information I needed in order to grow up and be like him.

My father's life seemed so much more exciting than my mother's that I thought it only logical to make him my hero. He seemed to be other people's hero too: they had elected him President of the Jamaica Jewish Center, the UJA, the Zionist Organization of America, State of Israel Bonds, you name it. In the synagogue, where our family went for every Shabbat and holiday service, my father was like the Big Man on Campus: not only did he do the Torah reading, he sat in one of the thrones on the bimah or he busied himself in the congregation, helping people find their place in the Siddur, handing out yarmulkes and talesim, while praying with the loudest voice.

There were wonderful bonuses associated with being small-daughter-of-the-Big-*Macha*. I got to sit in the front row in the sanctuary. I could set the table for the Men's Club bagel breakfasts, or work the Center's switchboard. And occasionally, I was taken along to conferences where my father was presiding, speaking, or being honored.

One of the great thrills of my young life happened at the Jewish War Veterans convention of 1945 which was held at Grossinger's hotel in the Catskills. I was almost six. My father was J.W.V. County Commander that year, so he got to sit up on the dais and I got to sit on his lap. Next to us was a withered old man who seemed lost inside his J.W.V. uniform. I don't remember which war he was a Jewish veteran of, but I vividly remember my father introducing him as 98-years-old, the most ancient person I had ever met.

The old vet took my little hand in his dry bony grip and said, "Bunny, you must always remember this moment because you just shook the hand that shook the hand of Abraham Lincoln."

I never write about my father because I don't want to have to give him credit for that memorable encounter or for the other special events of my childhood. He didn't go out of his way to make them happen; he never went out of his way for anyone. He got credit for so much because he himself seemed so important that just being with him made you feel special.

Somehow I learned how to be fathered by this man. You had to come into his world and do things his way if you wanted to have him at all. You learned that you were adored when you were smart and cute, but never when you were inconvenient. You didn't notice that he wasn't around much, except when your mother cried and begged him to stay home and accused him of giving more of himself to his Jewish organizations than to his wife and child. For you, it was enough to be his pet, his mascot, his creation.

Only years later did I understand that he gave to me not so that *I* would have, but in order to show the world what *he* had to give. Even the Bat Mitzvah was ultimately for him. Lauded as an extraordinary lay teacher, the triumph was his before it was mine. The patriarch of the Jewish community had shown his minions that he could teach his Yentl Torah.

I never write about my father because I would have to describe the good memories, as I just have, and then he would sound like a better father than he was. And then, I would have to set the record straight.

I would have to point out that the reason I remember everything my father did with me is because he did so little:

He read bedtime stories to me twice. One was Charles and Mary Lamb's narrative adaptation of Shakespeare's *Mid-Summer Night's Dream*. The second was a remarkable week-long installment reading of stories by Arthur Train, called *Tut and Mr. Tut*, the adventures of a British lawyer and his assistant. I must have been about 8 years-old at the time.

In those years, my father administered a couple of alcohol rubs when I was sick. While I was vomiting he helped support my head over the toilet. I remember feeling ashamed that he had to see me this way.

When I was about six, my mother talked him into going with us to the Bronx Zoo. In a snapshot taken that day, I am wearing a leopard-skin coat that my Uncle Herman the furrier made for me. My father joked that I would be mistaken for a baby leopard and claimed by a leopard family as one of their own, and then he would have to climb in the cage and rescue me. Back then, I believed he could.

He taught me how to swim when I was five. When I was 7, he took me horseback riding and taught me to canter. That winter, I went ice skating with him for about an hour. Two or three times in mid-childhood, he took me along with my uncle and cousin to see the Brooklyn Dodgers play in Ebbets Field. He made me feel proud that I understood the game, knew the players and even kept track of the innings in my souvenir program.

I'll never forget our ride on the ferris wheel at Coney Island. On the first turn, I felt so terrified that I asked him to make them stop the motor and let me off. He wouldn't do that, but he put his arm around my shoulders and told me to chant one phrase over and over again to myself until the ride was over: "Uuuuup and dowwwwwn, round and round," he intoned in a sing-song voice, a litany of calm, like his daavening. I've used his mantra to cope with anxious situations many times since then. But my father never again took me to Coney Island.

That's it. Those are my memories of life with father from birth to age 15. If I'm lucky the good days add up to a month all together. Maybe I never write about my father because I might count up the good days and find they don't even amount to a month's worth overall. Then I would have to move on to the rest of the memories which would reveal my brilliant, dashing Daddy to be another kind of father altogether.

If I were to examine the Other Father more closely I'm afraid I would forever destroy the mythic Daddy, the man I once thought perfect. But as long as I do not write about him at all, I can keep the two images separate, grouse about the man I came to know from age 15 onward, and keep the childhood Daddy, the mentor Daddy, the Jewish sage, safe in the bell jar of memory.

The Other Father was another story. I came to know him, and to be disappointed by him, during my mother's illness and after she died. Without her there to cover for him, to run interference, to neutralize his absences with her luminous presence and his selfishness with her love, I had to start facing who he really was.

February 3, 1955. It was an ordinary school night except that my mother was not home; she was in the hospital. After supper, my father took me into his study, closed the door, and offered me one of his Luckies. I knew something terrible was coming. Until then, I had only smoked behind his back. His gesture told me I was about to be addressed as an adult.

"Your mother has cancer," he said. There was no preamble; he prided himself on being direct and to the point. "The doctors have told us that she has less than six months to live. You'll have to be very helpful and very brave."

That was it. And that matter-of-fact attitude marked his behavior after we brought her home from the hospital to die slowly and painfully in their bedroom. During the whole ordeal, he took care of things in his no-nonsense, efficient way. There were treatments and medications, arrangements to be made, a housekeeper and nurse to hire. No time for reflection. No room for sad feelings, or ceremony or quiet despair.

"We all die sometime," he'd say.

But not this righteous, kind Jewish woman who sacrificed for everyone. Not my mother.

"No use complaining about what we can't help."

But you can help me get through this. Talk to me. Hug me.

"The best thing we can do is to go on with our lives."

And he did.

April 20, 1955. She died during the night. There were tears in his eyes when he woke me. I wouldn't say he *cried* but they were, to my knowledge, his first tears. He let me go in and kiss my mother goodbye. Then he shifted into his lawyerly mode, making phone calls, giving us assignments, and complaining about how much detail was involved in dying. Even the modest requirements of a Jewish burial, he said, were too elaborate for him. "Don't do any of this for me, I just want to be cremated."

(Twenty-seven years later, he was cremated—according to his wishes, and against Jewish law.)

Our week at home sitting shiva was interminable for him. I remember his impatience with the daytime inactivity, the constant flow of visitors and the mountains of food accumulating on the kitchen counter. Only during the evening memorial service did he come into his own. He led the prayers.

One night, only nine men showed up. "I can say the prayers." I cried. "I want to be counted."

I meant, *I want to count.*

I meant, You cannot exclude me just because I am a girl. I am a good Jewish scholar; I am my father's intellectual heir.

I protested: Surely, for a mother's Kaddish a daughter can be counted in the minyan. It's *our* house. It's *our* minyan. God will understand. Daddy, *you* understand.

"It's not allowed," said my father.

He called the synagogue and asked them to send us a 10th man.

May, 1955. My father gave away my mother's things. At 15, grieving, I did not think to petition for a hope chest of her clothes, or her paintings, or the books, china or jewelry that was precious to her. Unmindful that I might someday wish for concrete mementos of my mother's life, my father let people pick through her closets and drawers and take away her history.

Summer, 1956. I found out that my father sold our house and most of our furniture. He never asked me if I was ready, or how I felt about it. He never gave me the chance to say what objects had special meaning to me. It did not occur to him that I might think of the contents of our house as mine and hers, not just his.

Everything was sold before I knew about it. At first, I could not understand. And then I understood. He was getting married. He got married. They took an apartment. The apartment had one bedroom. There was a daybed for me in the foyer. I was in my freshman year of college. I didn't need a bedroom just for school vacations, did I? It was clear the new wife didn't want me around. What my father wanted wasn't at all clear to me anymore.

We used to have a kosher home; he insisted on it. But the new wife couldn't be bothered with kashruth, so after 56 years of kashruth, he just let it go. I began wondering about the other sacroscanct values he had taught me; which really mattered, and which would he just let go?

November, 1958. I called my father at the office and told him I was driving down from school. I would arrive in New York around 7 p.m. I had to see him.

Since I'd never before asked for a scheduled appointment, I thought he would deduce that I was coming to tell him something urgent. In a wild moment, I even thought he might ask me to have dinner alone with him. But he had a meeting that night. He instructed me to come straight to Rego Park Jewish Center and fetch him out of his meeting room. We would have our talk in an empty classroom and he could return to his meeting.

I drove for four hours and found him at the Rego Park Jewish Center. We sat down in an empty classroom. I told him I was pregnant, I didn't have the money for an abortion, I didn't know a doctor and I was terrified because it was illegal. He assured me that he'd take care of the arrangements. No moralizing. No scolding. But also no comfort.

He attacked the practical issues: who, when and how much. Then he returned to his meeting and I drove back to school.

Late one night, a few weeks later, I went to a doctor's office accompanied by my father and his wife. I hated having her there but my father insisted we might need a woman in case there were complications. She acted as if we were asking her to rob a bank. Then she played the martyred nurse. There were no complications. The abortion cost my father $350 but I paid him back.

It took me five years, but I paid him every penny.

I needn't dredge up other such recollections. You get the point. That's the Other Father, the one I have to reconcile with the good Daddy before I can fully understand myself and, most particularly, my relationship to Judaism.

In the years after my mother died, I felt betrayed by my father. Gradually, I withdrew from him, and he from me. This might have been a manageable psychological problem if it hadn't become an untenable spiritual one. That is, my connection to Judaism was inextricably bound up with my feelings for my childhood father. The Judaism I grew up in was a male-run religion presided over by a masculine God and personified by my Daddy. My religion *was* my father. Leave one, you leave them both.

I left my formal identification with Judaism when I broke away from the enchantment of my father and the masculinism of my faith. I reclaimed my Jewish identity over time in a process that I have described elsewhere (*Ms.*, July/August 1987). But I have yet to deal with Daddy.

The Other Father keeps getting in my way—just as Jewish men and their *mishigas* have gotten in the way for many of the contributors in this book. From these provocative chapters on all aspects of Jewish masculinity, it is evident that I am not the only one trying to decode Judaism and manhood. But I may be the only one here who is writing about her father for the first time.

I have this book to thank for helping me to begin.

INTRODUCTION: FROM THE POLITICAL
TO THE PERSONAL

I think it will be instructive to tell the story of the genesis of this book. But first, a word on Jewish genesis stories.

I once taught a course on biblical and classical cultures, or, as it was more commonly called, the Jews and the Greeks. This was a good number of years ago, while I was a graduate student in philosophy at the University of California at San Diego. One of the things we taught our first year college students was that historical consciousness was a distinctive Hebraic contribution to what we now call Western Civilization. The Greeks tended to think of eternal truths outside of and unaffected by the contingencies of the ebb and flow of time, a time stream which, if it had any effect at all on the most meaningful realities of the world, was more likely to be leading toward a decay from a Golden Elysian past than to any kind of progress in the future. In contrast, the Jews had a God who acted in and through history, and consequently a philosophy and theology in which eternal verities were progressively revealed through particular historical events. From this comes an idea of inherent significance in the progression of events, and a tradition of revealing meaning through narrative. In contrast to the Greeks, who opposed the art of the storyteller to that of the philosopher, for the Jews storytellers are philosophers. Jewish sages and texts teach through stories.

From the Jews, then, comes the idea of meaning in history. And it is as a Jew that I shall impart the meaning of this book through its history. But to look to the storyteller as a source of truth has other implications as well. For there are many ways of telling a story. Thus, truth resides not in a single monolithic truth inscribed in an impersonal universe, a truth simply to be read off as it stands by one who has insight, but rather in a multiplicity of interpretive tellings of the tale. Thus I shall tell the story of this book in several different ways, with different starting points and in different contexts.

A professor of mine once remarked that the distinctive Jewish faculty was memory. "Gedenk," we are told—"Remember." And this memory must be personalized—"*I* was brought out of Egypt," we say at the Passover Seder. I shall begin my telling with the immediately triggering event which led to this book and go on from there to situate it in other contexts. I remember one particular conversation as the proximate genesis of this book. About two years ago, I sat in a car in Los Angeles with a friend, Tom Mosmiller, who told me that he and a mutual friend, Clyde Franklin, were going to edit a special issue on Third World men for the magazine *Changing Men: Issues in Gender, Sex and Politics*. "Oh!," I said, "Why don't I edit an issue on Jewish men?" As a result, a few months ago issue number 18 of *Changing Men* appeared, a special issue on Jewishness and Masculinity I edited containing several of the pieces included here either in part or in their entirety. But behind that initial "Oh!" lies not only another tale, but several tales. One needs to understand something of the men's movement and men's studies, the contexts in which that conversation took place, and something of me and my history.

I saw this project as a way of bringing together the men of different communities, Jewish and feminist, between which I felt there was already considerable overlap and a great deal of as yet untapped potential for mutually beneficial exploration of common themes. Between the conversation and the publication I had written a call for papers, and gone first to the library of the Program for the Study of Women and Men in Society at the University of Southern California, where I was teaching at the time, to get the addresses of whatever feminist publications I thought might carry the call, and then across the street to the library of Hebrew Union College to do the same for Jewish publications. I sent out the call and waited for the results, which when they came were most gratifying, as I believe readers of this book will discover.

I have been consciously working on men's issues for many years, first as a participant and then activist in the emerging men's movement, and then in the nascent field of men's studies as a teacher and scholar. As an undergraduate in the late sixties and early seventies, I had shared with many men an exposure to the women's movement which raised questions in my mind about the social construction of masculinity as well as femininity. While some men's relations to feminism were formed in reaction against it, for others of us feminist critiques of patriarchy seemed to explain much of all of our lives. Women seemed to be developing a new sense of sisterhood, while we men still seemed to be jousting with each other in traditional ways. Might men too not benefit from a reexamination of society's expectations of us? I joined a men's consciousness-raising/support group while a graduate student in San Diego, and my first exposure to the organized men's movement came in 1978 at the First California Men's Gathering, which I and most of the other members of that group attended together.*

One scene at that first California men's weekend made a lasting impression on me, and continues to provide me with a fundamental orientation

* For those to whom the "men's movement" may be a strange concept, some explanation is in order. In general sociological terms the movement's history can be traced through the impact and fusion of the feminist and gay movements. Individual men, of course, came to the movement through many other routes as well, such as through personal experiences of family loss, perhaps a divorce or a father's death or absence, or because of a life stage identity crisis, or perhaps through involvement in something like a peace movement which challenged traditional male norms. The principal organization currently embodying this movement nationally is the National Organization for Changing Men (NOCM), whose statement of principles defines itself as male-positive, pro-feminist, and gay affirmative. Prior to this organization, the movement existed as a series of annual conferences which the organization now sponsors on men and masculinity. Though small in numbers, NOCM and allied groups in the movement have had some impact, particularly in areas such as counseling and advocacy against men's violence, gay-straight unity work against homophobia, support for fathers, and producing a body of literature reflecting a new men's culture and men's studies scholarship. The leading forum for this literature within the movement has been the magazine *Changing Men: Issues in Gender, Sex and Politics*, originally titled *M.: Gentle Men for Gender Justice*. This men's movement should be differentiated from various groups often classified as "men's rights" groups, though this designation itself covers a broad range. The movement is sometimes referred to as the "pro-feminist" men's movement to accomplish this differentiation. While some groups usually put under the "men's rights" rubric are relatively politically non-controversial, simply offering support services for non-traditional fathers, for example, others see men as discriminated against in areas such as divorce, alimony, and custody proceedings, or the male-only military draft, and lobby for what they see as men's interests in opposition to women in these areas. It is the non- and anti-feminist stance of such groups, as well as their inattention to gay liberationist concerns, which make groups like NOCM want to clearly stand out as pro-feminist and gay affirmative, and leads to the classification as a different movement.

regarding the tasks facing men today. Breakfasts, at which everyone gathered, were over the weekend a time for general announcements to the gathering of about a hundred. At one breakfast, a man stood up and angrily complained that there were no workshops scheduled that day dealing with men's sexism and their relationships with women. For him, this was the key reason, and really the only justification, it seemed, for men coming together at a gathering like this. We needed to work on the damage we had done to women in all sorts of ways and figure out how to overcome and rectify sexist injustices. At this point another man jumped up and just as angrily proclaimed that we had just heard the politics of guilt, and he was certainly no longer going to be driven by such politics, as they were inherently destructive. He was there for himself, to get more in touch with his feelings as a man and learn to relate to other men in more satisfying ways, and for him this was the sole justification for such a men's gathering, for which he would be apologetic to no one.

It has become increasingly clear to me that, posed in either/or terms, the question as to whether pro-feminist men should be concerned solely with male privilege or male pain is unanswerable. The only way out is to see the latter as the underside of the former, to understand that in discussing the drawbacks of male roles we are discussing the many and varied prices of power.

The social, political, legal, and economic privileges men as a group have come at too high a personal cost. While this cost to men does not equal the cost to women of the power it purchases, it is nonetheless quite real. To take just the most oft-cited example, the injunction that "real men don't cry," one need only consider how all the performance pressures men labor under—whether on the job, in the bedroom, or simply among friends and family—combine with the inhibitions against releasing these pressures in any emotionally healing way to produce society's prescriptions for all the tension-related diseases men disproportionately suffer from: ulcers, heart attacks, high blood pressure, headaches, suicides, and eventually early deaths (currently averaging seven to eight years younger than women in the industrialized nations). But the reasons men continue to suffer this very real pain become comprehensible only if one understands the power this emotional restraint confers. By withholding information about oneself, one gains the upper hand. By appearing to be more rational, one appears more suited to wield authority. Men adopt self-destructive behaviors not because they are evil or stupid, but because society makes it appear in their interests to do so, by conferring very real power on those who conform to these norms. Hence, the only way to gain the capacity to heal male pain is to incapacitate male power. For men to practice feminist politics is then not the politics of guilt, but the politics of long-term enlightened self-interest, though one must be clear that in the immediate context it will be a politics requiring the surrender of one's power and privilege.

To my mind, the mission and message of the men's movement in social, political, and cultural spheres, and of men's studies in the academic sphere, is to validate and publicize this perspective.[1] In these contexts, it has become increasingly clear to me that we need to speak less about "the male sex role," and more about specific and varying male sex *roles* as they differ by race, class, ethnicity, sexual orientation, religion, age and other factors. Indeed, the failure to be more specific in these ways contributes to the inability of new ideas about men and masculinities, inspired by new feminist understandings, to make more headway into the population at large. Given the broad strokes with which the sketch of "the male role" is painted, men are left feeling that what is being said does not really apply to them. The desire to speak to everyone so dilutes the message that we end up speaking to no one. Every man can feel that *he* is above the caricatured stereotypes being criticized. We are simply not reaching men in ways which would enable them to identify with what is being said. If we could reach deeper into people's lives, into where their real sense of themselves resides, we could touch them in meaningful ways, and open up paths to change.

This question of one's sense of self, one's identity, is crucial. One of the most significant notions to emerge from what is loosely called the sixties is the notion of "identity politics," as it came to be called. As it emerged in American political discourse, this notion is partly rooted in the feminist ideal of "the personal is political," and partly rooted in a distrust of abstract political theory and an accompanying psychological bent to much of "new left" political practice. The old left tended to construct political theory on a universal and impersonal scale, with the individual then left to deduce one's role in this grand scheme. At one point, this produced a host of young people from middle-class families descending on factories to find jobs, a display of downward mobility which the working class people who were the presumed beneficiaries of this newly professed and proffered solidarity and largesse were often somewhat at a loss to understand. Against this, a segment of the new left declared that it was of paramount importance to first pose and authentically answer the basic existential question of personal identity—who am I? If correctly answered, one's politics would then follow from this understanding. Rather than having to fit or tailor oneself to an appropriate political mold, often against the grain of one's heritage or background, one's politics would flow naturally from one's determination and assertion of one's authentic self, or more precisely, one's identity as a member of certain groups. For what is asserted by the proponents of identity politics is not an abstract individualism, a voluntaristic assertion of self-definition chosen *ex nihilo*, but an assertion of self which at the same time situates that self in an identifiable historical community, a community no doubt much in need of change, but a community also embodying core values upon which new values and traditions may be built.

For the story, about trends emerging from the sixties, to be the story of *this* book, one would have to fill in the gaps about how gender and ethnicity came to be such crucial categories in the construction of identity politics, and one would also need to tell the tale of contemporary movements for Jewish renewal. This would take one from the days of the civil rights movement through the transition to black power, and the accompanying message to whites, many of whom were Jews, to go tend their own rather than others' gardens, as well as through various phases of the women's movement, from an initial declaration of the shared plight of all women simply as women to a greater recognition of the significance of difference. This is a longer tale which requires its own telling. I shall not go further into it here. I would add, however, that from one point of view, the need to be more specific about the multiplicity and variety of male identities may be particularly crucial for men. Compared to the mass scale of the women's movement, the men's movement is quite small, and if this were the only way to take the measure of a movement one would hesitate to use the same word for both. But one cannot reasonably expect a movement of the relatively privileged to attain mass dimensions. Even pro-feminist men would be unlikely to become active in a men's movement unless the issues were extraordinarily salient for them, a situation unlike a movement of the oppressed where the saliency of the classification is continuously forced on people by the dominant group (e.g., "*We* decide who is a Jew," said the Nazis). As a member of the dominant group one has the luxury of not being aware of one's categorization—one simply assumes one is being considered as an individual. While a significant number of women might gain gender con-sciousness simply *as women*, it is therefore unlikely that significant numbers of men will gain gender consciousness simply *as men*. For men as a dominant group, gender might become salient only as a supervenient category, a category following upon or expressed in conjunction with another category. Thus, in order to have an impact we must learn to speak not of men in general, but of black men, Jewish men, gay men, male workers, male parents, male elders, etc. My experience in the men's movement confirms that it is often precisely through such conjoint identities that men gain their strongest identification with the movement. I believe this accounts in part, for example, for the strong presence of gay men in the movement, whose core identity as gay men combines gender and sexual orientation, with one element having the further significance of membership in an oppressed group.

But the background story of general trends must converge with a more personal story about *me* before we arrive at these pages. No matter how powerful and important trends may be, they do not edit or write books. Indi-vidual people do. And so I come to the need to discuss and understand not just masculinity in general, nor simply my particular identity as an individual, but my identity as I live it in terms of gender and ethnicity, not just as a man, but as a Jewish man. To complete the task of self-understanding and definition, I would also have to situate myself vis-à-vis other categories, declaring and under-standing the significance of the facts that, among other things, I am also white, heterosexual, middle-class, and a host of other things. But, as they say, one thing, or in this case rather two things, at a time. For now, it should suffice that this is the first book to discuss Jewish men *as Jewish men*, that is to say, with conscious focus on this interplay of gender and ethnicity. There are, of course, innumerable books which are *de facto* about Jewish men by virtue of their exclusion of women, but this book is about Jewish men in quite a different and more self-conscious way. So, to put the question another way, why was I so captivated by a remark made by a friend a couple of years ago that it eventually led to this book?

As noted above, there are many ways in which I might describe myself, many communities with which I might identify. I find that the single identification coming closest to my core identity is that I am a child of Holocaust survivors. This seems my real peer group, the group with whom my identification is most powerful, the group where when I watch others of us speaking in filmed documentaries, I can often finish the sentence they start before they do. More accurately, I am a child of temporary Holocaust survivors. That is to say, though both my parents survived the war years, they died earlier than I believe they would have had they not suffered that experience. They survived, but only temporarily. We do not yet know how many others' survival is also temporary, and will not know until the last survivor of those years dies what we will judge to have been a "natural" death, unhastened by war traumas. I find this way of thinking about Holocaust victims more useful than the usual way, which closes the tally at the end of the war, because it establishes greater historical continuity between past and present, reminding us that the Holocaust is still very much in living memory, still continually relived in people's nightmares.

Given the centrality my Jewish identity has for me, it was inevitable that I would eventually turn my attention to the issue of Jewish masculinity. Indeed, I have come to understand that my Jewish identity, and in particular the circumstances of my upbringing as a child of survivors, played an important role in my initial sympathetic response to feminism. At a minimal level, the same factors were operating that are often invoked to explain the high proportion of Jews in various progressive political movements: elements of Jewish culture such as its commitments to justice and equality, its messianism, and its emphasis on intellectualism and ideas, and other more sociological factors, such as the particular marginality of Jews, the economic and social roots of anti-Semitism, and a historical sympathy for the underdog.[2] In my case vis-à-vis feminism, other factors were involved as well. For I found the feminist critique of mainstream masculinity personally empowering rather than threatening. As a child and adolescent, I did not fit the mainstream male image. I was an outsider, not an athlete but an intellectual, fat, shy and with a stutter for many years. The feminist critique of mainstream masculinity allowed me to convert my envy of those who fit the approved model to contempt. It converted males previously my superiors on the traditional scale to males below me on the new scale, for I had obviously shown premature insight and sensitivity in rejecting the old male model. I could pretend that others' rejection of me had really been my rejection of them.

Of course, I could not have admitted this at the time. To do so would have seemed effeminate, and confirming of my fears of others' worst judgments of me. I was especially vulnerable to feelings of not belonging because my European style upbringing and background in the United States had reinforced the outsider status Jews often feel, even when native to the culture. The immediate community of friends with which my parents surrounded us in Forest Hills, New York was so dominated by other survivors that I was in college before I had friends whose parents didn't speak English with an accent, and I found myself very unsure how to relate to them. Indeed, I had a German accent I lost only after starting school, having been born in Berlin and my family having emigrated to the United States a few years later. (To this date, I am not sure of my citizenship at birth, since I was born to then stateless refugees in what was the British sector of a Berlin still divided by the Allies.)

It took me a long time, well into my involvement with male feminism, before I realized that I would have to come out from behind my use of feminism as a shield against other men, protecting me from my fears of and hostilities toward them. In using my Jewish marginality as a vantage point from which to attack the mainstream, from which point the feminist critique of mainstream masculinity seemed to bypass me as a target, my ability to use feminist arguments had been purchased at the price of continuing alienation from other men, and hence from myself as well. Rather than use my Jewishness to avoid being categorized as a "real" man, "real" understood as a term of critique rather than praise, I have come to understand that I must reevaluate what it really means to be a Jew and a man, a Jewish man, in the contemporary world. This question is what motivated me in assembling this book. I felt compelled to know what was out there in terms of people's thinking on this question, in the hope they might enlighten me on my condition, and that we in turn might be helpful to others. It is clear to me that I am still very much in the process of working this question through, and that I have as yet reached no definitive answer or resting place. In the remainder of this essay, I would like to share where my reflections have taken me thus far in understanding myself as a male child of temporary Holocaust survivors.

●

The Holocaust continues to affect me. Though I of course experienced it only vicariously, primarily through the stories my parents told, my historical self-consciousness begins with this experience. The Holocaust was for me not an intangible, amorphous horror, but a concrete reality of names and places. The events recounted over the dinner table seemed immediate past history, and I came to identify with a collective suffering so strongly that when challenged by adversity I actually came to feel that *we* had already suffered enough, with a depth of feeling out of all proportion to my actual life experiences.

There was, however, a marked difference in the stories my parents told, or rather in the ways they told them, in part stemming from their markedly different experiences, but also in part stemming from their gender. While my mother's stories seemed to invite further questions, to be intended to reveal her and her life, my father's stories seemed told to tell a discrete tale, and that tale ended when he finished the telling. That part of his life seemed discontinuous with the present—he was reading from a book which was closed, or at least from a chapter which had ended. One of my regrets has been that I adopted my father's injunctions, and never asked my mother the questions she wanted asked, nor my father the questions he did not want asked, but I now feel should have been asked nonetheless.

My mother was a German Jew, who spent the war working as a nurse in a Jewish hospital in Berlin. To the astonishment which almost always greets my statement that this Jewish hospital functioned openly in Berlin throughout the war, my set response has become that apparently the regime felt they needed the hospital more than they hated the Jews. From her I heard stories of Eichmann walking through the hospital to fill his quotas for the transports to the camps which left from the adjoining courtyard; of her and her friends spending their salaries on too expensive haircuts (for who knew what tomorrow would bring) in fashionable Berlin, an area they reached by removing the yellow star from their coats when they left the neighborhood where they were personally known (for which act alone they could have been arrested, for the stars were supposed to be permanently sewn on, not simply held in place with pins as theirs were); and of survival in the final days of the liberation of Berlin, worrying first about the bombs and bullets flying around them, and later about their treatment by the liberating Soviet troops, who were at first understandably skeptical about claims that these were Jews they were meeting in Berlin, but who treated them royally when their identities were verified. My father was a Polish Jew who spent most of the war hiding and fighting in the forests near his hometown, often as part of a small band whose membership shifted, consisting at one point, as he put it, of "two communists, two bank robbers, and me." From him I heard stories of survival through courage and the use of one's wits, of hardships endured as he lived without a roof over his head for four years, and of the destruction of shtetl life.

I knew that my maternal grandfather was proud of the medal he had earned as a German World War I veteran, never believing that his country would *really* do to him the things people feared. He and his wife died in camp Theresienstadt, the supposedly model ghetto in Czechoslovakia. My mother knew the approximate date of her father's death, because one day she received from the camp a postcard from her mother dated June 26, 1944 (which I still have) with the usual form declaration of thanks for receipt of a parcel, but this time with the return address signed not simply Johanna Schüfftan, but Johanna

Schüfftan Witwe ("Widow"). I was told that my paternal grandfather was an Orthodox and respected man in the village, and that he kept silent when he learned that his son had started carrying a gun, something my father never told him directly, for he knew that he would not approve. (Many years later I stood with my father in an airport in Germany, where there was a visible presence of security guards, young men with machine guns in German uniforms, about the same age my father had been in the war. My father's discomfort at being unarmed was so strong I could almost see his fingers twitching, so strong that I felt it too, feeling disarmed for the first time in my life. Though I have never carried a gun, I can still remember the world of difference between simply not having a gun, and being unarmed.)

My father learned what I believed was his father's silence, and I in turn learned it from him. When my father died six years ago, almost ten years to the day after my mother, I concluded the eulogy I gave at the funeral by saying:

> One reason I feel the need to speak is that my father left so much of his life unspoken. Those of us who knew him best learned to measure the depth of the loss he felt for my mother by how difficult he found it to speak of her these last ten years, and we learned to gauge the hardships he went through in his life by how rarely he spoke of them. But what is left undone in one life is left for others to complete, and the mitzvah of speaking of my father's life should begin today.

I should like here to continue this mitzvah, this meritorious act, of speaking of my father's life, but I must do so with today's, not yesterday's, understanding of this male silence. While I then heard his pain in this silence, and still do, today I have a greater understanding of the pain this silence also causes others. As Adrienne Rich eloquently and aptly wrote in the first paragraph of her essay "Split at the Root: An Essay on Jewish Identity":

> Trying to be honest with myself, trying to figure out why writing this seems to be so dangerous an act, filled with fear and shame, and why it seems so necessary. It comes to me that in order to write this I have to be willing to do two things: I have to claim my father . . . . and I have to break his silence, his taboos; in order to claim him I have in a sense to expose him.[3]

Some silences are maintained to enable the nonspeaker to listen to the world. Others are maintained to compel the world to listen to the nonspeaker. Such is the male silence of which my father and I and our fathers before us partook. Relieving ourselves of the obligation to communicate and disclose our feelings and desires, others are forced to be inordinately attentive to us so that they can decode our muted messages, or simply not learn what we choose to keep hidden. The silence of my father's pain was also the silence of his power.

As I argued above, to ask which is more real is to ask a meaningless question. To understand is to see them as one and the same.

Just as the silence of "the strong silent type" is in a sense not a silence at all, but a way in which the voice of authority speaks all the more powerfully for not having to speak at all, so too does his strength conceal a weakness. For this strength is a male strength, the strength of the warrior, a strength called upon when battle lines are drawn. And here is its weakness, for when battle lines have not been and need not be drawn, it seeks to draw them so that it may be brought into play. For an exquisite expression of this mindset one need only recall Hamlet's soliloquy, endlessly cited and recited as an expression of *the* quintessential existential dilemma, but more properly understood as an expression of the quintessential *male* existential dilemma, where "not to be" is "to suffer the slings and arrows of outrageous fortune," but "to be" is "to take arms against a sea of troubles and, by opposing, end them." This is the psyche of the male warrior, who feels that he will not exist if he takes off his armor long enough to acknowledge his pain, perhaps because in that moment he fears he will be defenseless when attacked, or perhaps because he fears he will not be able to support his own weight without his external skeleton, and who seeks troubles to oppose and conquer in order to don his armor and affirm his existence.

For many years, missing the link between this strength and this weakness, I could not reconcile different aspects of my father. While his heroism in the war and his forcefulness as an aggressive businessman were undeniable, at the same time he seemed afraid to become involved in all the routine controversies of daily family life. Impending disagreement brought from him not argument or even discussion, but withdrawal into silence. We learned to respect, honor, and obey this silence, not to even raise issues which might upset him. I have come to see this "respect" as disrespect, as not giving him his due as an adult, instead treating him like a fragile child in need of protection. I have also learned from friends who are adult children of alcoholics that this kind of reversal of the parent-child relationship, where the children come to parent their parents, is all too common when the parents have been unable to heal their own wounds, and the children have come to feel these wounds as their own.

Only after his death did I really come to understand that his was not a courage which could face life's ambiguities, where ongoing interpersonal problems are resolved through the compromise of give and take, where one must often accept long-term irresolution, but a courage which requires as its precondition the drawing of battle lines across the field or the bargaining table, with clearly delineated antagonists, and with the promise of a clear winner and a clear loser at the end of the engagement. And since such is not the stuff of life, certainly not where ongoing familial love and intimacy are involved, he could not really be engaged with us, nor we with him. Problems had to be denied rather than faced, for when the rules of engagement demanded full battle regalia at the first hint of trouble, one could not risk acknowledging this hint for fear of unleashing the dogs of war on the family. But I came to this understanding at the price of considerable pain and disillusionment which I still feel, for it was only after his death that I learned that he had been unable to tell me of his dissatisfactions with me that I did not suspect existed, but were expressed in the provisions of his will, and which we would never have the opportunity to hash out and perhaps resolve. And I had played my role as well in this denial of engagement, in the perpetuation of the distance between us. To decipher his silence would have required decoding skills I did not have, skills men on the whole do not have, for the ability to read such hidden messages are the survival skills of the oppressed. I had accepted this distance from my father, in our shared fear that closing the distance would mean closing battle. I find today that my inherited tendency to prefer still but stagnant to invigorating but potentially raging waters still inhibits my relationships. For someone who makes his living with words, I too have at times been remarkably silent. And non-verbal communications remain relatively unheard by me.

My father and I related to each other in all too common male fashion, afraid to cross each other's boundaries. Thus, when my mother died, in a real sense I felt I had lost both my parents, for in so many ways she had been my access to him, playing the mediator's role women often play in men's lives. When I first grew a beard at age nineteen, I heard from her but not from him how upset he was by it, for it upset his image of his clean-cut son. Thus, the distance between us easily widened in the years after her death, for we no longer had our go-between to bring us messages across the divide. Instead, we took turns complaining to my younger sister that we could not talk to each other.

The most significant single piece of news my mother ever brought about my father was the most closely guarded secret in our family. My father had an artificial leg. As a result of a wound received toward the end of the war (I still don't know the circumstances), his leg had been amputated below the knee. I don't know if my father had ever wanted his children to know this. I learned of it when I was somewhere around eight years old, I think. My memory is uncertain. I had asked my mother why my father sometimes limped—I knew enough not to ask him. She came to my bed that night to give me the answer, and it was to be our secret, that I knew. At least it explained why he never went to the beach or played ball like the other kids' dads. After that I was expected to make things easier for my father by not making him have to walk so much, bringing things to him whenever possible, but all the while not doing it so obviously that he might suspect the reason. (I still find it awkward letting people know when I may have done a small kindness for them—it feels right to me that such things be kept secret.) It was many years later that he was brought home from work one day after his artificial leg had broken in an accidental fall. I was sent to bring down from my parents' bedroom upstairs a small suitcase which contained a spare, a suitcase which had always simply been declared invisible. That night he told my mother that perhaps it was time to tell the children of his leg. She told him they had known for years. I never heard a word from him about it. This was never to be discussed, never hinted at. I really believed that many people who I am sure knew did not. I still expect people who knew him to be shocked reading this, and I frankly have no idea who will and who won't be. When, at his funeral, someone barely hinted at his "handicap" as part of their praise for him, we were enraged at this betrayal.

When brute facts are so massively denied, mere unpleasantries have no chance of being heard. When a man suffers so long and deeply in silence, his children would feel criminal if they were to add to his burdens. I know my mother felt many of the same pressures. She took pills so that she would not reveal the pain of her rheumatoid arthritis when he came home, while her doctors spent years trying, not very successfully, to convince my father not to deny the reality of her illness. But my father was never a man to let mere facts stand in the way of his opinions. I remember when my mother was on what was to be her deathbed in an intensive care unit in the hospital after a heart attack, when my father told us what a good sign it was that while the EKGs of the other patients were wildly fluctuating, hers was steadier. I didn't have the heart to tell him this was a sign of weakness, not the stability, of her heart. His strength of will was much admired, by me and others, and it brought him through many difficult situations, but it also formed a wall around him. He would have been described in many ways as a "self-made man," particularly in his business success. Part of the gap between us was that in many ways I preferred the man he was before he remade himself, a man who was at precious times still much in evidence, a man of old world charm and uncomplicated pleasures, the Srulek Brod of Lezajnsk, Poland, who was increasingly overshadowed by the Sam Brod of Great Neck, New York.

Some of our differences had to do with my Judaism being different from his. Having felt the healing power of mourning my father, I have come to the conjecture that much of his rigidity here stemmed from his having been denied the opportunity to mourn his. His parents, and many of his family, friends, and community, were brutally murdered at a time when, in the struggle to defend his own life and those of others, he did not have the luxury of mourning. The normal maturation process, where father and son go through a period of difference and then later find reconciliation, was cut off for him. When I moved toward another kind of Judaism, he could not understand this as simple difference. For him, it appeared as a betrayal of those who had died, for I do not believe he ever fully made peace with having abandoned his father's Orthodoxy for a Conservative Judaism in the United States. Rather than celebrating his successful adaptation to new circumstances, I believe he assuaged his guilt for denying the faith of his forefathers by telling himself he had to change out of necessity, and as compensation drawing a line and promising himself and them he would go this far and no farther. Thus, in my bending or extending this line I was not simply finding *my* own way. As the fruit of his labors, the fruit by which he would be judged, I was breaking *his* promise. To fully bridge this gap between us would furthermore have required undoing generations of inter-Jewish conflict, for I tended more toward the intellectual strain of German Jewry with which I identified, largely through my mother, rather than the traditional Jewry of my father's Polish background, and these two tendencies of East versus West have all too often viewed each other with disdain. Much more could be said, but those are tales for another time.

•

      Friends and colleagues who know my writing will recognize this as the most personally revealing piece I have published. When I set out to write this, I knew it would have to be more personally written than most of my writing, but I frankly did not expect to spend as much time as I have dealing with my own life history, and particularly with my relationship with my father. I find myself reminded of an old favorite essay by Robert Benchley on "How to Get Things Done," which I shall use as the final route through which I will tell the story of the genesis of this book. In it Benchley explains that he makes a list of things he needs to do, but cleverly puts what is *really* the most important item toward the bottom of the list. Working on the principle that anyone is capable of doing any amount of work, provided it is not what one is *supposed* to be doing at that moment, Benchley ends up procrastinating on the things at the top of the list and doing what is at the bottom instead. Thus, he has tricked himself into doing what he needed to do. I may have similarly tricked myself. When I wrote the section of this essay following the excerpt from my father's eulogy, it was late at night, or rather early in the morning, in September with the fall chill of the North-eastern United States in the air, just as it was when I wrote the eulogy six years earlier. I felt again the healing effect I had experienced then. I had been afraid to write about my relationship with my father, still feeling the fears I wrote about above, feeling that, given the anger I still feel toward him, to so fully engage with him again would be to do battle with him again, jeopardizing the closeness I felt I had come to through my mourning. In my bad faith with myself, I had at one point even convinced myself that these fears inhibiting my writing were really only appropriate feelings of respect for the dead. Yet I have found it worth the risk, and rewarding to have done so. In thinking about writing this piece, I had put the more intellectual earlier part of this essay at the top of my list of what needed to be done, and the more personal writing at the bottom. Perhaps I have successfully tricked myself into doing what I truly needed to do, à la Benchley. I must however confess that given all the other issues I must deal with in my personal life, if I really have to fool myself into writing a book on each one, though I do have some confidence in my abilities to be prolific, the prognosis for my personal growth does not seem promising. On the other hand, I can find grounds for optimism in the thought that having now become conscious of my self-subterfuge, the detour may not be necessary in the future.

In any case, having never been all that much a fan of the recent genre of new men's confessional writing, I shall cease being self-indulgent, aware that good therapy may still produce bad art. I shall instead let the reader turn to the essays in this book, which conclude with a non-confessional piece of mine on male Jewish feminism. I shall not here attempt to summarize or synthesize the ideas the other authors develop in these pages. I prefer on the whole to let the essays speak for themselves. Furthermore, at the beginning of each of the four sections of this book the reader may find a brief introduction which highlights distinctive features of each contribution. They cover a wide range of issues from many different perspectives, from scholarly exegesis of Jewish texts, both sacred and profane, to intensely personal recollections, from literary criticism to social activism. The authors are male and female, young and old, devout rabbis and committed secularists. They all contribute greatly to our under-standing of the experiences of Jewish men, and meanings of Jewishness and masculinity.

H. B.

Notes

1. See Harry Brod, ed., *The Making of Masculinities: The New Men's Studies* (Boston: Allen & Unwin, 1987).
2. See Percy S. Cohen, *Jewish Radicals and Radical Jews* (London and New York: Academic Press, 1980).
3. Evelyn Torton Beck, ed., *Nice Jewish Girls: A Lesbian Anthology* (Trumansburg, NY: The Crossing Press, 1984), p. 67, reprinted in Adrienne Rich, *Blood, Bread, and Poetry: Selected Prose 1979-1985* (New York: W.W. Norton, 1986), p. 100.

I.
REAL MEN DON'T EAT KOSHER:
ON JEWISH MALE IDENTITIES

Lori Lefkovitz's "Coats and Tales: Joseph Stories and Myths of Jewish Masculinity" takes up several themes which later contributors return to in other contexts, including the significance of sexuality, in particular heterosexual virility or potency, in establishing masculinity; anxieties created by historically changing standards of masculinity, standards changing both because of changes in the larger non-Jewish world in which Judaism survives and changes internal to the development of Jewish traditions; and the significance of Jewish familial relations involving males, both intra- and inter-generational.¹ The biblical figure of Joseph is shown to be an extremely important representative model for Jewish men.

The author's autobiographical reflections in "To Be or Not to Be Larry Bush" highlight the necessity of understanding the interconnections between the two dimensions of what Eric Erikson described as identity: one's personal sense of self, and others' confirmation of that sense of self. When identifiable social forces pressure us to keep our identities to ourselves, we are impelled to publicly proclaim who we are.

In probing his answers to the question "What Do Men Want, Dr. Roth?" Barbara Gottfried's examination of the male protagonists of Philip Roth's writings illuminates various dichotomies which frame discussions of Jewish masculinities: the "nice Jewish Boy" versus the "Jewboy," in Roth's work and in the minds of many others often synonymous with "the scholar vs. the rake," assimilation versus ethnicity, boyhood (and being a son) versus manhood (and being one's own man), and impotence versus potency and pleasure, the linkage between the latter two concepts being especially noteworthy.

The title of Joshua Hammerman's "A Young Rabbi" poses its

question: how do young men come to be recognized in a tradition whose image of wisdom is the bearded old man? Like the other essays in this section, it asks the reader to look with new eyes at the images of Jewish men which form our traditions and inform our actions.

Note

1.   For an excellent treatment of the significance of relations between brothers in Judaism, see Arthur I. Waskow, *Godwrestling* (New York: Schocken, 1978).

Coats and Tales: Joseph Stories and Myths of Jewish Masculinity

Lori Lefkovitz

Joseph, as he is represented in *Genesis* 37-50, is a relatively complex figure whose heroism finds expression not only in the grand acts of vision and planning that save his family and all Egypt from famine, but also in the more incidental details of his beauty and chastity. While the Joseph of Hebrew Scriptures is not without his character faults, his beauty and chastity have unambiguously positive connotations. In medieval midrashic literature,[1] in the Koran, and in subsequent art and fiction, however, texts find it increasingly difficult to reconcile Joseph's heroism with his chastity. The beauty that is sexually unproblematic in the biblical story becomes effeminate in later renderings of Joseph, and what has come to be remembered as the "coat of many colors" is reshaped accordingly. In my brief reading of several trans-figurations of Joseph, I will suggest that these reinterpretations reveal something of the changing image and self-image of the Jew, and that a negative image of the Jew's masculinity and sexual vulnerability developed in correspondence with a developing image of the Jewess as sexually overpowering and insatiable. Both exaggerations derive from messages implicit in Scripture and both have had sorry consequences for the stereotype of the Jew in Western culture.

The Bible tells the history of the world, and each person wants a story. Soon after Eden, however, the world becomes too populous for each person to be fully included in this important text, and the narrative must choose among equal sons of the hero. The Bible is then punctuated by genealogies and tales of sibling rivalries as brothers and the mothers of sons vie for the important position of next in line in the future of the chosen people. Perhaps because they may have been a relatively small, militarily weak, and young people, the early Israelites favored myths that reverse the usual rule of primogeniture.

In Hebrew Scriptures, it is not the older, stronger, more masculine son who inherits the future. Instead, in the cases of Isaac and Ishmael, Jacob and Esau, Joseph and his brothers, later King David and his brothers, and Solomon and his brothers, it is the younger son, often the child of the more beloved but less fertile wife, the physically smaller, less hirsute, more delicate, more domestic son, the son closer to the mother, a hero of intellect rather than of brawn, who will be chosen by God over his brothers. In most cases this son is the mother's rather than the father's favorite. An awareness of this pattern may have contributed to an image of the Jews as a feminized people ruled by their women.

In this regard the biblical Joseph, characterized as an instrument of divine will, is typical. Singled out equally as an object of love and an object of envy, Joseph's status as hero is plainly a function of his having been pre-selected for a special role in *Genesis'* narrative history; while everything in his personal story numbers him among the type of the biblical hero (a beloved son born of a "barren" favored wife; the attempt on his life; the move to a position of political power . . .[2]), Joseph's acts of pride compromise him in the eyes of the reader. Joseph is a complex hero in part because his human ambitions and faults are necessary to actualize God's plan.

Jacob gives Joseph a fine striped coat. This detail in the story would seem superfluous, but added to Joseph's dreams of power and to the detail that Joseph tattletales on his brothers, the reader sympathizes with the brothers' jealousy. Even Jacob is slightly annoyed by his favorite son's pretentiousness. When Joseph tells his prideful dreams, Jacob rebukes him, asking if Joseph really expects his parents and brothers to bow down before him (*Genesis* 37:10). Jacob encourages Joseph to join his brothers on the day that the brothers will concoct the story of Joseph's death, and the coat that was his gift comes back torn and bloodied to haunt Jacob as "proof" that his son has been slaughtered by wild beasts. Joseph is thus more sinned against than sinner, and the rest of the narrative is generated by the injustice of the brothers having sold Joseph into slavery.

The fact of Joseph's beauty occurs as a single line in the text that serves only to explain why Potiphar's wife lusts after him. Once more Joseph's garment, this time left behind in his flight from the seductions of Potiphar's wife, is the material sign of a lie: it "proves" that Joseph came "to insult" his lord's wife. Again Joseph is unjustly punished—this time by imprisonment—but once in jail, he has the opportunity to prove himself a reader of dreams. In the context of the false readings of Joseph's clothes, Joseph distinguishes himself as a true interpreter, and eventually earns his release from prison because of his inter-pretive powers. The day does come when his brothers bow down before him. However extraordinary we may suppose Joseph's beauty to be, Joseph knows his brothers, but they do not recognize him. His identity is withheld for narrative suspense, and the brothers are allowed to prove the fullness of their repentance. Jacob descends to Egypt, and these episodes end happily, God's promises and Joseph's prophesies alike fulfilled.

Although Joseph is God's pawn, his personal heroic qualities are evident: he is wise, chaste, loyal to God, to his own people, and the Pharaoh; he is a skillful politician (he manipulates both Pharaoh and his brothers to get what he wants) and a skillful administrator (he manages Egypt so well that he acquires people and property for his lord, transforming a system of private land ownership into a feudal economy). What is it about the Joseph story that so troubled later readers as to necessitate that Joseph's beauty—incidental in the Bible—would become his most remarkable and memorable trait?

A midrash glosses *Genesis* 37:2 ("Joseph, being seventeen years old . . . being still a lad"): "It means, however, that he behaved like a boy, pencilling his eyes, curling his hair and lifting his heels."[3] Joseph, thus rendered immature, effeminate, and vain of his beauty, deserves the treatment that is plainly unjust in the biblical account. Indeed, this commentary invents a crime that fits the biblical punishment: Joseph is made guilty of slandering his brothers, claiming that they are lustful. God exacts vengeance by inciting "a bear," that is, Potiphar's wife, against Joseph himself.

In traditional commentaries and later literature, much is made of Joseph's beauty. Jacob loves Joseph best not only "because he was the son of his old age" (37:3), but also because they share beauty ("his features resembled his" *MR* to 37:3, Freedman, pp. 775 ff.), an interpretation derived from a pun latent in the Hebrew. Other rabbis (*MR* to 39:6) and the first-century Jewish historian Josephus comment that Joseph inherited great beauty from his mother Rachel *(Jewish Antiquities* 2:9).[4]

In the Bible, however, Joseph's beauty is a vehicle only to present the lusts of one woman and the chaste virtue of the hero; in one midrash, Joseph's exaggerated beauty provokes all of Egypt's noblewomen to lust, and Joseph's heroic self-control is multiplied exponentially. The "problem" of Joseph's chastity motivates rabbinic expansions in two directions. The first, as we see, is to call Joseph's manhood into question; the second is to make Potiphar's wife repulsive. We are told in the *Midrash Rabbah* to *Genesis* 39:16 that she "speaks like an animal," that she let Joseph's garments "grow old in her keeping, embracing, kissing, and fondling them," and that she went great lengths in her seductions: "she went as far as to place an iron fork under his neck so that he would have to lift up his eyes and look at her" (*MR* to 39:25).

In the biblical story, Joseph's innocence of the charges of Potiphar's wife are known only to the reader; Joseph leaves prison because Pharaoh needs him. There are midrashim that are less able to tolerate an unjust accusation remaining undiscovered, and these suggest that if Potiphar had believed his wife, then Joseph would have been killed rather than imprisoned. Potiphar is given an additional line: "'I know that you are innocent,' he assured him, 'but (I must do this) lest a stigma fall upon my children'" (*MR* to 39:20). And Joseph is rewarded with Potiphar's vestures of fine linen, not because he is prepared to save the kingdom, as the Bible has it, but because "his body had not cleaved to sin." For these rabbis, the politics of the body had become more important than the politics of the state.

As much as these midrashic stories betray the rabbis' uneasiness over Joseph's chastity, others go to great lengths to assure the reader that chastity is a great virtue; in so doing they protest too much. Joseph's self-control is made to go beyond the lusts of one noblewoman: "The Egyptian women, daughters of kings, desired to gaze upon Joseph's face, yet he would not look upon any of them. He therefore merited both worlds, because he entertained no impure thoughts about them." An alternative tradition elaborates: "You find that when Joseph went forth to rule over Egypt, daughters of kings used to look at him through the lattices and throw bracelets, necklets and ear-rings, and finger-rings to him, so that he might lift up his eyes and look at them; yet he did not look at them." Again, just as the rabbis marvel at the self-discipline of their hero, they feel obliged to account for it: "R. Huna said in R. Mattenah's name: He saw his father's face which cooled his blood. R. Menahema said in R. Ammi's name: He saw his mother's face, which cooled his blood" (also recorded by Ginzberg, Vol. 2, pp. 52 ff.).

Writing in first-century Alexandria, the Jewish philosopher Philo betrays still greater unease in his treatment of Joseph's character. In spite of the Bible's nuanced characterization of Joseph, to Philo, Joseph is principally a man of carnal lusts. In Philo's *Allegorical Commentary*, an exposition of the Bible aimed at Jewish initiates,[5] Philo places Joseph in an allegorical scheme that presents Egypt (a standin for contemporary Rome) as the type of the body and its passions. To paint Joseph as wicked, all body and pleasure, Philo omits those biblical episodes and comments uncongenial to his thesis. He is warning his Jewish readers against the sins of materialism. In *De Josepho*, a work directed to sympathetic Gentile readers, Philo indicates that he recognizes that Joseph's character is open to other readings. In this work, Philo approves of Joseph. In the former account, Philo depicts Joseph as vain and spurious; in the latter, Joseph is lordly. Philo's English language editors collect the descriptive language in which Philo depicts Joseph: "prepared to subordinate truth to expediency of falsehood; . . . eager for vain glory, self-opinionated, presumptuous, swollen-headed with vanity . . . Joseph is the lover of the body and its passions, the champion of the body and externals, fond of luxury. From his mother he inherited the irrational strain of sense-perception . . . .".[6] A unique passage, *Allegorical Interpretation* 3:237-242, praises Joseph for controlling himself with Potiphar's wife.

Midrash constructs several explanatory fables. In one, a she-bear (again, Potiphar's wife) is arrayed in expensive jewels; the crowd declares that whoever is brave enough to attack her may keep the jewels. The wise man looks at her fangs, not at her attire. In another, a man who is "pencilling his eyes and curling his hair" declares, to the amusement of the crowd, that he is a man. "'If you are a man,' the bystanders retort, 'here is a she-bear, up and attack it.'" If Joseph were a man, he would not apply make-up to his face; if Joseph were a man, he would attack the woman.

These rabbis are clearly troubled by Joseph's chaste beauty, but inasmuch as he is a sacred hero, they fear articulating their doubts too directly. The blunt phrasing is put in the mouth of a woman: "A matron asked R. Jose: 'Is it possible that Joseph, at seventeen years of age, with all the hot blood of youth could act thus?'" (*MR* to 39:10). While Rabbi Jose confidently replies that the Bible is clear on the matter, another rabbi finds reason to argue that Joseph's intentions, at least, testify to "hot blood": "On examination he did not find himself a man" (*MR* to 39:10), and in a footnote, a modern editor explains: "He actually went in to sin, but found himself impotent" (*MR* to *Gen.* vol. 2, Freedman, p. 811). Joseph is an ambivalent figure because his beauty and innocence strike the rabbis as unnatural and effeminate; they expand the text in an effort to naturalize the hero.

The Koran, which scorns narrative as a vehicle for religious teaching, chooses to develop but one sustained narrative, Sura 12, "the fairest of stories," the story of Joseph.[7] Intolerant of divine injustice or deception, the Koranic version departs from the biblical account in order to clarify the morality of the story. Allah frequently interrupts himself to make meaning and moral explicit. Western preference for narrative suspense and ambiguity might prejudice us against this version of the story, but the Koran's departures from the Hebrew Bible indicate that Mohammed was no less troubled than the rabbis by Joseph's chaste beauty.

More prophetic than the biblical Jacob, the Koranic Jacob discourages Joseph from telling his dreams lest his brothers "plot against him" (12:5). While the biblical Jacob urges Joseph to follow after his brothers, the Koranic father is more anxious and reluctant: "a wolf may devour him" (12:13). The coat, designed to justify this fear, is returned to Jacob "with false blood"; no mention is made of its being torn. Seeing the coat whole, Jacob is not deceived by his sons. Later, at the home of Joseph's Egyptian lord, the coat, which is dropped in one piece in the Bible, is ripped off his back by his master's wife. The tear, displaced from the first coat, is replaced here. Just as the whole coat bore witness to the brother's lie, the torn one testifies to Joseph's honesty. Joseph could not have been the aggressor as he was clearly running away from the woman's advances. A witness of the fold explains that because the coat is torn from behind, Joseph speaks the truth (12:26-28).

The Koranic story, otherwise more concise than the biblical version, adds several details about Potiphar's wife: "She verily desired him, and he would have desired her if it had not been that he saw the argument of his lord" (12:24). Thus, Joseph is transformed into a man with natural sexual desires. The Koran sees a double problem: if Joseph's innocence is proved by the torn coat, why is Joseph imprisoned? And if Potiphar's wife is proved guilty, how does she survive the women's gossip in court? The Koran explains that Potiphar's wife invites the women to dine and equips each with a sharp knife and blood oranges:

> 31. And when she heard of their sly talk, she sent to them and prepared for them a cushioned couch (to lie on at the feast) and gave to every one of them a knife and said (to Joseph): Come out unto them! And when they saw him they exalted him and cut their hands, exclaiming: Allah Blameless! This is not a human being. This is no other than some gracious angel.
>
> 32. She said: This is he on whose account ye blamed me. I asked of him an evil act, but he proved continent, but if he do not my behest he verily shall be imprisoned. . . .

The women see Joseph and bleed. While Potiphar's wife is not vindicated in the eyes of posterity, a silent consensus is reached among the court women as Joseph's beauty justifies lust. Joseph prefers imprisonment to submission and warns Allah: "if Thou send not off their wiles from me, I shall incline unto them and become of the foolish" (12:33). Thus, once more, Joseph's beauty is exaggerated and his natural urges are clarified. "And it seemed good to them (the men-folk) after they had seen the signs (of his innocence) to imprison him for a time" (12:35). If Joseph had remained free, his sexual urges would have proved too strong.

Finally, the Koran adds a third coat to Joseph's wardrobe. Jacob's metaphorical blindness (the prophet does not know what has become of his son) is relieved when Joseph sends his coat home with his brothers. Jacob wipes his eyes with it, and his vision is restored. The third coat comes to reveal that which the first tried—but failed—to conceal. Thus, the deceptions that motivate the biblical story are not tolerated in the Koran, which makes every sign a readable vehicle for divine justice.

In spite of his simplifying effort to elucidate meaning, Mohammed, like earlier Jewish exegetes, betrays an anxiety over Joseph's masculinity and accordingly elaborates upon both Joseph's beauty and the extent to which he must have been tempted. While the Bible shows no concern over either male beauty or "healthy" male sexuality, over time male beauty became suspect if it were not used to seduce women. As the ethic of machismo became normalized, vigorous sexuality became a more important heroic trait than spirituality. The biblical Joseph's chastity therefore leads later interpreters to doubt his masculinity; by exaggerating Joseph's beauty, these writers virtually deprive him of beauty, imagining an effeminate man who is not a model to emulate.

When Henry Fielding came to write *Joseph Andrews* in the eighteenth century, his title character is also exemplary for his chastity, but he learns to be a "real man." Fielding attempts to solve the "problem" of Joseph's beauty by balancing Joseph's spiritual nature with an equally strong animal nature. Although this Joseph also refuses the seduction of a noblewoman, he is saving himself for a more deserving heroine. By the time of the Byronic hero of Romanticism, the suggestion of virility, even of sexual wildness, was a requisite quality of heroism. A man represented as a beast would become a more appealing hero than the fine gentleman. The Joseph figure, vain of his talents and always in fancy coats, had increasingly less to recommend him in the eyes of readers who preferred physical strength and sexual power.

Historically, it has not been the Jewish man, but rather the Jewish woman, who has been portrayed as sexually powerful. The myth of female insatiability, an *inability* to be satisfied, has long been a male stereotype of the female.[8] It is a sexual stereotype. Hebrew Scriptures develops such a characterization and Freud perpetuated it with a vengeance. The Jewish woman has been its special victim. As lover or as mother, the Jewish woman has been imagined as a monster of misguided sexuality. The contemporary version of this duality consists of, on the one side, Portnoy's hungry Jewish mother and, on the other side, that brunt of many a Jew joke, the Jewish American Princess. While the one is all appetite, the other is all restraint. Yet both eat their men alive. Both are all *desire*.

This characterization may derive from the Bible. Women in biblical literature are overinvested with sexual power, and Eve is the first instance. In a striking counterfactual, the first woman is born out of the belly of a man. Eve is tempted to knowledge by an erect snake. While the story blames woman for tempting man, in an act of symbolic displacement, clearly it is the symbol of male sexuality that tempts the female. The punishment is appropriately backwards in this story of sexual reversals. Woman is cursed with excessive desire of man, while man must lord it over her. This is a story that betrays anxiety with respect to female creative powers (as it is from the mother's belly that all life really comes) and fear of feminine seductive powers. Female sexuality threatens man's Edenic peace, and it must be controlled for all eternity.

In the Bible, women play many roles. She may be chaste wife, special mother, adultress, alluring clever woman friendly to Israel, or enemy harlot threatening to Israel. But no matter whether her role is as heroine or villainess, her power to create or destroy is sexual. Each time a woman enacts her role, a man is rendered powerless, and the text's fear of emasculation conveys the secret message that one must contain she who, if unleashed, wields a threatening weapon.

The barren mother is a case in point. All of the matriarchs, Hannah, and the mother of Samson, obey this narrative convention. As in the case of Rachel before the birth of Joseph, in all of the cases of a loved barren wife, God intervenes to remove the curse of barrenness, and a miraculous birth follows. The special child will be a hero and will hold a special place in the history of Israel's redemption. But in each case the birth is conditional: God removes barrenness and enters into a pact with the mother of the hero. She will bear a remarkable son, but she must consecrate the son into the service of God. Like the other favorite sons, Joseph leaves home in his youth in order to actualize the divine plan and carry forward the narrative.

What is the hidden message of this scenario? God functions principally as Creator. The text reasserts the prerogative of the Divine to create whenever heroes have birth stories, first by insisting that man alone is insufficient to impregnate the mother of a hero; and second, by depriving the female of her full creative powers, allowing her to be the receptacle of such remarkable seed only if she renounces claim to its issue by affirming her willingness to give the son to God by allowing him to leave her.

The ordeal of bitter waters described in the *Numbers* 5 reenforces the same message. If a jealous husband suspects his wife of infidelity, she swallows a muddy mixture and submits to the priest's curses. If she is guilty, she will either die, or perhaps equally devastating, be barren thereafter. If she is innocent, she will be fertile and have children. We thus discover that there are two antithetical interpretations of the barren wife: her barrenness may be read by all who know her as proof that she is either the ultimate wicked woman guilty of sexual crimes, or conversely, the ultimate good woman destined to someday bear heroes.

Whether supremely evil or supremely virtuous, a barren wife carries frightening implications: she emasculates her husband. In the one case, she is public proof that her husband is a cuckold, and in the other case, she becomes the second principal party in a contractual arrangement with God. God and woman enter into a pact which guarantees her right to bear a son, who will ultimately belong to God, the Father. This arrangement twice erases the human father, first as impregnator, and second as authority over the child's destiny. The myth of the ineffectual Jewish father persists to this day.

Thus, in variant stories in which the barren mother bears the father's youngest son, the rule of primogeniture must be broken. Her child, the weaker, more domestic, prettier, more feminine son carries on the line in preference over the stronger, older boys in the family. The rule of femininity prevails. Again, female power is imagined to be extreme. What Israel fears is that it is a "feminized" people.

The epitome of sexual powerlessness is, of course, the rape victim, and Hebrew Scriptures offers us several such victims. The only daughter to the matriarchs and patriarchs is Joseph's sister, Dinah, and her story is the story of a rape. While the Bible's narrator objects that Shechem ought not to have done such a thing, the story's larger point is that Dinah's brothers, Leah's sons, overreacted in their acts of vengeance. In midrash Dinah becomes the most wicked of women. From her story we learn "why man must master his wife, that she go not into the marketplace, for every woman who (like Dinah) goes into the marketplace, will eventually come to grief." Every woman who is said to "go out"—and the list includes Leah, Jael, and Dinah—is immoral, a designing prostitute (*MR* to *Gen.* 34:1). In the Bible, Dinah's brothers are said to remove her from Shechem's house, but according to one midrashic account, the men must drag her by force because "when a woman is intimate with an uncircumcised person, she finds it hard to tear herself away" (*MR* to 34:25). The Jewish male thus expresses his anxiety about control in the larger world, and he expresses those fears in terms of his relative sexual potency.

Delilah, Jael, Tamar, Esther and Judith exemplify the final category of women who act. Jael is typical. During Deborah's rule in Israel, it is not the female judge herself who destroys the enemy General Sisera, but rather Jael, Deborah's double in the bedroom. All of these heroines achieve their victories in the bedroom. The bedroom is that battlefield where men always lose.

Jael lures Sisera into her tent and, surprising Sisera and reader alike, instead of being penetrated by him, she penetrates him, driving a tent peg into his temple, until it "reached the ground" (*Judges* 4:21). One midrash cited by Ginzberg only allows Jael this uncommon strength after she has relations with Sisera seven times, once for each verb in the relevant verses. Thus, she exhausts him, though the writer of the midrash has no worry that she may have been too tired herself to lift the hammer.

Esther defeates Haman lying down because her husband misinterprets Haman's posture. Haman appeals to Esther for mercy in a prostrate position, and the king wrongly imagines that Haman is making sexual advances upon his wife. Jael chops off Sisera's head. Judith does the same to Holofernes. Delilah blinds Samson and cuts off his hair. Blindness and haircuts are literary symbols of castration (exemplified in the Oedipus story). The men who recorded these central narratives display a shocking fear of "losing their heads" because they lust after woman. In granting women these superhuman powers, the texts betray an underlying terror of female sexuality. And it is this terror of powers that no real woman possesses that has long justified the oppression of real women.

Mythology and history imagine false power to justify oppression. The black slave was imagined to be a man of brutal sexual impulse, so he had to be shackled lest white women be harmed. Jews have been imagined to control banks and governments before they were victimized. Woman too needs to be enchained if a little perfume is all it takes for a man to lose his head.

The powerful Rebecca of *Ivanhoe* stands trial for witchcraft because, as Sir Walter Scott demonstrates in his novel, medieval Europe imagined the Hebrew beauty as a creature of dangerous sexual allure. Conversely, Joseph has been a paradigmatic male Jew in the popular imagination. He remains an ambiguous hero whose talents entail flaws. Even as Joseph is an interpreter of dreams, so too he is a dreamer. Even as he is exemplary for his chastity, so too he is vain and boastful. He is less than a full man: a mama's boy, a braggart, his father's pretty darling, derided and defeated by his stronger brothers. He is a bit of a fop, who is too self-righteous to be seduced by the most powerful woman in Egypt. His strength is not physical: it is vision, calculated management and prudence, rather than brawn, that are his saving features.

These motifs echo in twentieth-century popular culture. Jewish women are represented as overpowering and not easily satisfied. The Jewish man is said to make a good husband: he does not drink, does not tend to domestic violence, is submissive, domestically responsible, is perhaps too loyal to his mother, but is also faithful to his wife. His mother dresses him in fine coats which his wife will tear from his back. This mythology urges the Jewish man to assert himself, to free himself of the Jewish woman. Perpetuating the Joseph myth does neither the Jewish man nor the Jewish woman much justice, as it places excessive weight on female sexuality with consequent loss of male sexual potency. Joseph and this balance need to be redressed.

Notes

1. *Midrash* names rabbinic stories that were collected and anthologized over hundreds of years as commentaries to the Bible. Those that I will quote from here were collected between 200 and 1200 C.E. Because I am interested in the general attitudes conveyed by these stories rather than in the variety and differences among them, I quote from the sources without the discrimination that would otherwise be appropriate. My sources are: H. Freedman and Maurice Simon, eds., *Midrash Rabbah*, vol. 2, *Genesis* (New York: Soncino Press, 1983), hereafter abbreviated *MR*; and Louis Ginzberg, *The Legends of the Jews* (Philadelphia: Jewish Publication Society, 1974).
2. Cf. Lord Raglan, *The Hero: A Study in Tradition, Myth, and Drama* (London: Metheun, 1936).
3. Freedman and Simon, eds., *MR* refer us in a footnote (p.774) to a midrash on the story of Cain and Abel in which Abel (not entirely a blameless victim in midrash) is criticized, like Joseph, for

"pencilling his eyes, curling his hair and lifting his heel," 1:xii.

4. H. St. J. Thackeray et al., eds.,*Josephus*, Vol. 4 (Cambridge, Mass.: Loeb Classical Library, 1926-1965), p. 173.

5. E.R. Goodenough, *An Introduction to Philo Judeus* (New Haven: Yale University Press, 1940), p. 77.

6. H. Colson et al., eds., *Philo* (Cambridge, Mass: Loeb Classical Library, 1949-1961), index.

7. My translations of the Koran are taken from Mohammed Marmaduke Pickthall, trans., *The Meaning of the Glorious Koran* (New York: New American Library, n.d.).

8. Cf. Robert Scholes, "Uncoding Mama: The Female Body as Text," in *Semiotics and Interpretation* (New Haven: Yale University Press, 1982).

To Be or Not To Be Larry Bush

Larry Bush

In the 1976 French film, *Mr. Klein,* directed by Joseph Losey, a Parisian art dealer is mistaken by the occupying Nazis for a Jew of the same name. Throughout the movie this gentile Mr. Klein hunts his Jewish counterpart in order to disavow him, but the Jewish Mr. Klein cannot be found. Several surreal elements in the film suggest that the Jew does not exist, that Mr. Klein is stalking himself. By the end, he hunts himself right onto a transport train bound for the concentration camps; without ever reconciling himself to it, Mr. Klein finds his identity.

The point is not that Mr. Klein is a Jew, somehow "latent" or assimilated. Rather, the film delivers a message like that of the Jewish proverb, "If there's a fire at your neighbor's you too are in danger." It calls to mind German pastor Martin Niemoller's famous statement of guilt—the guilt for oppression that is absolved only by resistance. "In Germany," he said, "they came first for the Communists, and I didn't speak up because I wasn't a Communist. . . . Then they came for the Jews, and I didn't speak up because I wasn't a Jew." The trade unionists and Catholics were next, then the Nazis came for the pastor himself. "By that time there was no one left to speak up." Niemoller, now 90 (and active in the West German peace movement), ended up in Nazi camps for seven years.

Curiously, he didn't name homosexuals as being on the hit list.

•

I have discovered my Mr. Klein, though he's better named Mr. Clone—and our relationship is almost as bizarre as that in the movie. Nearly a year ago I had a short science fiction story about human cloning, "Designer Genes," accepted for publication in *The Village Voice*. What was simply a neat victory for a fiction writer became a quasi-mystical experience when my editor called, shortly after, to request that I alter my byline, for another Larry Bush had just had an article accepted, too.

He was a Washington-based writer. He had no middle initial, and his legal name was Larry, not Lawrence or Laurence. His article was a collaboration with Richard Goldstein about antigay backlash. He was gay.

The news was a blow to my writer's ego, often gratified soley by a byline. ("The Other Larry Bush" somehow doesn't sastify.) It was a threat to my future, as some antigay editor might withhold work or publicity from me without ever communicating his reasons. Worse, and more deeply set in me, was a recoil reaction: *I don't want people to think of me that way!* (I'm a married man!)

Yet how could I express even a shred of such homophobia to an editor at the famously progay *Voice*? I took a deep breath and said, That's okay, I don't want to change my byline. Though I have a middle name, Dana, and my legal name is Lawrence, all of my publishing has been done as Larry Bush, and the readership of *Jewish Currents*, the magazine of which I'm assistant editor, knows me as Larry Bush, so Larry Bush I'll remain.

She suggested that they print biographical blurbs with each piece.

His ran first. Front page. Biographical blurb or not, my phone began to ring: Congratulations, Lar . . . Hey, uh, how come you're writing on *that* subject? . . . Is this Larry Bush? Reverend William Sloane Coffin just made a very important statement supporting gay rights. Think you could cover the story?

I began to kibitz my wife, Susan: maybe we should send an announcement to my mother's friends and to everyone in my high school yearbook assuring them it's not me?

●

I am nine years old, a cute kid, and I go into a public bathroom in Long Beach, Long Island, to use the toilet before my family leaves the beach. The tile floor is sandy and cool but thankfully not sticky on my bare feet. Perusing the stalls for an empty, I see just one set of feet sticking down in the row. I choose my spot and sit down with my bathing suit around my knees.

Then this guy walks into my stall without knocking: a tanned lifeguard of a man, very handsome. He's holding a pocketknife, blade out, and before I can speak he starts to fiddle with the toilet paper dispenser and says he's a maintenance man. Only he's not dressed as a maintenance man, he's wearing just a bathing suit. Embarrassed, I try to rush my bowel movement.

Suddenly he's holding his penis, swollen and enormous, at my eye level. "Why are you doing that?" I ask, scared shitless.

"Because I like you," he says.

How did I get out of there? Am I afraid to remember? Perhaps someone else came and scared him off. I think that's what happened. Did he intend to use his knife on me? Maybe he was just into exposing himself. Maybe I just got up and pushed past him. I don't remember.

My parents were trudging toward me across the sand with all our beach gear. I made a beeline for my Dad. "There was this really weird guy in the bathroom . . ."

He smiled—with mischief and concern—and said to Mom, "Larry just met his first queer."

●

My hope had been that this other Larry Bush was more a gay activist than a gay journalist and that his appearance in the *Voice* would be a one-time-only. But the bio with the antigay backlash piece eliminated that hope. This guy had a Fund for Investigative Journalism grant to research the treatment of gays in the armed forces. He was a columnist for two gay newspapers. He soon began contributing regularly to the *Voice*. In our competition for who would become *the* Larry Bush, he was winning hands down.

I clung to my name for dear life. For political reasons: "You know, when they used to ask Charlie Chaplin if he was Jewish, he would say he refused to answer that question for as long as anti-Semitism was rampant. In fact, Chaplin was only fractionally Jewish, if at all—I'm probably more gay than that! So I'm not going to disavow this gay Larry Bush's struggle. If some editor holds it against me—*Er zol einemen a mieseh meshuneh* (he should meet a strange death)!"

Or for mystical reasons: "This other Larry Bush has been placed in my world for a reason. He's here to remind me that it's not the byline and the egoism and the fame that count—it's the content of your work. I needed to learn that lesson so badly—my ambition is so thick-skinned—that the lesson became a corporeal reality in my life. Hence, my clone."

Or I struck up an attitude of nonchalance, particularly as my side in the name-game scored some points: a contract for a novel, to be published in September 1982. "We're in different worlds. He's a gay journalist writing on gay subjects—how widely known can he become in this homophobic world? And I'm a fiction writer (maybe my book'll sell, hm?), or a journalist writing on Jewish subjects. He won't become known to my readership, and I probably won't become known to his."

On November 19 Larry Bush struck back with a vengeance. He had an article on gays and the Moral Majority—in *The New York Times*.

●

My family name, when my father was a child, was Babushkin. His elder brothers legally changed it to Bush when they entered a pharmacy business so that they wouldn't seem quite "so Jewish" in any given encounter — wouldn't be accused of being clannish and hateful of non-Jews; of being specially talented and therefore too influential in certain spheres of business; of being oversexed and subhuman, a corrupting force in decent society; so that they wouldn't be persecuted, perhaps even beaten up, on the streets of America.

That was the America of the 1920s when the Ku Klux Klan had four million members. And today, how many does the Moral Majority claim? Larry Bush, the coarse threads of hatred that bind the KKK with the MM bind us to each other. For how many years could you not be at one with your own name? How many stereotypes have you had to sidestep in your attempt to be, and to be accepted as, a whole human being?

●

As a kid I was a good athlete. I was never a wimp. No one called me faggot. No one called me cocksucker.

But I wasn't an asskicker, either. I enjoyed playing potsie and jump rope with the girls almost as much as playing fungo with the boys. I liked having sensitive conversations with friends. I liked eating lunch quietly at school, without having milk cartons flying overhead, and when the rowdiness of the fourth-grade boys' table made that impossible, I sat with the girls.

There was a test that boys administered to each other: look at your nails. Look at the sole of your shoes. Sit and cross your legs. If you extended your hand rather than looking at your nails by folding them onto your palm, you were a girl. If you bent your knee in rather than out while looking at the bottom of your shoe, you were a girl. If you sat knee to knee rather than heel to knee, you were a girl.

I was a girl in all three tests.

My brother—who liked to wrestle with me in bed—would tease me because my ass wiggled when I walked. My brother—who recruited me into "The Body Club," a group of boys who inflicted pain on each other ritual-istically, for fun—made up humiliating names for me like Fluffy and Fakky Cuddlekins Jr.

The girls in school, who regularly elected me Most Popular because I was cute, smart, and nice to them, nicknamed me Cupcake.

No one called me faggot, but I was *younger* than all of them—admitted to school at four and a half, hanging around with my brother's friends, always the aspiring innocent, always the willing victim. Gentle but slow with girls. Quick to cry. Thank God I had a great outside jump shot in basketball and could handle a bad hop like Brooks Robinson. So the misconceived jokes ("Take Bromo, homo, and wake up feeling yourself") and careless exclamations ("You suck") were rarely aimed at me.

Yet now, as a dry-boned adult, I walk the streets, ride the subways, meet my public, with the fear of being considered homosexual shaping my posture, wardrobe and facial expressions. I'll carry a dirty canvas shoulder bag rather than a nice leather one—better to be considered an overage hippie than a queer. If I cross my legs (knee to knee) on the subway, I'll be sure to match it with a sober, "masculine" look on my face. Meanwhile, the brown corduroy jacket that I bought last autumn hangs in my closet, nearly new, because it ends above the waist.

This terribly confining self-consciousness is similar to that which I feel carrying books past a construction site (there goes an egghead) or parading my white face in a black neighborhood (there goes a gentrifying honkie) or reading a Jewish magazine in public (there goes a Zionist Imperialist). It is an embarrassment that confines my eyes to the stained sidewalk and polluted sky. Whatever happened to the bravado of my real hippie days, when I wore my hair down my back and purple drawstring pants? Or reaching further into memory, whatever happened to the joy of being a boy who loved other boys, who giggled himself to near insensibility with boyfriends, who acted like he owned the streets? How is it that the subtle warnings about being effeminate have completely overwhelmed the warmth and pleasure of same-sex bonding?

●

There is another self-consciousness about gay people that I encountered while dialing Larry Bush's phone number in Washington, D.C., to get his approval for the concept of this article. It is the watch-what-you-say kind of dealing with any member of an oppressed group, the "You must forget I'm gay/ you must never forget I'm gay" dialectic. In certain "liberated" circles, the world is turned upside-down. I feel guilty about my heterosexuality. I feel impossibly pressured to behave "independently" toward my wife. I feel obsequiously delighted by acceptance of friendship from gay men and women.

At our wedding two years ago, Susan and I prefaced our home-made ceremony with an explanation of why we were marrying. "How can we sanction an institution," we self-consciously asked our 180 guests, "that has historically been a means of securing women as the property of men; that breeds conformity and consequent isolation, the isolation of people's real selves; that perpetuates myths and yields disillusionments; that is denied to or made difficult for certain groups in our society?"

"Certain groups"—even after we answered our own doubts by asserting the untraditional (and traditional radical) values that (we hope) inform our relationship, a lesbian friend was quick to criticize us. We should have specified just *who* those "certain groups" are, she said. Unless we actively help make gay people visible, we are actively keeping them invisible. Sexual preference is not "irrelevant"—it's political.

But Larry Bush, on long-distance telephone with me, offered no such painful lessons. Instead, he was full of praise for my willingness to risk being identified as gay, and full of appreciation for the humor of the whole affair. Then again, he had no time to teach lessons—early on in our conversation his other phone rang and he put me on hold. Fifteen seconds later he returned with the report that a man had called simply to curse him as a faggot bastard.

"You must forget I'm gay/you must never forget I'm gay."

●

But when a gay man (was he gay, or was that my father's conception of child molesters?) exposes himself to me, I'm to understand? When a lesbian separatist reviles me for breathing, I'm to understand?

I'm trying to understand. Recently I edited an article for *Jewish Currents* by a 22-year-old German woman about her experiences in Action Reconciliation, a volunteer group (inspired by Martin Niemoller's Confessing Church) of young Germans who choose to "atone" for Nazi sins—sins for which they cannot logically be held responsible—through "good works" in countries and among peoples that were ravaged by Nazi Germany. This woman had toured the U.S. as a speaker under the auspices of the Anti-Defamation League, encountering Jewish audiences that were emotional and sometimes hostile. In their hearts, if not in their heads, she wrote, they always assumed that a "victim-victimizer" relationship existed between them and her. And she would never question that assumption, not even when Jews discovered their vast store of anger in her presence, at her expense—not, she wrote, "for as long as understanding can be and needs to be gained from it."

I'm trying to understand. Jewish history helps.

●

Larry Bush helped even more.

He is a remarkably eloquent, thoughtful, and sensitive man of 36—young to be what we Jews call a *tzaddik* but old in experience. Some of that experience, which he shared with me for a couple of intense hours on November 30, consists of an enormous struggle to possess his as his own.

Until 1978 he was a tenured civil servant of high rank with security clearance, a speechwriter for Nixon and Ford, and, on the side, under a pseudonym, a gay journalist. (Eat your heart out, Tricky Dick!) Then he allowed a letter protesting anti-gay biases in *The Washington Post* to be printed over his real name. Immediately he was stripped of assignments at work . . . and then of his staff . . . and then of his office. Left with just his nameplate, he went free-lance.

As to the enviable achievement of appearing in the *Times*? The local paper where his parents live reprinted the article. Practicing Mormons, the Bushes face excommunication if they maintain contact with their apostate son.

Next on the agenda for Larry Bush are pieces in *Atlantic Monthly* and *Newsweek*. "The Eisenhower melting pot era is back with us," he told me in explanation of his success. "The residual tolerance from the Kennedy era is over. But there are many, many people who remember just how miserable the Eisenhower era was. And they're starting to realize that gay people are very much a part of the forces that want to hold onto tolerance and diversity in American life. I'm therefore given certain opportunities . . ."

Opportunities to fetch lots more harassment calls, no doubt. While I've been fearful of losing my name, he must be terribly afraid of gaining his. Yet his fears are paltry compared to his love for the gay community: a community-in-birth, that is just gaining the breathing space to search out questions for itself. It is a community, says Larry Bush, that offers America profound lessons about transforming oppression into strength; about the humanism that communal self-discovery can bring.

To me this is poetry, not rhetoric. But it is poetry that I can read only in translation—with empathy bounded by ignorance. The gay world is largely invisible to me, except in caricature. As with black culture, as with women's culture, as with working-class culture, as with my own Jewish culture—I am kept from it, and it from me, in both subtle and overt ways, so that my own search for self-determination should be routed toward self-indulgence and nihilism.

But we're not going to let that happen so easily. Larry Bush, I am rooting you on.

What *Do* Men Want, Dr. Roth?

Barbara Gottfried

It has become a truism of gender studies that gender is socially constructed, that though most people are born biologically "male" or "female," we are not born "masculine" or "feminine," but trained to those gender identities by the input of parents, teachers, siblings, and peers, not to mention TV, movies, teen magazines, advertising, and the world of fashion. To paraphrase Simone de Beauvoir, "one isn't born a man, one becomes one." Thus, "masculinity" and "femininity" may be succinctly defined as "patterns of sexuality and behavior imposed by cultural and social norms."[1]

At the same moment that gender studies has become a legitimate field of academic concern, ethnicity, or ethnic studies has also moved inside the academy. In both cases, marginalized groups (women and ethnic minorities) have forced a reevaluation of the way we see the naturalized world which decenters and destabilizes it, offering instead a more fluid, pluralistic perspective. Like gender, ethnicity is socially constructed, not, like distinguishing racial features, inborn. As Michael J. Fischer recently put it, "ethnicity is something reinvented and reinterpreted in each generation by each individual, something puzzling, over which he or she lacks control. It is dynamic, not learned or passed from generation to generation."[2]

The nexus of ethnicity and gender, or, more specifically, "Jewishness" and "masculinity" is central to the work of Philip Roth. For Roth, whose own relation to "Jewishness" is many-sided and fraught, "being Jewish" is an expression of what Mark Schechner finds an almost "tribal," "primitive," and arcane ethnicity,[3] whereas "Jewishness," according to Roth himself, is a question of style, the primarily verbal manifestation of that ethnic identity. As Roth recently replied in answer to a question about the "struggle with Jewishness" in his "Zuckerman" trilogy:

> The Jewish quality of books like mine doesn't really reside in their subject matter. Talking about Jewishness hardly interests me at all. It's a kind of sensibility if anything: the nervousness, the excitability, the arguing, the dramatizing, the indignation, the obsessiveness, the touchiness, the play-acting, above all, the *talking*. It isn't what it's talking *about* that makes a book Jewish—it's that the book won't shut up. The book won't leave you alone.

Won't let up. Gets too close . . . I knew what I was doing when I broke Zuckerman's jaw. For a Jew a broken jaw is a terrible tragedy.[4]

The critic and essayist Alfred Kazin sees Philip Roth as a second generation Jewish writer. For Kazin, Saul Bellow and Bernard Malamud, with whom Roth is often grouped to form a triumverate of Jewish-American writers, actually differ from Roth because they are first generation writers whose novels are "celebratory," whereas Roth writes about "the self-conscious Jew, newly middle class," whose identity, "though established, is a problem to himself."[5] What Kazin means, in part, is that by the second generation, Jews had successfully assimilated into the American mainstream, but that they were not entirely comfortable there largely because they are ambivalent about the loss of ethnic identity. As Roth himself puts it,

> I have always been far more pleased by my good fortune in being born a Jew than my critics may begin to imagine. It's a complicated, interesting, morally demanding, and very singular experience, and I like that. I find myself in the historic predicament of being Jewish, with all its implications. (*RMAO*, p. 20)

In both his fiction and essays, Philip Roth explores what it means to be Jewish and male in late twentieth-century America. His novels focus on the struggle of his protagonists, urban, intellectual, second generation American Jews, to define their masculinity over against a prototype of American maleness, which is desirable from the point of view of assimilating into the American mainstream, yet antithetical to certain elements in their ethnic make-up. In effect, Jewish men are white, but they're not: outwardly they are assimilated, but inwardly they are more aware of differences than similarities, and those differences are most pronounced in relation to gender characterization. Thus, for the Roth "hero," the nexus of Jewishness and masculinity is crucial, yet paradoxical, precisely because "Jewishness" contributes what the Roth "hero" most respects and yet most loathes in himself; what makes him, at one and the same time, both superior and inferior to what is defined as "masculine" in America.

For Roth, gender and ethnicity first come together explicitly in his early working drafts of *Portnoy's Complaint*, *The Jewboy* and *The Nice Jewish Boy*. These terms delineate for him the limits and limitations of Jewish masculinity:

> the "Jewboy" (with all that word signifies to Jew and Gentile alike about aggression, appetite, and marginality) and the "nice Jewish boy" (and what that epithet implies about repression, respectability, and social acceptance . . . [were] the Abel and Cain of my own respectable middle-class background. (*RMAO*, pp. 35, 37)

or, as he might have put it, "the Dr. Jekyll and Mr. Hyde of my childhood." In his later novels, the "nice Jewish boy" and the "Jewboy" grow up into what David Kepesh, in *The Professor of Desire* thinks of, after reading Byron and Steele, as the "scholar and the rake."[6] Though these two novels, *Portnoy's Complaint* (1969) and *The Professor of Desire* (1977), and at least one of the four novels written in between them, *My Life As A Man* (1974), suggest there is something inadequate in the dichotomies into which their male protagonists feel themselves split, they are so centrally concerned with Jewishness and masculinity, the battle between the "Jewboy" and the "nice Jewish boy," that they can virtually be read as deconstructing the relationship between gender identity and ethnicity. Ultimately, what these novels reveal is both the projective dynamic of Jewishness and masculinity for Roth's protagonists, and the damage it does to the male and female characters (and real men and women) who figure in that dynamic.

In all of these novels from what I call Roth's "middle period" the action is constructed as a parody of the classic *bildungsroman*, or novel of education. The "hero's" task, in this male-centered genre, is to grow from son-ship into his "life as man," to educate himself ethically and morally to take his rightful place in the world. But the problem for Roth's protagonists is that though they, as good Jewish sons, would seem to have had everything anybody could want or need to grow up good and true, manhood, or, in the gender terms we're working with here, full masculinity, eludes them. Or, the novels would seem to suggest, perhaps it is precisely because they are "good Jewish sons" that the achievement of a relatively unproblematic masculinity is at stake.

In *Portnoy's Complaint*, the earliest and most purely comic of these middle novels, Alexander Portnoy attempts an ersatz psychoanalytic reading of his impotence and patent failure to "become a man." What "makes men of . . . boys," or so Alex Portnoy believes, is the capacity to "be bad—and enjoy it![7]" Or, in other words, to be able to stop being a Jewish mother's well-behaved son and let the Jewboy in himself go. In the context of the novel this primarily means eating what is forbidden, whether it is unkosher meat, or lobster, or an "unkosher" woman, a *shikse*, without guilt. But for Roth, "the joke on Portnoy is that for him breaking the taboo turns out to be as unmanning in the end as honoring it" (*RMAO*, p. 19). As Maurice Charney explains it:

> A guiltless, spontaneous sexuality becomes the ideal of the guilty, who seem to forget that it is their guilt that endows forbidden sexuality with such exciting resonance. It is only through guilt that sex can be felt so intensely, since guilt makes sex a cultural, ideational, cognitive artifact and not simply a physical transaction.[8]

That everything is rendered in sexual terms in Roth—particularly retribution and guilt (which are translated into impotence and the inability to enjoy the sexual act as a sexual pleasure)—points to the fact, as Charney suggests, that Roth is writing in a particular post-Freudian moment in which the nexus of sexuality and psychology has become a privileged discourse. It is, ultimately, the "manhood" or "masculinity" of his protagonists which Roth explores, and the novels suggest that the crucial criterion in the test for manhood, the measure of all things, is the successful negotiation of one's sexuality in a potentially hostile, impotence-inducing world. Guilt isn't really the issue, partly because Portnoy's *modus operandi* is projective, rather than transformative, but finally because transgression, whether dietary or sexual, and its attendant guilt, doesn't really get at the heart of Portnoy's complaint. What "unmans" Portnoy is not guilt, but his inability to choose between the conflicting claims of Jewishness (of either the Jewboy or the nice variety) and a more mainstream masculinity.

In Alex's version of the failed "family romance," it is not simply that his mother is domineering and a nag, obsessive, and potentially castrating (she holds a knife over the six-year-old Alex because he will not eat), but that his father, his masculine role model, has already buckled under to the power of his mother:

> —if my father had only been my mother! and my mother my father! But what a mix-up of the sexes in our house! Who should by rights be advancing on me, retreating—and who should be retreating, advancing! Who should be scolding, collapsing in helplessness, enfeebled totally by a tender heart! And who should be collapsing, instead scolding, correcting, reproving, criticizing, faultfinding without end! Filling the patriarchal vacuum! (*PC*, pp. 44-45)

But what does Alex mean by "should"? According to Barry Gross, Alex derives his notions of proper American gender identity from the radio shows blaring throughout the Portnoy dinner hour, where:

> [the] fathers are men with . . . deep voices who never use double negatives . . . Jack Armstrong, the All-American Goy! . . . [whose son]—David or Ricky, Henry Aldrich or Oogie Pringle knows how to take motors apart . . . and isn't afraid of anything physical. (*PC*, pp. 163, 170)

Thus, the difficulty for Alex lies in the conflicting messages he gets about masculinity from the "Jewishness" within his home, which, he claims, in training him to be a perfect "little gentleman," is preparing him for homosexuality, rather than masculinity; and the "goyishness" or, if you will, the "American-ness" beyond it. Indeed, Alex goes so far as to suggest that his pursuit of *shikses* has less to do with Gentile women as "forbidden," or with himself as an appetitive "Jewboy," than it does with the idea that possessing a *shikse* will make him more like the *shkotzim*, their brothers, those "engaging good-natured, confident, clean, swift, and powerful halfbacks for the college football teams" (*PC*, p. 163). Ultimately, he concludes that sex with "nice" *shikses*, like his college girlfriend, Kay Campbell, whom he tellingly calls "The Pumpkin," or Sarah Abbott Maulsby, whom he even more baldly calls "The Pilgrim," is a means for him of appropriating their "Americanness," "as though through fucking I will discover America. *Conquer* America—" (*PC*, p. 265). To be truly American in these terms is to reject one's ethnicity and its more fluid gender possibilities in favor of assimilation and its more rigid conception of American maleness. But Alex's resentment of the strictures of assimilation and his hostility toward the dominant culture are evidenced in his italicized emphasis on "conquering" and dominion.

Doth Alex protest too much? The problem for Alex is that he is, precisely, his parents' son, and while that has proven emasculating, the American alternative doesn't really appeal to him either:

> All they [Gentile men] know, these imbecile eaters of the execrable, is to swagger, to insult, to sneer, and sooner or later to hit . . . also they know how to go into the woods with a gun, these geniuses, and kill innocent wild deer . . . stupid *goyim*! Reeking of beer . . . home [they] head, a dead animal strapped to each fender so that all the motorists along the way can see how strong and manly [they] are. (*PC*, pp. 89-90)

This is, precisely, the attitude of many women (and some men) I know toward the pretensions of what passes for "masculine" in American culture; but for Alex, this eschewing of what the dominant culture defines as masculine is as devastating for himself, his relationships with women, and those women themselves, as his need to get out from under the "Jewishness" which has nourished these alternative values in the first place. De-masculated in the American [male] realm, he tries to reconstruct his masculinity by lording it over those whom he can dominate, American women, or, if you will, *shikses*.

Thus, Alex's portrayal reveals not simply a fundamental conflict between ethnicity and assimilation, but more pointedly, the traces of that conflict as it is mapped on to gender construction and identification. In effect, Alex experiences one cultural system of gender in conflict with another; and what his "complaint" underscores is both the anxiety this conflict produces vis à vis gender identity, and the appropriative and destructive force that displaced anxiety has for those others, especially women, who come into contact with it. Thus, Alex's impotence, which is what has driven him to Dr. Spielvogel's couch to make his complaint in the first place, derives from the impossibility of either reconciling, or abdicating, the conflicting claims of Jewishness and

[American] masculinity. But realizing this is no solution, nor is projecting his insecurity all over the place. As the doctor responds to Portnoy's complaint in the novel's open-ended last line, "'Now vee may perhaps to begin'" (*PC*, p. 309).

The problem for David Kepesh in *The Professor of Desire* and Peter Tarnopol and his fictional persona Nathan Zuckerman in *My Life as a Man*, as for Alexander Portnoy, is that while they have excelled at [Jewish] son-ship, that regency has somehow not prepared them for finding any kind of satisfaction, emotional, sexual, even creative or intellectual, in adulthood. All of these novels are marked by their protagonists' seeming success in their work (Portnoy is the Assistant Commissioner for Human Opportunity in New York City, Peter Tarnopol—like Roth himself—has written an award-winning novel while still in his twenties; David Kepesh moves from outstanding student to college professor) and failure in their emotional and/or sexual lives.

My Life as a Man foregrounds the narrator/author struggling to come to grips with the recalcitrant materials of "life." The novel is divided into two parts, "Useful Fictions," which includes two stories, "Salad Days" and "Courting Disaster," and a long "autobiographical narrative," "My True Story," all of which, we are told in a "Note to the Reader," are "drawn from the writings of Peter Tarnopol."[9] Like Portnoy, Tarnopol feels compelled to tell his story, or, more precisely, shape it into texts for interpretation, as a means, retrospectively at least, of coming to terms with what he sees as a failure of manhood. He has allowed a disastrous marriage to reduce him to making the desperate gesture of donning his wife's undergarments to express his sense of emasculation at her hands. But neither through psychoanalysis, nor through his recuperative attempts at writing "Useful Fictions" can he finally blot out that devastatingly undone image of himself because he cannot acknowledge his own complicity in the destructive dynamics of his marriage, nor the hostility, even misogyny, that has fueled that collusion.

For Peter Tarnopol, as for Alexander Portnoy and to a lesser extent David Kepesh, there are two basic questions: "How did I, a 'nice Jewish boy' with a youth so full of promise, make such a mess of my life?" and "What can I do to get out of this nightmare of frustration and impotence?" In *My Life as a Man*, Tarnopol seems to shift the blame for his predicament away from the claustrophobic Jewishness of his childhood that Alexander Portnoy finds so unmanning, placing it instead on the combined highmindedness of the 1950s, and a literary education in the classics of Western civilization. But in moving from Freudian psychoanalysis to pop sociology, Tarnopol is still looking for someone or something to blame other than himself, when it seems clear, to this reader anyway (and the coyly complex structure of the novel would seem to bear this out), that if he has "been undone," it is because he has all by himself been "courting disaster."

Though he doesn't insist upon it to the extent Portnoy does, Tarnopoi's "Jewishness" is implicitly present in both his "useful fictions" and his "true story" since virtually everything his protagonists do can be read not as autonomous actions, but as re-actions to that crucial element of their childhoods. In "Salad Days," the most light-hearted of the novel's stories, Tarnopol's fictive persona, Nathan Zuckerman, chooses Bass College because its image is so patently unlike those of growing up Jewish in Camden, New Jersey:

> It was the pictures in the Bass catalogue of the apple-cheeked boys in white bucks crossing the sunlit New England quadrangle in the company of the apple-cheeked girls in white bucks that had in part drawn [him] to Bass in the first place. To him . . . beautiful Bass seemed to partake of everything with which the word "collegiate" is so richly resonant . . . (*MLAM*, p. 12)

Bass, in other words, is an emblem not simply of "collegiality," but of acceptance into the heretofore alien world of gentile America. And, as a student in Miss Caroline Benson's English honors seminar, Nathan is taken to task for his "relentless use" of the word "human,"

> human, character, human possibility, human error, human anguish, human tragedy. Suffering and failure . . . were "human conditions . . ." (*MLAM*, p. 18)

which Miss Benson finds "redundant" and "mannered," but which Nathan finds absolutely necessary because for him it replaces the insistent litany of his childhood: " 'Jewish' character, 'Jewish' anguish, 'Jewish' tragedy . . ."

The story ends ominously, before, as the narrator puts it, Nathan, "looking for trouble, would find it—" (*MLAM*, p. 31). In Tarnopol's next "useful fiction," "Courting Disaster," Nathan Zuckerman explains that he is drawn to the woman who ends up making his life hell because her [gentile] background is the very opposite of his own comparatively sheltered and loving [Jewish] upbringing against which he is reacting (*MLAM*, pp. 93-94):

> Not only that she had survived, but *what* she had survived, gave her enormous moral stature, or glamour, in my eyes: on the one hand, the puritan austerity, the prudery, the blandness, the xenophobia of the women of her clan; on the other, the criminality of the men [her father has raped her]. (*MLAM*, p. 71)

But in eschewing Jewishness in favor of the "moral" challenge Lydia represents for him, Nathan gets less, rather than more than he bargained for, "squander[ing] [his] manhood," as he himself concludes, on a woman he seems to have chosen out of his own perversity (rather than hers, as he would have it) to fulfill rather than defy that favorite dictum of Jewish parents, "Never marry a *shikse*."

Finally, "useful fictions" having failed to root out his despair, Peter Tarnopol attempts to tell the "True Story" of the "nice civilized Jewish boy" (*MLAM*, p. 193) who gave up the nice civilized Jewish Dina Dornbusch because she was "rich, pretty, protected, smart, sexy, adoring, young, vibrant, clever, confident, ambitious— . . . [but] a girl still," and he's decided that what he really wants is "a woman" who has lived and suffered to make him "humanish: manly, a man" (*MLAM*, pp. 182, 176). Like Portnoy, what Tarnopol here implies is that the experience of having grown up "a nice Jewish boy" is somehow not conducive to the development of a "full" masculinity, and that the only way for him to compensate for the deficiencies of his [Jewish] boyhood is once again to take on a *shikse* in defiance of his parents, through whom he can tap into American masculinity and become "a real man" by American standards.

Tarnopol is established at the beginning of "My True Story" at the Quahsay Colony, a foundation-supported artists' retreat where, after six months' contemplation, he has decided to compose an "autobiographical narrative." Close to a third of the way through that narrative, after he has described his relations with his sister and brother and self-consciously reproduced their critiques of his "Useful Fictions," then detailed his post-marital relationship with Susan Seabury McCall, Tarnopol attempts to approach the central and most disturbing part of his "true story," his marriage to Maureen, by beginning with a critique, fueled by his own special animus, of the sexual politics of the 1950s. According to Tarnopol, masculinity in the fifties is defined as "Decency and Maturity, a young man's 'seriousness,'" but what underlies it is "the myth of male inviolability . . . male dominance and potency," whereas femininity is characterized by "female dependence, defenselessness, and vulnerability" (*MLAM*, pp. 172, 175, 174). The net result of these gender definitions is debilitating for both sexes, since neither marries for positive reasons; rather, women feel the necessity of marrying, both financially and emotionally, and men feel the obligation to do so because they have all the power in the "great world" while "it was only within marriage that an ordinary woman could hope to find equality and dignity" (*MLAM*, p. 172). Thus, according to Tarnopol, women were set up by the ideology of the 1950s as the perennial helpless victims, and men became their all-powerful victimizers. But Tarnopol takes issue with this dynamic (and we can hear Roth responding to feminist critiques of his work), suggesting (with Hegel) that ultimately, it is the "master," or victimizer, who is enslaved to the victim and unable to break the chains of his "bondage" (*MLAM*, p. 176).

In offering his readers a scathing critique of marriage in the fifties, Tarnopol momentarily steps out of the persona of autobiographer and attempts to extrapolate some larger understanding of (as he presents it) what happened to him as an instance of a much more widespread cultural phenomenon. But his demystification of fifties marriage rites is ultimately more self-serving than self-illuminating. Though he goes on for another 150 pages in the paperback edition trying to figure out how and why he could have become so "enslaved," he never adequately explains it. Yet, oddly enough, Tarnopol ends up exactly where he thought he wanted to be: in taking on Maureen, he indeed purges himself of any pretensions to being "a nice civilized Jewish boy," beating her when he cannot get the best of her in any other way, thereby achieving an "American" standard of "masculinity" by aping his real American male counterparts, her abusive father and the first of her two former husbands. Ironically, however, just as for Portnoy, "breaking the taboo turns out to be as unmanning in the end as honoring it" (see above, p. 4), Tarnopol finds that physically abusing Maureen "unmans" him, rather than enhances his masculinity. Whereas Portnoy's pursuit of *shikses* would seem to be motivated by his love/hate relationship with his mother and his unvoiced fear that marrying a Jewish woman will do to him exactly what his mother has done to his father, that is, emasculate him, Peter Tarnopol chooses a *shikse*, seemingly because she *will* emasculate him, making that choice a kind of perverse self-fulfilling prophecy with regard to women. Thus, though they would appear to be oppositely motivated, Tarnopol's attempt at reconciling Jewishness and masculinity is really no different from Alexander Portnoy's, nor any more successful; for both, the net result is impotence and frustration rather than a successfully negotiated masculinity.

Roth has described his male protagonists as "clay with aspirations," and claimed that his intention in his novels has been "to show the frailty of men" rather than to "demonstrate cause for male chauvinism [sic]."[10] The difficulty with this claim, however, is that "the frailty of men" and the "cause for male chauvinism" are rarely mutually exclusive, "frailty" often fueling male chauvinism, especially in the form of turning on those even less powerful, particularly women. Roth's "heroes" are part of the twentieth-century tradition of non-heroes: neither enfranchised, nor attractive, they are failed sexual acrobats and guilt-ridden neurotics, the conflict between their "Jewishness" and the dominant ideology of American machismo compounding the collapse of their masculinity. But it would seem in Roth's work, that because his protagonists are "frail," or de-masculated in one realm (the realm of the American male), they attempt to reconstruct their masculinity by oppressing those they can have power over, *shikses*; or, in other words, the women who "belong" to those American males, and can therefore be used, as their powerless representatives, to get back at those supposedly powerful males. Thus, though the inadequacies, neuroses, guilt, and obsessions of Roth's protagonists would seem to be offered in mitigation of their misogyny, the dynamic is more complex, and more destructive of those caught up in it than Roth's remarks would suggest. But, as Roth works through the nexus of Jewishness and masculinity from *Portnoy's Complaint* through *My Life as A Man* to *The Professor of Desire*, he moves away from any easy projection of blame or guilt to a fuller comprehension of his protagonists' sexual politics, and their complicity in their own emotional/sexual dilemmas.

Early in *The Professor of Desire*, while a student at Syracuse University, David Kepesh comes across Macaulay's description of Addison's collaborator, Steele, as "a rake among scholars, a scholar among rakes," and takes it as a "prestigious justification for [his] base desires" (*PD*, p. 14). Like so many of Roth's protagonists, Kepesh feels himself split between the demands of "the Jewboy" and "the nice Jewish boy": he lives in his head, yet his body clamors for [sexual] attention, and it seems virtually impossible for him to reconcile what he experiences as the conflicting demands of "temptation" (*PD*, p. 1), or "appetite and aggression" on the one hand, and "repression, respectability and social acceptance" on the other (see above, p. 3). The characters who surround David in the novel are paired to play out that conflict (his "nice" parents versus the scatalogical Herbie Bratasky; the loving, but ordinary Elisabeth versus the uninhibited Birgitta; repressed, respectable Schonnbrunn versus "rapacious" Baumgarten;[11] nurturing Claire versus "sensual[ly] abandon[ed]" Helen). Yet David's sense of the necessity of choosing only exacerbates the conflict: it is precisely because he sees himself as someone who must make a series of either/or choices, constructing his life out of decisions between what he seems to think are opposite extremes, permissible or forbidden, that he is a professor(er) of desire, a wishful, rather than a satisfied, participant/observer. Indeed, like *Portnoy's Complaint* and *My Life as a Man*, *The Professor of Desire* suggests that there is something inadequate in the dichotomy into which its male protagonist feels himself split, and Kepesh, like Portnoy, Zuckerman, and Tarnopol before him, ends up going to destructive extremes before coming up with even a potentially workable solution (which, however, is more than any of his predecessors have managed).

In all three of the novels, but progressively more explicitly, so that it is clearest in *The Professor of Desire*, the female figures the protagonists encounter challenge male control, and the easy, dichotomous categories into which those protagonists feel themselves split. Because these novels are all either first-person narratives related by their male protagonists, or "omniscient," narratives allied to the point of view of the "hero," the reader never knows what the female characters think: their subjectivity is erased, unrevealed, hidden. But, for the male protagonists they both attract and threaten, the female figures seem to represent some kind of challenge to their masculinity, calling into question male complacency, power, and control. Thus, the female characters become, in this male-centered discourse, the projection of the protagonists' own doubts about themselves, implicitly posing the questions those [male] protagonists force female figures to represent: what is masculinity, what *do* men want? For David Kepesh, as for Alexander Portnoy, Nathan Zuckerman, and Peter Tarnopol, those questions are not so readily answerable as he might like.

After a childhood immersed in the rich pageantry of Jewish life at the Hungarian Royale, his parents' small all-kosher hotel in the Catskills, and a stint as an actor earlier in his college career, one of whose specialties was the imitation of some of the more colorful characters connected to the Royale, David Kepesh has become a "sober, solitary, rather refined young man devoted to European literature and languages" (*PD*, p. 9). Like Portnoy, David remembers his mother as the more powerful of his parents, her competence and conscientiousness legendary, his father's dependence on her a given of his childhood, though poignantly appreciated. But unlike Portnoy, David remembers his childhood as happy and loving, and neither condemns nor vilifies his parents for their differences from accepted gender definitions, nor for their too great love of him. Yet like Portnoy, Nathan Zuckerman, and Peter Tarnopol, the choices David makes, his intellectual interests, the girls he chases, point implicitly to a turning away from the Jewishness of his background. But with David, there's a difference: the animus is gone, and he makes his decisions less in reaction to his parents, whom he loves without any sense of blame or disenchantment, or out of rebellion against a smothered childhood and adolescence, than from his own needs and desires. Still, again like Portnoy, Zuckerman, and Tarnopol, though he turns away from the "nice Jewish boy" model of masculinity, with its underpinning of social acceptance, he finds the "American" alternative no more palatable. Like his only male companion in college, the homosexual Louis Jelinek (also Jewish), he eschews dormitory living because he considers its "rituals of [male] camaraderie ... contemptible" (*PD*, p. 15), thus separating himself from "American" masculinity and community as well as from the "nice" Jewish masculinity and community of his background. As with Portnoy, the remaining alternative would appear to be the "Jewboy's" pursuit of appetite; but it hasn't worked for Portnoy, and it doesn't work for Kepesh either.

After college Kepesh is awarded a Fulbright to study Arthurian legends and Icelandic sagas in England, a boon for the nice Jewish boy in him, but he almost immediately overthrows all his good intentions, involving himself in a menage a trois with two Swedish girls he is soon living with. When Elisabeth can no longer take the emotional pressure of the triangle and returns, broken, to Sweden, Kepesh continues his liaison with her friend Birgitta, all the while assuring Elisabeth of his love, and fantasizing about marrying and having children with her. But, when in the midst of hitchhiking around Europe with Birgitta at the close of his fellowship year he lets her know he plans to return to America without her, she packs her knapsack and leaves him to his regrets:

> And then gently, so very gently (for despite being a girl who moans when her hair is pulled and cries for more when her flesh is made to smart with a little pain, despite her Amazonian confidence in the darkest dives and the nerves of iron that she can display in the chancey hitchhiking world, aside from the stunning sense of inalienable right with which she does whatever she likes, that total immunity from remorse or self-doubt that mesmerizes me as much as anything, she is also courteous, respectful, and friendly, the perfectly brought-up child of a Stockholm physician and his wife), she closes the door after her so as not to awaken the family from whom we have rented our room. (*PD*, pp. 45-46)

Kepesh pays her the kind of tribute he would perhaps like to have paid to himself. For him, she is someone who has reconciled her sexual predilections and her upbringing, the Swedish, and female, equivalent of the Jewboy and the nice Jewish boy, and is thus powerful and in control, whereas he feels he must choose between the two. And, in deciding to return to the States to pursue an academic career without "temptation," he underscores his failure to reconcile what he experiences as basic, yet unassimilable, aspects of his character.

Not surprisingly, Kepesh finds that graduate school alone is not enough to sustain him, and when he first meets Helen Baird he is attracted to her in ways that resonate with his assessment of Birgitta:

> I begin at last to relinquish some of my suspiciousness, to lay off a little with my interrogations, and to see these passionate performances as arising out of the very fearlessness that so draws me to her, out of that determined abandon with which she will give herself to whatever beckons, and regardless of how likely it is to bring in the end as much pain as pleasure . . . It appears then that the capacity for pain-filled renunciation joined to the gift for sensual abandon is what makes her appeal inescapable . . . this beautiful and dramatic young heroine, who has risked and won and lost so much already, squarely facing up to appetite (*PD*, p. 56, 59).

As the "heroine" of "passionate performances," Helen is at the center of her own drama, and, like Birgitta, though unlike David, she is capable of giving herself over wholly to whatever is at hand. But, at least from David's perspective, there is a difference between them: while Birgitta acts autonomously and participates in David's fantasies only incidentally (she has plenty of her own to occupy her both before and during the relationship), Helen is a "dramatic heroine," who, though she thinks she consults only her own tastes, in fact fulfills roles in relation to men rather than for herself. Though they marry despite hesitations on both sides, their marriage is doomed, finally, because while Helen cannot let go of her fantasies, David can no longer hold on to his in the face of day-to-day existence, his masculinity undercut by the "passionate performances" that had once so stimulated it.

After the collapse of their marriage, Kepesh is temporarily on his own in New York, and he fills a small part of the lack of female companionship with a faculty colleague, Ralph Baumgarten, who, though he happens, like David, to be Jewish, is, like Birgitta and Helen before him, "someone on the friendliest of terms with the sources of his excitement, and confidently opposed to—in fact, rather amused by—all that stands in opposition." (*PD*, p. 126). But David is ambivalent about Baumgarten, just as he has been about Birgitta and Helen: though he is attracted by their capacity for giving themselves over to sensuality without guilt, for him the "Jewboy"/"nice Jewish boy" dichotomy can no longer be resolved simply by favoring one side of the equation to the exclusion of the other.

Soon afterwards, Kepesh meets Claire Ovington, the first woman to whom he has been attracted since the end of his marriage. Unlike the sensual and exotic Birgitta and Helen, Claire is very much an all-American girl, complete with parents who would appear to be just like those on the radio shows Alex Portnoy so enjoys, but whose alcoholism and constant fighting, more like the destructive macho of the "real American" fathers in *My life as a Man*, reveals the underside of the American dream. Several months into their relationship, David describes Claire to his analyst in terms very different from those he has used to delineate the fascinations of Birgitta, Helen, and Ralph:

> "She is to steadiness," I tell Klinger (and Kepesh, who must never, never, never forget), "what Helen was to impetuosity. She is to common sense what Birgitta was to indescretion. I have never seen such devotion to the ordinary business of daily life . . . There's no dreaming going on there—just steady dedicated *living*" (*PD*, p. 149).

Though Kepesh refers to Claire as his "rescuer" and finds that her "sane" love has not only helped to heal him psychically, but returned him to intellectual productivity as well, by the end of their first year together, as they travel through Europe, memories of Birgitta disturb his equilibrium, heralding the waning of his passion for Claire. By the novel's conclusion Kepesh feels that it is only a matter of time before the man that he has become with Claire "will give way to Herbie's pupil, Birgitta's accomplice, Helen's suitor, yes, to Baumgarten's sidekick and defender, to the would-be wayward son and all he hungers for" (*PD*, p. 238). But he understands, as Portnoy, Nathan Zuckerman, and Peter Tarnopol have not, that if he is to be "robbed" of Claire and his life with her, he cannot look beyond himself for an explanation: "It always comes down to myself" (*PD*, p. 247). And, it is this acceptance of his own complicity in the failure of his relationships, his failure to reconcile either the Jewboy and the nice Jewish boy, or his taste for the exotic and his longing for the American, that sets him apart from Roth's earlier heroes.

Since *The Professor of Desire* Roth has published three short novels: *The Ghost Writer* (1979), *Zuckerman Unbound* (1981), and *The Anatomy Lesson* (1983) to which he added an epilogue, "The Prague Orgy," to make up the trilogy *Zuckerman Bound* (1985), and the recent *The Counterlife* (1987). All of these works feature Nathan Zuckerman, Peter Tarnopol's avatar, as their protagonist, but Peter has dropped out of sight, and Nathan has become a successful writer whose age (like that of Portnoy, Tarnopol, and Kepesh) is always the same as Roth's own. In returning to Nathan, Roth enlarges the focus of his concern, compounding the trials of Jewish son-ship and its attendant anxieties with regard to fathers and masculinity, with the difficulties of the figurative son-ship of the writer in relation to all of the fathers from whom he seeks approval for his work. When, in *Zuckerman Unbound*, Nathan's father finally dies, it raises rather than resolves the fundamental issues of son-ship:

> Is a Zuckerman without bounds or bonds finally done with the dependencies
> of tortured sonhood and ready to fully enter his Life as a Man at last—or a
> forlorn orphan alone in the dark? . . .[12]

Zuckerman himself doesn't seem to know, but his reappearance in *The Counterlife*, Roth's latest, and perhaps densest, meditation on his protagonist's dilemmas once again scrutinizes the relationship between Jewishness and masculinity.

In *The Counterlife*, Nathan must confront that scourge of midlife masculinity, impotence caused by medicine he must take for his overworked heart. At first he cannot do it, and projects his whole dilemma onto his brother Henry, who he has confide in him: should the staid dentist Henry give up his pleasure, recreational sex with his dental assistant, or submit to surgery which could alleviate his heart problem, thus restoring his potency at the risk of death? Henry undergoes surgery, and dies . . . Or does he? Perhaps, the next of the novel's four sections suggests, the cure for impotence in New Jersey is a "rebirth," or counterlife of renewed masculine and Jewish strength and vigor in Israel, where "the powerless, the scattered, the impotent Jews of the Diaspora are restored to potency by nationhood."[13] But projecting this solution onto Henry reveals Nathan's skepticism, and when he follows Henry to Israel five months later, he is unable to produce arguments either to persuade Henry to return to his family in New Jersey, or, on the other hand, to convince himself that Henry (or Mordecai Lippman, the novel's most vocal Zionist, or any of its other Jewish/Israeli fundamentalists) have the stronger side of the argument. Once Nathan leaves Israel, without Henry, the novel again shifts gears, and it is Nathan who must choose between impotence, or marriage to Maria and the possibility of fatherhood at the risk of death from heart surgery. Nathan chooses surgery, and dies, but in the manuscript Henry discovers in this apartment, Nathan survives, marries Maria, they move to England, and she becomes pregnant.

But Nathan cannot let well enough alone. Seemingly happy and centered, much the way David Kepesh is with Clair Ovington, he begins, while renovating his dream-house on the Thames, to find signs of English anti-Semitism in his wife's family, in the English upper crust, finally, in his wife herself, and in so doing, seems willfully to destroy at least one of his own chances at a counterlife, the counterlife of beauty and peace and pastoral simplicity with Maria. Instead, he chooses not choosing, preferring the rich limbo of polarized potentialities which has haunted Roth's potent/impotent Jewish "sons" all along:

> The burden isn't either/or, consciously choosing from possiblities equally difficult and regrettable—it's and/and/and/and/and as well. Life *is* and: the accidental and the immutable, the elusive and the graspable, the actual and the potential, all the multiplying realities, entangled, overlapping, colliding, conjoined—plus the multiplying illusions! This times this times this times this . . .[14]

At the end of his thirteenth novel Roth can finally say it: despite their agonies of self-doubt and self-laceration, despite their angst and their regrets, his protagonists are right where they want to be: in the thick of it, with all life's rich potentialities and counterlives still before them. If this sounds like perpetual son-ship, it is what the nexus of Jewishness and masculinity offers. "Alienated both from claustrophobic Jewishness and vertiginous Americanness,"[15] Roth's protagonists must "reinvent" their masculinity, and by extension, themselves, in the face of the inadequacies of both Jewish and American models, appropriating and projecting counterlives as best they can.

Notes

1.   Toril Moi, *Sexual/Textual Politics* (London and New York: Methuen 1986), p. 65.
2.   George Marcus and James E. Clifford, eds., "Ethnicity and the Postmodern Arts of Memory", in *Writing Culture* (Berkeley: University of California Press, 1986), p. 195.
3.   Sanford Pinsker, ed., "Philip Roth," in *Critical Essays on Philip Roth* (Boston: G.K. Hall, 1982), p. 123.
4.   Philip Roth, *Reading Myself and Others* (New York and London: Penguin Books, 1985), pp. 161-162. Further references to this edition will be included in the text.
5.   Pinsker, *Critical Essays on Philip Roth*, p. 106.
6.   Philip Roth, *The Professor of Desire* (New York: Bantam Books, 1978), p. 14. Further references to this edition will be included in the text.
7.   Philip Roth, *Portnoy's Complaint* (New York: Bantam Books, 1970), P. 138. Further references to this edition will be included in the text.
8.   Maurice Charney, *Sexual Fiction* (London and New York: Methuen, 1981), p. 124.
9.   Philip Roth, *My Life As A Man* (New York: Bantam Books, 1975), unnumbered page. Further references to this edition will be included in the text.
10.   Quoted in Judition Paterson Jones and Guinevra A. Nance, *Philip Roth* (New York: Frederick Ungar Publishing Company, 1981), p. 7.
11.   See Barbara Koenig Quart, "The Rapacity of One Nearly Buried Alive," *Massachusetts Review*, vol. 24, no. 3 (1983), for an elaboration of this characterization of Baumgarten.
12.   Quart, "The Rapacity of One Nearly Buried Alive," p. 606.
13.   Julian Barnes, "Philip Roth in Israel," *London Review of Books*, vol. 9, no. 5, 5 March 1987, p. 3.
14.   Philip Roth, *The Counterlife* (New York: Farrar, Strauss, and Giroux, 1986), p. 306.
15.   Hermione Lee, *Philip Roth*, Contemporary Writers Series (London and New York: Methuen, 1982), p. 45.

A Young Rabbi

Joshua J. Hammerman

I am 28 years old and a rabbi. Had I chosen to be a gymnast or tennis player, I would be considered past my prime. As a lawyer or computer engineer, I would be reaching the peak of yuppiedom. In my own eyes, I fret at how quickly the years pass while I helplessly watch my youthful vigor recede.

And yet, when I walk into my office each morning, I feel like a 17-year-old walking into a bar, fearful that some hulk of a bouncer will appear to check me for ID. I am a child in a profession where life begins at 60.

Being a rabbi at any age inhibits normal social intercourse, being a *young* rabbi compounds the problem acutely. I am an anomaly in a community where rabbis are expected to have gray beards and the all-knowing countenance of one who is nearing the end of life's tumultuous journeys.

I know that I am not alone; in many fields it is not easy to be young. In the two years since my ordination, I have left many a hospital room wondering whether the patients give their young doctors the same incredulous looks they often give me. A 30-year-old dentist tells me of the difficulties of starting a practice—he wonders whether people will be willing to entrust their sacred smiles to one so young. Another friend, a psychologist, labors to establish his professional reputation. I feel for him, as well as for all the young men who strain to reach the next rung on the corporate ladder, only to be quashed by someone older. I feel for those who fritter away a half-dozen precious years of youth at prestigious law firms, only to find that no partnership awaits them.

And yet my own position is particularly awkward. The awkwardness goes beyond the fact that I address doctors and judges by their first names while they call me by my title even when they are four decades my senior. It reaches beyond the fact that I commonly marry couples much older than I or that some of the more grandmotherly types I come across like to pinch my cheek. Wherever I go, age is an issue, for not only am I cursed by being young, I am cursed by looking young. When Ecclesiastes said, "Rejoice, O young man, in thy youth," he was not speaking to a convention of young rabbis.

I can understand why many of my rabbinical colleagues and classmates choose to pursue other advanced degrees before entering the pulpit, while others prefer to spend years of tutelage under the wings of established rabbis in suburbia. There are some who, like me, stand alone, unprotected and uneasy; but most are located somewhere out on the prairie, planting Jewish roots in places where most of the natives have never seen a rabbi before. But here I am, in a pulpit just a hop from New York, where people know what a good bagel—and a good rabbi—should look like.

If I seem overly energetic to my congregation, the quality is attributed to my age. My rather too apparent self-respect is something, they say, that will diminish "when I know better." Occasionally I am seen as being manipulated by one congregant or another; I am said to be easy prey because of my lack of experience. At a recent wedding, the father of the bride told me that I look more like a bookie than a rabbi. I made light of it (neither job, I said to him, is suitable for a nice Jewish boy), but I was sensitive to the anxiety underlying his remark. He was giving his daughter away, and the man who was going to put the stamp of God on the whole enterprise could just as easily be standing next to her— except that he's much younger.

My congregants ask themselves: How can this rabbi be mature enough to comfort mourners when he hasn't known a lifetime of personal grief? How can he advise parents about their children, when he hasn't yet reared children of his own? How can he counsel troubled couples, when he hasn't been married long enough to experience marital strife? How can he represent us before God when he hasn't been through our suffering, when he hasn't seen what we've seen? Can a rabbi who is not battle-scarred be truly a rabbi?

These anxieties have eased as the congregation has gotten to know me. But I'm not sure the congregants know that, if anything, I fear the consequences of too much experience. When I perform weddings, I want to sense the exhilaration I felt at my own. When I visit the sick or console the bereaved, I want to approach them, not as a trained professional, but as one who is in some way personally affected by their plight. I prepare for each funeral as if it were my first, for it was at my first that I was best able to share in the sense of raw, unadulterated grief that consumed the family.

It is sad that so many Jewish communities seem to insist that their rabbis shed their youthful innocence as quickly as possible, not understanding that, once the innocence is lost, the childlike sense of wonder and basic human empathy so essential to the job are also left behind. Once the rabbi loses his exuberance, even the most vibrant of communities becomes threatened with a similar stagnation. Perhaps early career burnout would be less of a problem among rabbis—and other professionals—if they didn't feel compelled to spend the first half of their careers trying to look older and the last half striving to regain the vitality of lost youth.

Still, my congregation has been very good to me, and I can only be grateful that they had the courage to employ me. They understand that I occasionally like to wear jeans and that I prefer Lionel Richie to Benny Goodman. And they are beginning to understand much more.

Many of them perceive that I am a rabbi precisely because I want to break down barriers such as the one I face, stereotypes that poison human relationships. As I see it, I am a spiritual leader simply because I want to refine my own spirit, to stretch myself, using the texts of my tradition for guidance, and, in doing so, possibly to inspire others to do the same.

If I remain a rabbi long enough, perhaps I will see the stereotypes crumble, and maybe someday there will be no barriers to honest, unprejudiced human contact in my little corner of the world. Perhaps. But by then I will be collecting Social Security, soaking up all the honor that comes with turning gray and casting nervous glances at the young, idealistic whipper-snapper of a rabbi skipping up the road.

II.
FATHERS AND SONS: FROM GENERATION TO GENERATION

Chaim Waxman's "The Jewish Father: Past and Present" presents a historical survey of Jewish fathers' roles, from the Rabbinic-Talmudic period through the Middle Ages and the Shtetl to the United States in the twentieth century and contemporary Israel and the Kibbutz, discussing both normative ideals and actual patterns of child rearing.

Gary Greenebaum, in "Learning Talmud from Dad, Though Dad Knew No Talmud" and Max Rivers, in "Growing Up Jewish and Male," offer brief vignettes of their early memories of being with their fathers. They reveal the tensions between the word and the deed in the transmission of the heritage of Jewish masculinity and describe how old memories take on new meanings when seen in a different light.

In "How to Deal with a Jewish Issue: Circumcision" Zalman Schachter-Shalomi shares his wrestling with the conflicts between the demand of the tradition that he inflict what will clearly be a painful experience on his newborn son, and his own personal fatherly feelings of horror at such an act. By the end of his multi-faceted meditations, his decision comes to seem inevitable.

Building on his experiences in counseling infertile couples, Michael Gold distinguishes two different and occasionally contradictory strands of thought within Jewish law and tradition for defining a father, what he comes to call the biological and the pedagogical perspectives. "The Real Jewish Father" offers several arguments that greater importance should be given to the ideal of the father as teacher and moral guide, rather than as mere biological sire.

Through an examination of certain literary texts, Robert Waxler, in "The Impotent Father: Roth and Peretz," argues that much of men's struggles with modernity can be understood as an attempt to find a moral substitute for the vanished patriarchal power of the father. In this dilemma lies much of the irony of the Jewish joke.

Doug Lipman's translation of Morris Rosenfeld's song "Mayn Yingele," literally "My Little Son," written in 1887, once again makes available to a wider audience a piece of Yiddish culture very popular around the turn of the century. One hears the echoes of a man's footsteps trudging home from the sweat shops of New York's lower east side to stand by his son's bed.

The Jewish Father: Past and Present

Chaim I. Waxman

INTRODUCTION

In Jewish history and tradition, the family is considered to be the most important institution for shaping ethnic and religious identity and transmitting Judaism's basic norms and values.[1] Indeed, the family and the synagogue are the only two institutions referred to in traditional Jewish literature as *mikdash me'at*, or "sanctuary in miniature," sharing the responsibility for handing down both Jewish law and Jewish values. The family has been the setting, if not the focal point, for much of Jewish religious tradition. And, in the view of many present-day observers, it is the institution primarily responsible for Jewish continuity.

In light of this emphasis, it is interesting to explore the role of the Jewish father in the Jewish tradition and the historical experience of Jews in different societies and cultures, and to see what elements in that role are particularly pertinent to contemporary Jewish life.

In every society, individuals have a number of different roles—they are male or female, parents, sons or daughters, husbands or wives, and so on. And role carries with it certain defined behavioral expectations that apply to all incumbents, and are internalized, through socialization, by everyone who belongs to the society.

Since roles are socially defined, they often vary from society to society and are subject to change within a particular society over time. Furthermore, in the process of social change, some roles may become less clearly defined than before, leaving the incumbents of such roles uncertain about how they are supposed to behave. If such conditions become widespread, the resulting anomie, or normlessness, can threaten the stability of the society as a whole. Such widespread anomie is, fortunately, very rare; but some uncertainty about roles is fairly typical during periods of rapid social change, and it is helpful, during such periods, to review society's traditional patterns and expectations.

Modern society has experienced a great deal of rapid social change, not only in the United States and the geographical West, but throughout the world. The role of women, particularly, has undergone dramatic change that bears heavily on marital and family relationships. Given the preeminence of the family in Jewish continuity, it is important to know how these changes affect not only the Jewish family in general, but each of its component parts. These pages will concentrate on both the traditional and the changing role of the Jewish father.

We begin by examining the role of the father in traditional Jewish literature—by reviewing how Jewish law and ethics define his duties, responsibilities, rights and privileges. It should be remembered, however, that real-life experience does not necessarily conform to the ideal set down in the normative literature. On the contrary, our knowledge of human behavior tells us that it is highly doubtful that actual performance ever lived up to these high standards. Nevertheless, it is reasonable to assume that in a highly traditional society, the general patterns of behavior reflect normative definitions, even if few individuals actually manage to live up to the ideal.

THE RABBINIC-TALMUDIC PERIOD

The Talmud is quite brief in its delineation of the duties and responsibilities of the father. One small passage in the tractate *Kiddushin* declares:

> The father is required to circumcise his son; to redeem him [referring to the first-born son, as per the Biblical passages in *Numbers* 18:15-16]; to teach him *Torah*; to assure that he marries; and to teach him a trade. Some say he must also teach him to swim. Rabbi Judah says, whoever does not teach his son a trade teaches him robbery (Babylonian Talmud, Tractate *Kiddushin*, p. 29a).

Rashi (Rabbi Solomon ben Isaac, 1040-1105), the famous commentator on the Bible and the Talmud, explains that Rabbi Judah meant that a father who does not teach his son a trade is as culpable as if he had taught him to steal, since without a trade, the son cannot earn money to buy food and must inevitably turn to robbery.

Reflecting the clear divisions between sex roles in traditional Judaism, the Talmud briefly notes that the father is required to clothe his daughter and provide her with all she needs in order to get married. Within Biblical and Rabbinic Judaism, study and trade and the public sphere were male provinces, while the female province was the home. According to several traditionalist Torah scholars today, the changes in modern society and culture make it not only permissible but imperative that women be as learned in Torah as men.[2] In that light, it is interesting to speculate whether the father is now obligated to teach torah to his daughter as well as to his son.

As indicated earlier, it cannot be automatically assumed that all, or most, Jewish fathers in the Talmudic period conformed with the normative prescriptions set down by the rabbis. On the other hand, there is a revealing passage in Tractate *Bava Batra*, which indicates that there were indeed some periods when fathers were the sole teachers of their sons:

> Rabbi Judah said in the name of Rav: Verily the name of that man is to be blessed, that is Joshua ben Gamla. Were it not for him the Torah would have been forgotten from Israel (Babylonian Talmud, *Bava Batra* 21a).

Apparently, there were times when the children's education was completely and solely the obligation of fathers, and Rabbi Joshua ben Gamla founded a school in order to provide for the education of fatherless orphans. In so doing, he did not free fathers from teaching their sons; he simply established the principle that the community was responsible for boys who had no fathers to teach them.

Except for obligations of fathers mentioned in the passage from *Kiddushin*, the primary focus of rabbinic discussions regarding the role of the father is more on the obligations and responsibilities of children toward their parents—obligations, first enunciated as the Fifth Commandment, repeated several times in the Bible, elaborated upon in many places in the Talmud, and the subject of lengthy discussions in rabbinic codifications and responsa literature throughout the centuries.[3]

When we turn our attention from the role of the father in traditional Jewish literature to his role in historic Jewish experience, we soon discover that very few of a growing number of studies dealing with historic Jewish communities include discussions of family life. The majority are concerned with the development and organizational structure of the communities studied, and their relations with other Jewish and non-Jewish communities. It is interesting to note that where discussions of family do occur, they are most likely to deal with the status of women in the community, leaving the status of men to be deduced from the more general discussions.[4]

It seems farfetched to suppose that the reason there have been so few historical analyses of the father's role in family life is that it was insignificant. The more likely explanation is that his significance was taken for granted, both by the strongly patriarchal communities themselves, and by the researchers studying them. This gap in our knowledge is not unique to Jewish communities; in fact, very little is known about the father role in general history. As John Nash points out, one reason why it is not easy to deduce the nature of child rearing in earlier times is that before the eighteenth century hardly anyone thought there was any reason to single out children as a special group of people.

"Even the extensive history of children by Aries gave few data on patterns of fathering (and little about mothering). It is more a social history of children as part of the economic system than a history of childrearing."[5]

As a result, we are forced to confine our analysis to two groups of historic Jewish communities—those in Arab countries during the Middle Ages, and those in the *shtetl*, the small town and village in Eastern Europe during the late nineteenth and early twentieth centuries. Only when we reach the twentieth century do we find more sources for analysis of the father's role in various Jewish cultures and subcultures.

THE MIDDLE AGES

The most complete and systematic historical study of the Jewish family is Shlomo Dov Goitein's multi-volume work, *A Mediterranean Society*.[6] Based upon documents in the Cairo *Genizah*, the large repository of discarded writings discovered in Egypt in the late 1800s, this work meticulously analyzes the Jewish communities in Islamic countries during the period known as the "High Middle Ages."[7] In contrast to many historical studies that rely almost exclusively on materials about the elite segments of the society, this one is based on documents that also reflect the middle and lower strata.

In the High Middle Ages, being a Jewish father, and especially having sons, "formed a prominent, central and, so to say, public component in a man's life to a far higher degree than is customary in our own society."[8] Reasons for having children were many: religious and moral, utilitarian, and egoistic. Marshall Sklare has referred to "*nachas fun kinder*," or joy from children, as a feature that distinguishes Jewish parents from other American parents.[9] Self-fulfillment through children, as expressed in the stereotypical American Jewish reference to "my son the doctor," was even more characteristic of the medieval Jewish communities of the Arab countries. A father would quite typically speak of "my son, the joy of my eye," and "the dearest to me of all mankind." Sons, both small and adult, were frequently referred to by their fathers as "the lovely flower," "the blossoming rose" and "muhja" ("lifeblood"). And "the most common word of endearment for son is *hamud*, 'delight,' so common that the Hebrew letter *h* stands, in memorial and other lists, simply for 'son of.'"[10]

A letter from a Tunisian Jew congratulating his brother in Egypt on the birth of his child underscores the central importance of having sons:

> Your letter containing the great news and joyful tidings about the blessed, blissful, and auspicious newborn has arrived. We had here much joy, music,

and congratulations gatherings because of this ... Yes, my brother, you are to
be congratulated, and very much so. May God bestow on me that both you
and he will live and may God make him a brother of "seven or even eight."
May God strengthen your arm through him and establish by him your
honored position and fulfull in your case: "Instead of your fathers there shall
be your sons, you will make them princes all over the country." May God
avert from you and from him the effects of the evil eye and may He never let
me hear anything undesirable about the two of you all my life.[11]

The birth of a daughter in these Middle Eastern communities was not
as auspicious an event as the birth of a son; nevertheless, it would be wrong to
assume that it was not a happy event. The *Genizah* documents indicate that
fathers loved their daughters deeply, and some actually preferred them to their
sons, possibly because it was acceptable to openly express affection for
them.

In keeping with the Talmudic mandate, fathers played the central role
in their sons' Jewish education and occupational training. Moreover, although
the letter of the law released them from this obligation when boys reached
puberty (Babylonian Talmud, *Ketubot* 49b), the *Genizah* documents reveal
that, in practice, fathers continued to educate their sons well into their
adolescence.

THE SHTETL

During the nineteenth century, the world of East European Jewry was
the *shtetl*, a community which, as Irving Howe points out, was not quite so
warm, loving and joyful as the one nostalgically portrayed in *Fiddler on the
Roof*.[12] Nor did it have the permanence implied in the anthropological study,
Life Is With People.[13] By the beginning of the twentieth century, the *shtetl* was
"a community in the process of disintegration, though the exact degree of
disintegration varied from region to region, from community to community,
and from group to group."[14] The majority of Jews in Eastern Europe lived in
cities.[15] Nevertheless, most East European Jews who immigrated to the United
States between 1880 and 1920, and especially those who emigrated before
1910, did come from *shtetlach*; and it is therefore valid to speak of a *shtetl*
culture with a shared religion, language, values, norms, institutional structure,
and sense of belonging.

Shtetl Jews fully internalized the biblical dictum that "It is not good for
man to be alone," and the injunction to "be fruitful and multiply." Marriage,
children and family life were among the most important values and institutions,
and it was the sacred responsibility of parents *tzu makhen fun kinder
mentshen*, to turn children into people.[16] By *mentshen*, they meant obedient,

respectful, and refined human beings—*sheyneh yidn*, fine Jews, who would bring honor to their parents. A child's responsibilities toward his or her parents lasted throughout their lives, and the obligation to care for elderly parents prevailed even when, as was often the case, they were reluctant to accept such care.

Marriage was not a matter of individual choice; it was carefully arranged by the parents, often through the intermediary services of the *shadkhen*, or matchmaker. Although it was assumed that "parents always want the best for their children" and children usually went along with a match, the now prevalent notion that the children had no say in the choice of their spouse and were often forced into marriages against their will is not quite accurate.[17] Since traditional Jewish religious law does not recognize a marriage as valid unless both the bride and groom agree to it, Zborowski and Herzog's observation that "those who object . . . succeed in winning their point," is undoubtedly correct.[18]

Sex roles, in general, and husband/father-wife/mother roles in particular, were clearly delineated in *shtetl* culture. The husband's major responsibility involved learning, economic pursuits or, more often, both. While it was true that many men devoted themselves entirely to sacred learning while their wives assumed economic responsibility for the family, this was not true for all, or even most, husbands and wives. Most husbands were either full- or part-time breadwinners, and women who were the sole providers were the exception, though many worked alongside their husbands out of economic necessity, and some worked so that their husbands could spend at least part of each day in sacred learning.

To his son, the *shtetl* father was a remote authoritarian figure and a rather formal teacher, but he was likely to be easygoing, emotional and indulgent toward his daughter, in whose life the mother played the more authoritarian role.

However, while the *shtetl* family was formally patriarchal, it differed sharply from the traditional non-Jewish European family in which patriarchy included the explicit subordination of wives and mothers. In the day-to-day activity of the Jewish home, the mother clearly played the major role, though she often held the father up to the children as the court of last resort. It was the mother who provided the children with affection. "The stereotype of the 'Yiddisheh mammeh,' familiar in many lands, has firm roots in the *shtetl*. No matter what you do, no matter what happens, she will love you always. She may have odd and sometimes irritating ways of showing it, but in a hazardous and unstable world the belief about the mother's love is strong and unshakable."[19] The father, by contrast was first and foremost the teacher; it is no coincidence that there has never been a parallel stereotype of the "Yiddisheh tatteh."

TWENTIETH-CENTURY UNITED STATES

Although there are no full-scale studies of American Jewish fathers, several limited studies include some enlightening examples. In analyzing the strongly patriarchal traditional Jewish communities, one might easily be led to believe that respect for the father is a function of religious tradition, that patriarchy and religious traditionalism go hand-in-hand. A study by Judson Landis indicates otherwise.[20]

Landis's study of Protestant, Catholic and Jewish families revealed that there was, in fact, a greater relationship between degree of religious observance and the closeness of sons and daughters to their fathers, than between such commitment and their closeness to their mothers. Apparently, the father's central role in establishing religious patterns was a factor in the respect accorded him.

At first glance, these data appear to support the assumption that respect for fathers is a function of religious traditionalism, and that a decline in one may be related to a decline in the other. Landis also found, however, that religiosity correlated positively with egalitarian parental roles, and that those families where either the father or the mother dominated were more likely to be characterized by religious indifference.

In this connection, an earlier study of Jewish and Italian boys in Boston is also instructive. In this study, Fred Strodbeck found that the value the boys placed on independence and achievement correlated positively with egalitarian parental roles.[21] Very dominating fathers, he found, were less likely than strong and assertive mothers to instill a desire for achievement in their sons. As Strodbeck sees it, this finding suggests an American adaptation of the Jewish father's traditional and historic role as the link between the family and the traditional Jewish community. As the Jewish community in America grew more secular, this role was reinterpreted, and it now manifests itself in the father's dedication to his work and to instilling the values of achievement in his children.

Whether or not one fully accepts Strodbeck's interpretation, the evidence concerning the socioeconomic achievement of American Jews[22] suggests that American Jewish fathers are, indeed, zealously dedicated to their work. Apparently, however, the price of this occupational striving has been a weakening of the father's role in the home. In the *shtetl* home, the father was always an authoritative presence, even if he was not there during most of the day. With the help of the mother, the children were constantly reminded of his importance and socialized to conform to the standards he set. They were taught that he was fulfilling the religious obligation of learning, and that they must honor his wishes that they internalize the norms and values of traditional Judaism. His economic work was seen as a means rather than as an end in itself; it supported the family and made it possible for them to maintain religio-cultural norms and values and be respectable members of the community.

CONTEMPORARY ISRAEL

The Jewish community in the United States is made up, for the most part, of third- or fourth-generation Americans, overwhelmingly of East European ancestry, and predominantly middle class.[23] Israeli Jewry is composed of two broad ethnic, or subethnic, groupings: the Sephardim, numerically the majority, whose ancestors came from Islamic countries; and the Ashkenazim, numerically a minority but socially and economically dominant, whose ancestors came from northern Europe and the Americas. Another significant subsociety, the kibbutz, is unique in its family patterns.

While it is generally asumed that there are many differences in the family patterns of Sephardim and Ashkenazim, there is little empirical evidence to substantiate this assumption. Virtually the only study of role differences in Israel's urban families was conducted by Rivka Bar Yosef, and it is based on limited samples from two ethnically and class-differentiated areas. The Ashkenazi sample was drawn from the middle-class neighborhood of Rehavia and the Sephardim sample from the lower-class area of Nahalaot, both in Jerusalem.[24] Bar Yosef's primary goal was to discover the patterns of authority in the respective family systems—how husband/father and wife/mother roles are ascribed, and the authority patterns of each. When it came to housekeeping, both groups demonstrated clear sex-role divisions. But in child rearing, there were both differences and similarities between the groups. For example, among both the Ashkenazim and Sephardim, the mother was seen as the dominant agent of primary socialization and the parent responsible for meeting the child's daily needs. However, distinct differences emerged on issues related to the children's education. When it came to choosing a school, 90 percent of the Rehavia parents made the decision jointly, whereas in Nahalaot only 50 percent did so (in the other 50 percent the decision was made by the mothers). Punishment was far more frequently the father's responsibility among the Sephardim of Nahalaot than among the Ashkenazi families of Rehavia, where it was likely to be meted out by mothers, or by both parents.

In sum, while Bar Yosef's study found some clear differences in roles between the two groups, three important facts must be kept in mind. First, the sample included only 85 families. Second, the subcultural and socioeconomic gaps between the two groups made it difficult to determine whether the differences were rooted in ethnicity or class. Finally, and most important, Bar Yosef's findings reveal fewer differences between the groups than overall similarities.

In another limited study, Shalva Weil interviewed a small number of Ashkenazi, Iraqi and Moroccan youngsters who were part of a larger sample of 168 children of various ethnic backgrounds, in order to see how their ethnic origins affected their perceptions of their families.[25] One finding was that in Moroccan families elder brothers seem to assume something of a father role in relation to younger siblings, whereas Ashkenazi elder brothers do not. Thus, in Moroccan families, the older brother often metes out punishment, and is therefore more feared than the Ashkenazi older brother. Conversely, Ashkenazi younger siblings are more likely than their Moroccan counterparts to turn to their older brothers rather than their parents when they have a problem.

Significantly, in their perceptions of family relationships, Ashkenazi children focused on their parents' trust in them and the attention they pay, especially to progress at school. The Moroccan children, on the other hand, emphasized family harmony especially among siblings, found their elder brothers to be unapproachable, and reported that they enjoyed the family Sabbath celebration and watching television together on weekday evenings.[26]

Among Israel's many ethnic Jewish groupings, the Yemenites, one of the oldest Diaspora communities, stand out for a variety of reasons.[27] Despite centuries of persecution, Yemenite Jews have remained staunchly traditional and religiously observant (except for a brief period around the turn of the eighteenth century), and the Holy Land has always played a central role in their religious and cultural life.[28].

In Yemenite Jewish families, the religious and cultural education of the son within the home always was the responsibility of the father, whereas the mother, usually illiterate, tended to the boys' physical needs. The father was generally strict and harsh. Sons spent many hours of the day in their father's company, engaging in many religious rituals, including daily prayers in the synagogue, circumcisions, Bar Mitzvahs and weddings, visits to the homes of mourners, and so on.[29]

On the Sabbath and holidays, fathers would test their sons' learning, filling in where they felt it was deficient. Since most formal education during the week was by rote, fathers would use the relaxed atmosphere of the Sabbath and holidays to explain and elaborate upon what had been learned in school.[30] Thus, the father was, first and foremost, a teacher to his sons. (There are virtually no references to any relationships between fathers and their daughters.)

THE KIBBUTZ

Although only a small proportion of Israelis live on kibbutzim, they enjoy a respected position in Israeli ideology, and their unique lifestyle has generated worldwide interest. Thus, the kibbutz is a magnet for social scientists the world over, and is probably the most studied social phenomenon in Israel. It should be borne in mind that kibbutz life is quite uncharacteristic of Jewish community life elsewhere, both historically and today.

On the other hand, something may be learned from an analysis of how the father role has developed in the kibbutz setting precisely because, in its early stages, the kibbutz was opposed to the nuclear family. This position stemmed from both the ideology of social revolution and collectivism that spawned the kibbutz, and the social purpose it was designed to serve. Implicit in the ideologies of the various kibbutz movements was a deep commitment to equality between the sexes.[31] Because the traditional family was seen as fostering and perpetuating sexual inequality, the collective took over many of the roles ascribed to parents, including the day-to-day care of children, virtually from the moment of their birth, as well as their education and socialization.

Unlike other children, for whom parental influence is dominant, at least when they are small, kibbutz children grow up with "an incredibly strong attachment to . . . peer group," to the point of "their willingness to give their lives for the boys and girls they grew up with. This is their deepest, most abiding attachment and the focus of powerful feelings about emotional events they have shared with their group."[32] In earlier years, the kibbutz strove not only to relieve parents of the more tedious aspects of family life, including child-rearing, but to eliminate, as much as possible, the institution of the family. Indeed, children normally address their parents by their given names rather than referring to them as "abba" (father) and "imma" (mother).

In recent years, however, traditional family patterns and sex roles have reemerged on the kibbutz.[33] Even traditional celebrations with extended kin groups are now quite common.[34] And even before young kibbutz children returned to sleeping in their parents' quarters instead of in children's houses, there was evidence of strong emotional and affectual ties between parents and their children. Describing in colorful detail the characteristics of child care in the kibbutz, the late Yonina Talmon-Garber indicated that this was because the main disciplinary aspects of child rearing is the task of the *metaplot*, kibbutz functionaries who care for children's daily needs rather than the parents:

> The petty quarrels and persistent disagreements which often pester parent-child relationships in other types of families are quite rare here. Parents endeavor to make the few hours their children spend with them as pleasant

and carefree as possible . . . Their main function is to minister to their childen's need for security and love. Both of them interact with their children in much the same way and play a common protective role. Fathers usually take a lively interest in their children and participate actively in looking after them. Mothers have closer contacts with babies and small children but fathers come into the picture very early. Sex of the children has no marked effect either.[35]

Although there is far less difference between father and mother roles in the kibbutz than elsewhere, some differences do exist even there. The mother is much closer to the children and their schools and is more likely to guide their cleanliness and health and, when parental discipline is applied, the mother more frequently takes the lead.

The father is less involved in these problems and the child may find him an ally in cases of exaggerated concern with them on the part of the mother . . . In the eyes of the growing child, the father emerges gradually as the representative of the Kibbutz and its values within the family, while the mother acts primarily as the representative of the family in the Kibbutz.[36]

In a comprehensive study of socialization practices, encompassing interviews with 300 preadolescents from kibbutzim and 300 from Tel Aviv, Edward Devereux and his colleagues found that city parents were more involved than those of the kibbutz in all aspects of discipline especially in meting out such punishments as temporary withdrawal of companionship or threats of physical punishment when children misbehave. But kibbutz parents were no less generous than city parents when it came to general supportive behavior; in fact, they were significantly more involved with helping children with their homework, for example. Devereux and his colleagues concluded that "the overall balance of the parent role in the kibbutz thus tends to be more positive and supportive."[37] But neither their data nor analysis dealt with comparative father roles and mother roles.

CONCLUSIONS

Depending on historical and cultural experience, there have been and are many variations in the roles of Jewish fathers, but we cannot assume that their role was or is radically different from that of non-Jewish fathers. Nevertheless, one fact does stand out. Until very recently, the Jewish father was expected to, and did, play a distinctive role as the educator of his sons. This duty, moreover, was fulfilled not merely by financing their formal education; he was also expected to socialize his children into the life of the Jewish community, and to represent its values and interests within the home. This educational component of the father's role appears to have been uniquely stressed in Jewish tradition and culture, and indeed was deemed essential to the religious and cultural survival of the Jewish people.

Perhaps the most concentrated manifestation of this role of the Jewish father is seen in the *Seder* ceremony, the most celebrated of all Jewish rituals among American Jews. More than any other holiday, Passover, and especially the *Seder*, is a family celebration. Everyone is expected to participate actively, and each role is clearly delineated in the *Haggadah*, a microcosm of the roles within the family throughout the year. The father is simultaneously the king, the leader of the service and, above all, the teacher. He transmits knowledge whether asked for it or not, as evidenced in recital of the portion of the *Haggadah* about "the four sons." He also teaches by example, and his children look to him to guide their behavior all through the *Seder*.

The Israeli philosopher, Eliezer Schweid, has succinctly summarized the family aspects of the Passover celebration:

> The family is the major theme of the holiday. It is realized through the family. And throughout, the holiday sustains the family because it makes real in an ideal fashion the unity of the family. Each family member has a role which indicates his place (status) within the family, and the family perceives itself as a unit when it fulfills a religious obligation (*mitzvah*) that transcends it. The family bond becomes, thus, a religious bond, and the religious bond a family bond.[38]

But, as Schweid points out, all holidays provide the family a way to express and realize the relationships among its members, thus binding them together and connecting them to the larger community and people.[39]

However, for most of world Jewry today, much of this dynamic no longer exists. There has been a major transformation in the structure of the Jewish community. In the past, the synagogue was the central institution of the organized Jewish community and there was an integral bond between the family and the synagogue. Since World War I, however, a dramatic secularization has transformed the synagogue into just one component among many in the Jewish community.

Formal Jewish education has also fallen to a record low, while secular education among Jews is higher than among any other group of Americans.[40] With Jewish fathers moving increasingly into the professions, and the Jewish community becoming increasingly secular, the historically unique role of the Jewish father has disappeared and Jewish fathers have become like other middle-class American fathers.[41]

It would appear that the prospects for reviving the unique role of the Jewish father range from dismal to nil.[42] However, a number of relatively recent developments and policy proposals regarding the Jewish family may have some bearing on these prospects. Ironically, the most significant of these developments is the change in the role of women. As Sheila Kamerman points out, the massive entry into the labor force of married women with young children is one of the most significant social phenomena in this century.[43] Women work today for the same reasons men do; that is, mostly to earn a living, and to achieve personal satisfaction. Thus, Kamerman argues, there is an urgent need to restructure the relationship between work and family life. While Kamerman emphasizes the impact on women, I would stress the positive impact of such a restructuring on men.

If, however, the traditional relationship between work and family life is restructured, a restructuring of the traditional sources of identity and status may ensue. There is increasing evidence that the traditional division of men's and women's domains has been unsatisfactory to many men as well as many women. Joint efforts to develop public and private policies, programs and services to strengthen family and community may yet provide the possibility for men to move beyond the occupational realm for their sense of identity and self-worth, as women move beyond the limits of the home to broaden theirs.[44] As American men, in general, reconnect with home and family, Jewish men may have the chance to retrieve their roles as Jewish educators for their children.

To the obvious question, "Where does one begin?" the answer is, "By doing something." Jewish fathers can begin by studying, in adult education groups and/or along with their children; by setting aside the Sabbath and holidays as meaningful Jewish family celebrations used to explore Jewish traditions within the family setting; by engaging, with their children, in Jewish community activities—in short, by thoughtfully sharing Jewish experiences with their children.

Notes

1. See Chaim I. Waxman, *America's Jews in Transition* (Philadelphia: Temple University Press, 1983), pp. 180-83.
2. Cf. Saul Berman, "The Status of Women in Halakhic Judaism," *Tradition*, vol. 14, no. 1 (Fall 1973), pp. 5-28; Chana K. Poupko and Devora L. Wohlgelerenter, "Women's Liberation—An Orthodox Response," *ibid.*, vol. 15, no. 4 (Spring 1976), pp. 45-52; and Warren Zev Harvey, "The Obligation of Talmud on Women According to Maimonides," *ibid.*, vol. 19, no. 2 (Summer 1981), pp. 122-30.
3. For a sophisticated and systematic analysis, see Gerald Blidstein, *Honor Thy Father and Mother: Filial Responsibility in Jewish Law and Ethics* (New York: Ktav Publishing House, 1975).
4. Cf. H. Z. (J. W.) Hirschberg, *A History of the Jews in North Africa,* vol. I (Leiden: E. J. Brill, 1974), pp. 183-90.
5. John Nash, "Historical and Social Changes in the Perception of the Role of the Father," in

Michael E. Lamb, ed., *The Role of the Father in Child Development* (New York: Wiley, 1976), pp. 68-69.

6. S.D. Goitein, *A Mediterranean Society*, vol. 3: *The Family* (Berkeley: University of California Press, 1978).

7. Idem, *A Mediterranean Society*, vol. 1: *Economic Foundations* (Berkeley: University of California Press, 1967). Introduction.

8. Goitein, *op. cit.*, p. 224.

9. Marshall Sklare, *America's Jews* (New York: Random House, 1971), p. 87.

10. Goitein, *op. cit.*, p. 225.

11. *Ibid.*, p. 226.

12. Irving Howe, *World of Our Fathers* (New York: Harcourt Brace Jovanovich, 1976), p. 10.

13. Mark Zborowski and Elizabeth Herzog, *Life Is With People: The Culture of the Shtetl* (New York: International Universities Press, 1952).

14. Bernard D. Weinryb, "Jewish Immigration and Accommodation to America," in Marshall Sklare, ed., *The Jews: Social Patterns of an American Group* (New York: Free Press, 1958), p. 15.

15. Arthur Ruppin, *The Jews of the Modern World* (1934) (New York: Arno Press, 1973), pp. 32-36.

16. Zborowski and Herzog, *op. cit.*, pp. 335-38.

17. *Ibid.*, p. 275.

18. *Ibid.*

19. *Ibid.*, p. 293.

20. Judson T. Landis, "Religiousness, Family Relationships and Family Values in Protestant, Catholic and Jewish Families," *Marriage and Family Living*, vol. 22 (1960), pp. 341-47.

21. Fred L. Strodbeck, "Family Integration, Values and Achievement," in A.H. Halsey, Jean Floud and C. Arnold Anderson, eds., *Education, Economy and Society: A Reader in the Sociology of Education* (New York: Free Press, 1961).

22. Waxman, *op. cit.*, chap. 6.

23. *Ibid.*

24. Rivka Weiss-Bar Yosef, "Role Differentiation in Urban Israeli Families," in Rivka Bar Yosef and Ilana Shelach, eds., *The Family in Israel* (Jerusalem: Akademon, 1969) (Hebrew).

25. Shalva Weil, "The Effect of Ethnic Origin on Children's Perceptions of Their Families" (Jerusalem: The Hebrew University, Department of Sociology and Social Anthropology, 1982) (unpublished faculty paper).

26. *Ibid.*, pp. 8-11.

27. See Yehuda Nini, *Yemen and Zion: The Jews of Yemen, 1800-1914* (Jerusalem: Hasifriyah Haziyonit [W.Z.O.], 1982).

28. The first of several waves of *aliyah* (immigration to the Holy Land) occurred in 1882. The most famous of these *aliyot* was the last, known as "Operation Magic Carpet," which carried the entire Yemenite Jewish population to Israel soon after the establishment of the Jewish State. See Itzhak Ben Zvi, *The Exiled and the Redeemed* (Philadelphia: The Jewish Publication Society of America, 1961), chap.4.

29. Yehuda Ratzaby, *The Yemenite Jews* (Tel Aviv: Israel Defence Forces, Department of Education, 1978), p. 36 (Hebrew).

30. *Ibid.*, p. 38.

31. Muki Zur, Tair Zevulun and Hanina Porat, *The Beginning of the Kibbutz* (Tel Aviv: Hakibbutz Hameuhad and Sifriyat Poalim, 1981) (Hebrew).

32. Bruno Bettelheim, *The Children of the Dream: Communal Childrearing and American Education* (New York: Macmillan, 1969), pp. 109, 256.

33. See Yonina Talmon-Garber, "The Family in a Revolutionary Movement: The Case of the

Kibbutz in Israel," *Studies of Israeli Society* (Israel Sociological Society), vol. 2: *The Sociology of the Kibbutz*, Ernest Krausz, ed. (New Brunswick, N.J.: Transaction Books, 1983); idem, *Family and Community in the Kibbutz* (Cambridge, Mass.: Harvard University Press, 1972); Menachem Gerson, *Family, Women and Socialization in the Kibbutz* (Lexington, Mass.: Lexington Books, 1978).

34.   Orit Ichilov and Shmuel Bar, "Extended Family Ties and the Allocation of Social Rewards in Veteran Kibbutzim in Israel," *Journal of Marriage and the Family*, vol. 42, no. 2 (May 1980), pp. 421-26. The reasons for this development have also been discussed and debated by Melford E. Spiro, *Gender and Culture: Kibbutz Women Revisited* (New York: Schocken Books, 1980): Lionel Tiger and Joseph Shepher, *Women in the Kibbutz* (New York: Harcourt Brace Jovanovich, 1975); Yaffa Schlesinger, "Sex Roles and Social Change in Kibbutz," *Journal of Marriage and the Family*, vol. 34, no. 4 (November 1977), pp. 771-79.

35.   Talmon-Garber, *op. cit.*, p. 269.

36.   *Ibid.*, pp. 269-70.

37.   Edward C. Devereux, Ron Shouval, Urie Bronfenbrenner, Robert R. Rodgers, Sophie Kav-Vanaki, Elizabeth Kiely and Ester Karson, "Socialization Practices of Parents, Teachers and Peers in Israel: The Kibbutz Versus the City," in Ernest Krausz, ed., *op. cit.*, p. 313.

38.   Eliezer Schweid, *Judaism and the Solitary Jew* (Tel Aviv: Am Oved, 1974), p. 43 (Hebrew).

39.   See Also Chaim I. Waxman, "The Sabbath as Dialectic: The Meaning and Role," *Judaism*, vol. 31, no. 1 (Winter 1982), pp. 37-44.

40.   Waxman, *America's Jews in Transition, op.cit.*, chap. 8.

41.   Cf. Lawrence H. Fuchs, *Family Matters* (New York: Random House, 1972), chap. 5, and *Fathers and Families: The Jewish Experience* (in press).

42.   Idem, "The Jewish Father for a Change," *Moment*, vol. 1, no. 3 (September 1975), p. 50.

43.   Sheila B. Kamerman, "For Jews and Other People: An Agenda For Research on Families and Family Policies," in Marshall Sklare, ed., *Understanding American Jewry* (New Brunswick, N.J.: Transaction Books, 1982), p. 149.

44.   Cf. Chaim I. Waxman, *The Stigma of Poverty: A Critique of Poverty Theories and Policies*, 2nd ed. (New York: Pergamon Press, 1983), chap. 5, 6.

Learning Talmud from Dad, Though Dad Knew No Talmud

Gary Greenebaum

Who are we as men? Who are we as Jews? As American Jewish men, we feel ambivalent about being American Jews. Perhaps most of all we feel conflict about being Jewish men. Our feelings are hard to sort out, difficult to understand. We are not sure who our role models ought to be. It is not clear to us what we want to be as American Jewish men.

The question "Who are we as men" makes sense only in the context of the 1980s, when men, challenged by the women's movement, have begun to rethink who we are and what we want. At last, we have become aware of our own longings as well as our own desires. It seems that some of us are only just now feeling our feelings, standing less behind intellectualized fabrications of who we are. We're stepping out of our homes and cars and offices to take a daylight look at what we *are* and not just what we *have*.

"Who we are as Jews" is a whole other question. Several men who attended the first San Francisco men's conference in 1985 said it was the first event sponsored by a mainstream Jewish organization they had attended in anywhere from five to fifteen years. One man said it was the first organized Jewish event he had attended since his Bar Mitzvah—well over half his life ago. Other men, who are involved in organized Jewish life, attended as the first event for them which dealt with issues of being men. However involved, or un-involved, or even alienated we may feel about Jewish life, our identities as Jews seem to continue to inform who we are as people and as men.

Who we are as Americans—as American Jewish men— adds another level of complexity to the mix. We were raised with the myth of the American male so strongly depicted for us that even when we know better, even when we can see its obvious drawbacks and limitations, we are strongly drawn to it, or at least some aspects of it.

When my brother and I were small, our father kissed us goodbye every morning when he left for work and kissed us hello every evening when he returned. If he took his leave of us in public, then he kissed us goodbye with the whole world looking on, and if we met somewhere, he kissed us then too. Sometimes it seemed a bother, but we indulged him. As we reached adolescence, we began to resist, and throughout our teen years, we refused to be kissed, first in public, then even in private.

He seemed to accept our decision cheerfully enough, and there seemed to even pass between us a sense that we all three knew that this isn't how men behave toward one another. In public, he would greet us with a hearty handshake. A safe substitute. Now, I kiss him in public. And give him a hug. And his body stiffens slightly, as though I am breaking some sort of sacred code between us. But I persist—in airports, at family gatherings, when he answers the door, and there I am. And when he stiffens, I want to shake him, and shout into his face—you taught me right the first time—we should hug and kiss, we want to and we need to. But he is the man who taught me what it means to be a man. He is the man who would tell me as he poured alcohol into my cut knees and elbows that babies cry, men don't. And when I would become so outraged, so angry at some injustice, or at how I had been wronged by the world if things weren't going my way, so frustrated that I was blithering, he would laugh and say, "You sound like Donald Duck." And when I started to grow up, he warned me, "You care too much. For other people. In the real world you will have to learn to watch out for yourself." And when it became clear that I was determined to become a rabbi, and not a businessman, it seemed, I'm sure, to him that my childish, dream-sense of how the world is and how the world ought to be was going to take precedence over a manly career—in business or in science. "All those years in school," he always says with a sigh and a shake of the head. "For all those years in school, you could have been a brain surgeon." And I always think, to myself, "A well-paid brain surgeon, you mean."

But I remember too, just after my mother died, that I was struck by how much my father knew about Jewish practices regarding death and burial. An assimilated Jew, such arcane practices seemed unlikely to be part of his Judaic knowledge. When pressed on why he knew so much, he admitted, as offhandedly as he could, that during all the years we lived in that small town in Iowa, whenever a Jew living out in the country, in some hamlet somewhere, would die, my father and several other Jewish men from our small city would travel to the little town, to insure that there was a minyan. He would travel a hundred, maybe two hundred miles, to pay respects to a man or woman he had never met.

And I remember, too, that whenever anyone we knew went into the hospital for surgery, it was always my father who went to the hospital to sit with the husband or wife or family during those excruciating hours when life hangs in the balance. He never asked if he was wanted, he only asked what time surgery was scheduled to begin.

How did I learn to care so much? For other people? Who taught me to watch out for others as well as myself? The same man who taught me not to cry. Who taught me basic Jewish values—taught them through his actions, for he did not know how to quote Talmud, and does not know what Midrash is. The same man who still cannot understand why I have become a rabbi.

My father taught me what he knew—about being a man, an American man, and about being a Jew. Sometimes garbled, sometimes contradictory, the messages sent to me by this most important man in my life left me with many spaces to fill in. But he taught me what he thought he was supposed to teach me, and he treated me as he had been taught to treat a son. If he had known Mishna, he would have taught me, "In a place where there are no men, strive to be a man." And he would have explained that being a man means being strong, resolute, knowing what is right, fearless. But his actions would have taught that being a man means being dependable, helping, caring, and involved.

Let me remind you of the story of Rabbi Zusya, who was told, "When you die and come before the Heavenly Tribunal, do not worry that they will say to you, 'Zusya, why were you not Moses?' Instead, they will require of you, 'Zusya, why were you not Zusya!'"

Growing Up Jewish and Male

Max Rivers

My earliest memory related to being a Jewish male happened when I was about three. I remember walking to my grandfather's Orthodox shule. (I was raised in the Reform tradition, which is why this incident stood out in my mind.) It seemed odd, all these grown-ups, all dressed up, walking together in a herd through the dirty city streets. In the clean, pristeen suburbs where we lived, grown-ups never walked. They drove everywhere. But I liked it. It seemed silly and out of the ordinary, like a party.

This festive mood changed abruptly in the dark, woody interior. Something mysterious and scary was happening as we entered the inner chamber. There was a low gravelly growl coming from men standing scattered around the main area of the room, swaying with their eyes closed, holding books and wearing what looked like beautiful white dresses over their dark suits. Occasionally, one or another of them would change his low moan into what sounded to me like a loud groan of pain and then would subside back into the group growl. I looked up at my father to see if he was going to help these men who were in such pain, but before I could figure out this mystery, another more confusing one swept over me.

I had been holding my mother's hand, and in such a strange place as this, that hand felt like my lifeline. Suddenly, my mother was drawn away from me, through a door that led up a dark flight of stairs. Other women were also moving in this direction, and as I had become accustomed to, I began to follow. But I was suddenly grabbed from behind and looking up, I saw my uncle holding me, laughing. I reached out to my retreating mother and was about to cry out when my father came up and wrapped me in one of the beautiful white dresses like the other men were wearing.

Up close, it was made of silk or satin, with crisp gold embroidery, and lots of silky soft tassels to play with. Then a satin cap was put on my head. I had never before been permitted to wear anything so soft and sensual. I remember looking up at my mother's retreating form, while fingering the tassels and holding onto the silky cap, then looking to my father's outstretched hand and feeling a tremendous conflict. One which it seemed must be resolved immediately, which was of immense importance, and of which I had almost no understanding.

That is where my memory ends, except for a flash of another image. I am sitting next to my father, surrounded by the moaning swaying men dressed darkly and draped in shining white talises. I crane my neck to see my mother up in the balcony, peering down at me through wooden bars. I remember that it seemed like something was very wrong with this separation.

I looked up at my father and at the other men, and back at the women cloistered away, looking for some sign that they too saw the injustice or felt the indescribable wrong that seemed so apparent to me. But seeing no such validation, I did something with those feelings. I have come to believe this kind of dilemma is often the case with little children. When their innate sensibility is contradicted, and the adults (or sometimes other children) around them don't seem to agree, they make the assumption that something must be wrong with them. And some precious part of them gets stored away forever (or until such time as it is brought back up into the light, and reclaimed). And this is just what I did.

It wasn't until recently that I uncovered this incident of my own Jewish history. I was seeking to reestablish a connection with the Jewish community after some twenty years as a self-described "anti-Semitic Jew," and in following that path I attended a service at a Reform synagogue that had rewritten their prayer book to remove sexist language.

As the service began, the cantor, a woman, came out and, before beginning, removed a beautiful white silk talis from its case, kissed the tassels, and draped it around her shoulders before taking her place in front of the congregation. I found myself staring at her the whole service. I felt myself fighting back tears the whole service long, and on the quiet ride home, I could feel something inside, healing.

Somehow, during that service I came to realize that what I had done with the wrong that I'd felt thirty years ago was to take it on myself. If I felt something was wrong, but neither my mother nor my father seemed to even notice, then it must be something wrong with me. It must be right to separate men and women in this way, for men to pray out in the open, clothed in silk and satin, while women hid behind bars. And my feeling bad about that must be a flaw in me.

But seeing a woman and a talis together, proudly praying, leading prayer, brought back that little boy's feelings of rage and disempowerment. And gave back the man a little of his faith in his feelings for justice and equality.

How To Deal With A Jewish Issue: Circumcision

Zalman Schachter-Shalomi

You have been involved in a natural birth and are now the parents of a baby son. You did it at home, or in surroundings that resembled a home setting as much as possible. You incorporated everything that has to do with gentleness and tried to avoid all violence. Now as your son is about to become eight days old, you have to make a decision. Will he be circumcised or not? And if the answer is yes, will there be a traditional *Bris* (ritual Jewish circumcision) or not? You wish you did not have to take your baby, a new person who loves and trusts you, and inflict the trauma of an operation on him. Yes, *inflict* is the word, let's not make it pretty.

You have already been through some of the literature and have weighed the possible medical advantages which might accrue as a result: reduced probability of cervical or uterine cancer in your son's future mate; the hygenic benefits to the child himself; and so on. But it does not add up, and you are in conflict.

Parents, relatives, and friends are exerting pressure with their expectations of a *Bris*, and you yourself would also love to have a celebration for family rejoicing, if only you did not have to do it in this form. You associate circumcision with barbaric customs practiced by uncivilized people, and you wish you didn't have to participate in such a brutal procedure.

At a deeper level there are other conflicts. You espoused and followed natural methods for the birth. You believe perfection lies in following the natural flow. Had God-Nature wanted boys to be without prepuces, they would be born that way. But your hesitation about your own son is balanced by your expectations of others: if the child were somebody else's, you would probably expect him to be circumcised. You find that your objections to circumcision are not absolute.

You are experiencing the pain and discomfort for your child in anticipation of his pain, the same way parent always have, telling their children, "It hurts me more than it hurts you." The anticipation is yours only; the baby is not caught in the anxiety because he does not know what is in the offing. You do, and this nagging discomfort makes you want to be past the experience.

Conversations with other parents confirm your feelings: they too felt as you do before the *Bris*. And so it has always been, and must be—that the mother and father sense a tightening in themselves up to the moment and even a little while after. It is a difficult, gut-wrenching experience, and all Jewish parents of a son must face it because it's an unavoidable feature of the Jewish landscape. Usually the decision is yes, but it's not arrived at without soul searching, hesitation, questions, or anguish. When it's over, though, it almost always turns out that it wasn't so bad after all.

After the *Bris*, one father said, "I felt I was being asked if I would allow *myself* to be circumcised, as I am now, as an adult. Shivers ran through me at the thought of the pain. But when I remembered the labor pains my wife endured when our son was born, I felt ashamed. I answered yes to the question. I thought, yes, I want to."

"My child is not someone to do this to!" a mother said. "The feeling came right out of my guts. No one has a right to do this to MY CHILD! Then I heard an echo . . .! '*Whose* child?' Do I own him or is he mine to care for until he is old enough to care for himself? Do I have the right to make a decision which might lead him *away* from his birthright, or is that a decision only he can make when he is old enough?

"While I was pregnant I felt the need to get in touch with my roots. I can go back only three generations on my father's side and fewer on my mother's. Then I gave birth and my son was here. I felt the roots extending all the way back to Abraham. It was a connection that came out of my body. It occurred to me that men could never experience labor and birth and the knowing that came with it. I knew that women have a secret that men cannot share. Maybe, I thought, the *Bris* is a secret for males which we cannot share. It was painful, but I felt I had to let go and allow my child to be initiated this way so he could belong to the world of Jewish men."

After the *Bris* of her son, another mother reported: "I had a lot of trouble letting this happen. As it turned out, I don't think it was really so bad on my baby. He's made worse faces with colic. Somehow, I felt he was sealed into his body by the *Bris* and the pain. Before, he was sort of in and out, not yet fully grounded. Since the *Bris*, he has become a person.

"There was another reason I decided on the *Bris*. All the men in my family have always been circumcised and I didn't want my son to be the first one who was not. Also, I didn't want my son to have a strange-looking penis. Somehow, my son's uncircumcised penis would make me think of him as an outsider. All my life I have wanted to have a big *Mishpoche* (family circle)— uncles, aunts, cousins. Some of my friends had, and I envied them. When all the people of our Havura, and relatives and other friends came and helped us celebrate, I felt my baby had connected with a *Mishpoche*."

Covenant is a large word in Judaism. We have made a contract with God. He will be our God and we will be His people. For Jewish men, the sign of this Covenant is circumcision. The word circumcision remains a medical term and confuses the issue; henceforth, we'll call it by its Hebrew name: *Milah or Bris Milah*.

Bris Milah is the seal, the sign of the Covenant. We are not the only ones who have this sign. Since it is a Covenant made with Abraham-Ibrahim, it is also a sign and commandment given by the *Shariya* for Muslims. We have it in common, though there are differences in the timing and form of the rite. Muslim and Jew are both connected to God in this way.

MY SON, MY SON

As a father of sons, I too have experienced the anguish of such decision-making. When my youngest son was born, I recorded my inner experiences with the thought that they might be helpful to others:

> My son is almost a week old. I sit at my typewriter, improvising thoughts about the *Bris*. As usual, my thoughts arrange themselves along the four dimensions of doing, feeling, knowing, and being. It is a habit of mind.

> *Doing:* Begin with history, going back to Egypt, where circumcision was practiced. Why did Abraham circumcise in the oak groves of Mem-Re? Because it was Mem-Re who gave him advice concerning circumcision. Circumcision had made sense in ancient Egyptian spirituality; it was one of the ways high consciousness and great knowledge were transmitted. Who knows to what extent *Milah* influences culture?

> Perhaps something destructive and "macho" gets refined by a *Bris*, directing a man away from pure instinct and toward prudent judgment. I scanned my life and saw how many times I had made decisions contrary to the urgings of my instincts, difficult decisions which turned out for the best and were right. Was this because of *Milah*?

> Maybe Freud was right about the dominating power of the libido: if so, it makes sense to take that absolute power away from the penis. I want my child to have this advantage over instinct.

> So much of what happens in sex is covenantal. Perhaps this is why Covenant has to be imposed on this organ from the very first.

> Then I think of the *mohel* (ritual circumciser). Much depends on him: who he is; what he does; what tools he uses; how self-conscious or assured he is. His emotional state is important. What feelings or tensions will he telegraph to the baby? Will he love the baby at least a little bit, and hold him firmly and warmly enouth to make him feel safe?

> I imagine the *mohel* and a thought begins to take shape in the back of my mind. If the world will be cruel to my son, and sooner or later we will all feel pain, let me mercifully and gently introduce him to it myself, rather than leave it to someone who did not love him before and will not love him after.

The thought occurs to me to be the *mohel* for my son.

I look into the future and want to see a world in which there are Jews. The world is richer because of us, more civilized. I want my children and grand-children to live in a world in which Jewish questions are being asked, like the one that exercises me at this moment and makes me consult my world of ethics and morals to make a life decision.

Abraham was not satisfied to perform circumcision on the advice of Mem-Re alone. He wanted God to command him. Oy! How strongly I relate to his desire at this moment. I feel and know that I cannot do this to my child for idealism alone. I cannot take the whole responsibility on myself. All my good notions are not enough. There is a moment of risk: what if the knife slips? All the catastrophic possibilities arise as risks I fear to take alone. I can't do it by myself. I need God's command. By way of answer, an image rushes through my mind in which I see my penis, from which my son came, and my father's penis, from which I came, and all the penises of all the fathers back to Abraham and the moment he received God's command: " . . . every male among you shall be circumcised; the foreskin of his penis shall be cut off. This will be the proof that you and they accept this covenant."

Feeling: "Lonely" and "connected" are the words that come to mind. Foreskin (*Orlah*), a stopped-up dullness, is removed, leaving a penis sharply exposed, vulnerable yet intimate when caressed, standing erect, full of con-sciousness. We have been taught to cover our private parts, but privately we know we have a *Bris* which connects us with others. Marked forever as a Jew.

Taking a child to the *Bris* is a sacrifice. It is a death that is not fatal. It is the first time my child will get close to being a sacrifice, his first at-one-ment and holymaking. All the other nonfatal deaths that will occur are contained and made safe in this one.

Why do this to a child who has no control, instead of waiting for him to do it himself? The Jew says, "Because it is better so, and I as parent take responsibility." There is an aspect of being Jewish that goes beyond a mere private matter between a soul and her God. My father *wanted* me to be Jewish, and my children and my children's children, all the way to the end of time. And so do I.

Of all the tests of my loyalty, this test of the *Bris Milah* is the hardest. Yet there can be only one outcome. All my cells know it. I feel my refusal to participate would deny my son the option of a vital Jewish life.

Then I look at my son and my resolve weakens. In the here and now, there are not enough reasons to do the *Bris*. My baby *is*, flesh of my flesh and blood of my blood, while the history resides only in my feelings—the same feelings that program me to protect my child.

What would I do if a deranged cultist were to sneak in and circumcise my son for the sake of his private madness? I would destroy him. I am not an absolute pacifist when it comes to protecting my children. And yet it is I, Zalman as *mohel*, who am about to do this unspeakable thing to my child.

Knowing: In my world of thoughts, the pros and cons endlessly cancel each other out. Inclinations toward culture and against brute instinct are cancelled out by a natural sense that the baby is already perfect as he is. Thoughts in support of the *Mishpoche* and the clan are cancelled out by the messianic vision that we are all one clan and there is no need for such divisions for the good of humankind.

But bigger thoughts roll to the center of my awareness, thoughts of the limits of my understanding and the finiteness of my mind. Be humble vis-à-vis God and your ancestors, these thoughts say, the tradition is *ancient* and *collective*, and you are only *one*. One Jewish man among all Jewish men. And so too is your son.

My thoughts move full circle. The *Bris Milah* of my son is inevitable. And I myself shall perform it. Myself. My son.

Being: As God exists in relationship to humans in his AM-NESS ("I AM THAT I AM"), so in some smaller way do I stand in relationship to my son. In the am-ness of being as father, I sired him with sperm from my body, and shall protect, provide for, and prepare him until he becomes himself, on his own, to be whatever it is he will be. As my own *Bris*, among many other experiences, helped to shape my being, so shall his.

I cannot end these observations about the *Bris* of our sons without addressing a very great question—what about our daughters? What ceremonial act initiates them into the Jewish Covenant with God? The fact is that there is no Jewish female equivalent to a *Bris* (nor would any reasonable person suggest that a rite of excision by instituted). The roots of this situation lie in the patriarchal past, where our heritage begins. Tradition, of course, carries great importance in the unfolding of our lives, but we must also be concerned with the present. Judaism is evolving, is attempting to meet the needs of real people here and now. The reality is that we must discover or allow for the revelation of a ritual for girls that will serve the convenautal function performed for boys by the *Bris*.

The Real Jewish Father

Rabbi Michael Gold

A woman came to see me with a difficult question. She had married her current husband when she was eight months pregnant. The man who impregnated her denied paternity, and her new husband has been raising the baby as his own. Now their son was five. The woman asked, "How can I tell him that daddy's not his real father?"

As a rabbi, I wondered what kind of Jewish perspective I could give her. The very wording of the question raises an issue as to the meaning of fatherhood. Is the "real" father simply a biological relationship? Or does "real" fatherhood entail some ongoing responsibility toward the child? If so, what responsibilities? What insights does Judaism offer about fatherhood that could help answer these questions?

Judaism sees fatherhood as central to the Jewish man's understanding of his obligations to his community and to God. The first commandment of the Torah is "be fruitful and multiply." The rabbis of the Talmud understood this commandment as being incumbent on men but optional for women. Jewish law saw a man who was not a father as somehow incomplete. At eighteen, a man was expected to marry; if he did not have children within ten years after marriage he had to find another wife to fulfill his commandment. A man without children could not sit on the Sanhedrin, the central Rabbinic decision-making body during the Second Commonwealth. For a man to die childless was a great tragedy; in biblical times his brother was obligated to marry the widow and raise children in the dead man's name.

The question is, what do these Rabbinic rulings mean by fatherhood? It should be noted that in our popular culture, including movies and other media, fatherhood is a purely biological relationship. A man has all the rights as the father if his sperm conceived the child. His subsequent relationship with the child is often irrelevant. One well-acclaimed motion picture showed a man reappearing in his young son's life after a four-year disappearance. He then took "his" son from the couple who had been raising him. In another movie, a woman introduced a young girl to a very surprised man and told him, "Guess what? You're the father." Tears welled up in the man's eyes as he held the child close and said, "My daughter." Never mind that he had not seen the woman since he had impregnated her.

A similar message was disseminated in our society by a recent Supreme Court ruling. It required the biological father's consent for an adoption proceeding, even if he was unaware of the existence of this biological child. I have been involved in advertising for biological fathers who were fugitives from the law in order to seek their consent for their child to be adopted. The message is once again clear: when it comes to fatherhood, biology is everything.

It should be noted that ethically our society does not condone simply siring a child with no further responsibilities. Paternity does entail a legal responsibility to at least physically provide for that child. The father's responsibilities are in the material realm: food, clothing, shelter, education, medical care, etc. How often do we picture a man coming home to a noisy house full of children and telling his wife, "I worked all day to bring home the bread, you keep the children quiet." Fatherhood in modern life entails two major tasks: being a sperm donor and a bread winner. Too often the mother takes responsibility for the spiritual end of child raising while the father is concerned with the physical.

This emphasis on the biological and physical in modern fatherhood will be the backdrop of our study of Judaism. We will show that there are two different, and occasionally contradictory, strands within Jewish law and tradition. The first strand is biological, emphasizing the importance of a man siring a child. Yet there is a second strand, which close scrutiny will reveal as more important in Jewish thinking. That strand is concerned with a father as mentor rather than as progenitor, as teacher rather than as provider.

At first glance, the emphasis of Judaism seems to be on the first strand, with the expectation that a man will fulfill the mitzvah of "be fruitful and multiply." As mentioned, procreation is considered a man's mitzvah. In fact, the Mishnah teaches:

> A man should not neglect the commandment of "be fruitful and multiply" unless he already has children. The school of Shammai teaches, two sons. The school of Hillel teaches, a son and a daughter since it says "male and female he created them." If a man marries a woman and lives with her ten years, and they have no children, he cannot neglect it any longer . . . A man is commanded to be fruitful and multiply, but not a woman. (Yebamot 6:6)

This Mishnah is based on the story of Abraham and Sarah in the Torah. According to the Torah:

> Sarai, Abram's wife, had borne him no children. She had an Egyptian maidservant whose name was Hagar. And Sarai said to Abram, "Look, the Lord has kept me from bearing. Consort with my maid: perhaps I shall have a

son through her." So Sarai, Abram's wife, took her maid Hagar the Egyptian—after Abram had dwelt in the land of Canaan *ten years*—and gave her to her husband Abram as concubine. (Genesis 16:1-3)

The major problem for the Bible was Abraham's inability to have a child: Sarah's infertility was a secondary concern. Abraham's problem was solved by a surrogate mother arrangement. At least he would have his own biological child. The Torah and the Talmud seem to support the contention that a childless woman may be sad, but a childless man is a tragedy. If a wife cannot have children, the husband should take another wife. It is a biological definition of fatherhood.

However, when it comes to Abraham's son, Isaac, the picture becomes murkier. Isaac and Rebecca, like Isaac's parents, were also an infertile couple. However, they waited a full twenty years before their children were born. The Talmud questions this, and comes to the conclusion that Isaac knew he was the infertile one. (Yebamot 64a) The Talmud does equivocate on this, saying perhaps that both Isaac and Rebecca were infertile. Yet this Talmudic passage raises the question of a man who desires to be a father but has his own fertility problem. In fact, that same page rules: "If a man marries a woman and dwells with her ten years without children, she should leave but she still receives her marriage settlement. For perhaps he was not worthy to be built up through her."

The Torah recognizes the existence of an infertile man, but sees his situation as particularly tragic. The proof of this is the law of levirate marriage. If a man dies childless, his brother has an obligation to marry the widow and raise up children in the dead brother's name. If he refuses, he must participate in a ceremony called halitza, which in biblical times was considered a disgrace. (See Deuteronomy 25:5-10 for a detailed description.) The story of Judah and Tamar demonstrates the sin of neglecting this levirate duty and leaving a man with no seed. No parallel ceremony exists for a woman who dies childless.

A number of other laws in Judaism demonstrate a concern with blood-lines, genetic heritage, and the proper identification of the biological father. Only he can pass on to his son the status as a Kohen or Levi, much to the disappointment of adoptive fathers who are Kohenim and Leviim. Similarly, a woman who is divorced or widowed from one husband must wait ninety days before remarrying in order to insure that there is no confusion as to the biological father of a subsequent child (Eben Haezer 13:1). Many rabbis have outlawed artificial insemination by donor because of confusion about paternity. (Other rabbis, however, have permitted the procedure.) Judaism is concerned with establishing accurate biological ancestry and teaches that a child never loses his or her biological identity.

Jewish law seems to support the biological trend, indicating that every effort must be made to give a man his own biological offspring. I remember once speaking at an infertility conference regarding the issues of adoption and surrogate motherhood. I definitely prefer the former. One man in the audience told me, "Rabbi, all that is fine. But by adoption I cannot fulfill the biblical mandate of 'be fruitful and multiply.' By impregnating a surrogate mother with my sperm, I can." In a technical sense, he was correct.

Yet, Jewish tradition is not quite so simplistic. There is a hint of a non-biological trend in the law of Levirate marriage mentioned above. This law concerns a man who dies childless. It should be noted that, when his brother marries the widow, he has children who are called by the name of the dead brother. There is a biological connection, but it is indirect. In Levirate marriage *one man has provided the sperm, another man is called the true father*.

We see hints of this separation between the biological parent and the "true" parent at other places in the Bible and Talmud. We already read of Sarah choosing Hagar as a surrogate mother. Sarah's exact wording to her husband is: "consort with my maid, perhaps I will have a son through her." Here, one woman provides the womb and the ovum, but another considers herself the mother. Unfortunately, it did not quite work out that way, since a quarrel broke out between Hagar and Sarah, with Hagar and her son being cast out into the wilderness.

The story of Michal, wife of King David, worked out better. Michal was punished by God for chastising David: she was told that she would never have children. Yet, later the Bible mentions her five sons. The Talmud remarks on this contradiction, "Merab (Michal's sister) gave birth to them, but Michal raised them, therefore they are called by her name. This teaches that the one who raises an orphan in his home, Scripture considers him as if he gave birth to him" Sanhedrin 18b). True parentage is once again separated from biology. The pasage continues with a similar statement, "Anyone who teaches the son of his companion Torah, scripture considers him as if he gave birth to him."

There are other examples where one person provides the sperm or egg, another raises the child, and the later is called the true parent. In the Bible, Rachel has children by her handmaiden Bilhah. In the Talmud, Abbaye often quotes the wisdom of his mother, who was really his foster mother. A second trend seems to be emerging from Jewish tradition, which we can call the pedagogical trend, one that puts greater emphasis on raising a child, guiding it and teaching it, without reference to biology.

This pedagogical strand in Judasim is most clear in a fascinating Mishnah, dealing with the commandment to return a lost object:

> (If a man finds) a lost object of his father and a lost object of his teacher, his teacher's comes first. For his father only brings him into this world, while his teacher teaches him wisdom to bring him into the world to come . . . If his father and his teacher are bearing a burden, he should remove his teacher's first then remove his father's. If his father and his teacher are captured, he should redeem his teacher first and afterwards redeem his father. (Baba Metzia 2:11)

This Mishnah is clear, the most important role a man can play in the life of a child is teacher and mentor, not sperm-provider and progenitor. Masculinity is bound up with helping a child function in society, and providing that child not only with book knowledge, but with values and a world outlook. A man can be a mentor to a child, whether he is the biological father, adoptive father, grandfather, stepfather, foster father, teacher or friend. Jewish tradition sees the one who raises the child and guides the child as the one who deserves to be called "father."

The emphasis on the spiritual rather than the physical can be seen in Jewish law regarding the obligations of a father toward his child. Six obligations are delineated in a statement in the Talmud: "A man is obligated regarding his son to circumcise him, to redeem him, to teach him Torah, to teach him a trade, to find him a wife, and some say, to teach him to swim" (Kiddushin 29a). All of these obligations are spiritual or educational, not material. We see that the primary role for a man is to be a mentor, not necessarily a provider.

In fact, Jewish law had difficulty finding a source for the obligation that a man must physically provide for his minor children. There is a long dicussion in the Talmud whether such an obligation is mandated by the Torah or not. The rabbis finally ruled that a man certainly does have such an obligation, but it falls under the laws of charity.

> R. Elai stated in the name of Resh Lakish who had it from R. Judah b. Hanina: At Usha it was ordained that a man must maintain his sons and daughters while they are young. The question raised: Is Torah law in agreement with this statement or not? Come and hear: When people came before Rab Judah he used to tell them, An ostrich bears progeny and throws them upon (the tender mercies) of the townspeople. When people came before R. Hisda he used to tell them, Turn a mortar for him upside down in public and let one stand (on it) and say: the raven cares for its young but that man does not care for his children. (Ketubot 49b)

The moral expectations of the rabbis are clear: a father must provide for his children. Yet, the passage also states that there is no clear biblical source for this ruling. Jewish law is far more clear when it describes a man's role as mentor than when it discusses his responsibilities as provider.

Thus, we see two almost contradictory trends in Judaism, one that stresses biology and one that stresses pedagogy. Which is more important? We have already seen the law that a man should not stay in an infertile marriage more than ten years, a law which stresses the biological imperative. Historically, this particular law has fallen out of practice in the Jewish community; the codes mention it, but say that today it should not be enforced. The emphasis seems to be on the sanctity of marriage and maintaining a marital relationship even without children. Rabbi Joseph Solovechik has said that the mitzvah of "be fruitful and multiply" can be fulfilled through adoption.

Jewish ethics seems to prefer the pedagogical trend: Jewish masculinity is proven through being a spiritual parent and a mentor. By exploring biblical theology, perhaps we can see a reason for this. In particular, let us explore the difference between the animal kingdom and human beings regarding the biological imperative.

For animals, biological survival of the species is of ultimate importance. In the long term, an individual animal's life takes on importance only in terms of the survival of the species. From a biblical perspective, there is no intrinsic holiness to an individual animal's life; that is why the Bible permits the killing of animals for food or to offer sacrifice (but not for sport and not wantonly). Of essence is the survival of the species. That is also why Noah was commanded to take two of each species, a male and a female, onto the ark. When animals were created, they were blessed by God and told "be fruitful and multiply." Survival of the species is the essence of their task on this earth. We can say that animals live by a biological imperative.

To the biblical view, humans live on a qualitatively different level than animals. Their divine imperatives are different. That is what is meant by the verse "And God created man in His image." God's blessing to human beings is different from that to the animal kingdom. "Be fruitful and multiply, fill the earth and subdue it; and rule the fish of the sea, the birds of the sky, and all the living things that creep on earth" (Genesis 1:28). The human imperative goes beyond procreation and species survival. We must "fill the earth and subdue it." We can identify this with creating a culture, a society, and a civilization across the face of the earth.

Humanity's ultimate purpose is not merely biological, it is technological and sociological. Human beings have a responsibility to pass on technological knowledge, cultural forms, and spiritual values to a new generation. When an animal has a biological offspring, it has fulfilled its divine imperative. When a human being has a biological offspring, the task is only beginning. That is why Jewish tradition values the "teacher" over the "father." That is why masculinity and fatherhood are ultimately proven in the realm of pedagogy, and not biology.

We are going through a period of profound changes in the roles of men and women in Jewish life. Even the Orthodox community is not immune from these changes. Among these changes is a reevaluation of our definitions of masculinity and femininity. We are moving away from the animal concept of manhood being proven simply through biology, toward a view of man as nurturer and teacher. The time has come to emphasize that in Judaism the true father is not merely the donor of sperm, but the mentor.

Such emphasis could have a profound effect, not just on the Jewish community, but on society as a whole. Consider, for example, the recent painful Baby M case. An infertile couple hired a surrogate mother to have a baby using the husband's sperm. After the baby was born the mother sought to keep her, sparking a controversial custody court case and a national debate on the ethics of surrogate motherhood.

In my mind, the whole surrogate controversy grew out of this biological trend in our society. Men have great difficulty giving up the idea that their sperm will conceive the child they raise. Adoption is certainly less controversial and less risky than surrogacy. Yet, my own experience has taught me that men have a particularly hard time with adoption as well as artificial insemination with donor sperm. It would be healthy for our society to emphasize the pedagogical trend, that one need not be a biological father to be a father.

The pedagogical trend could also remind men what their primary responsibility is as a father. Physically creating a child is not enough; neither is physically providing for that child. A man must teach that child. He must also be a role model in his personal life. The six responsibilities of a Jewish father mentioned earlier cover not only religious rituals, not only the teaching of marketable skills, not only the teaching of survival skills, but the teaching of religious values. Too often men leave these responsibilities for their wives as they busily try to earn a living.

Jewish tradition would teach that a man can fulfill his obligation to father a child through raising and teaching that child, through being a spiritual rather than a biological parent. This emphasis can be seen in another Talmudic passage: "'Such as have no successors and fear not God' (Pslams 55:20) R. Johanan and R. Joshua b. Levi (dispute the meaning of the passage.) One says whoever does not leave behind a son. The other says whoever does not leave behind a disciple" (Baba Batra 1116a). The passage implies that a man who fears God can replace himself by having a child or having a student.

With this background I can explain my answer to the woman who came to see me. The true father, the one who deserves to be called "daddy," is the man who raised this child since birth, who is teaching and guiding this child into adulthood. Yet, the child does not lose his biological identity; there is another man whose sperm conceived the child, and whose genetic make-up helped form that child.

The child should be told the truth from the youngest age in a casual and nonthreatening way. Even children of four or five will enjoy the story of their origins, of how mommy became pregnant from one man, and how she later married the man who is "daddy." One man is the biological father, the second is the "real" father. Judaism's lesson is that the child should be called by the name of the latter.

The Impotent Father: Roth and Peretz

Robert P. Waxler

For Philip Roth, life in the late twentieth century is a bad Jewish joke, not so much because Jewish mothers smother their sons through domestic repression (a popular reading of Roth), but because Roth himself, the eternal Jewish son, cannot discover the power of fatherhood. Roth's continuous grappling with the modern inability to find the roots of this power is of primary concern to him and has always been a motive force within his work.

When, for example, Roth claims: "For myself, I cannot find a true and honest place in the history of believers that begins with Abraham, Isaac and Jacob," he is not simply declaring an inability to make a leap of faith, but is announcing a failure to discover his place within the patriarchal tradition of Judaism. In fact, Roth's texts seem to be informed by an almost obsessive desire to discover how a Jewish son becomes a father in a world without any strong model of an authentic father.

For Roth, the problem of fatherhood is connected to the problem of creating and maintaining an ethical civilization in opposition to the confused and often brutal forces of nature. The erosion of the patriarchal tradition may lead to the modern sense of freedom, but it also leads to a breakdown in ethical laws and an increase in criminal activity. In his novel *Letting Go*, for example, Roth suggests that the akedah—"Isaac under the knife, Abraham wielding it"—simply implies that justice is an illusion because there is no authentic father: Abraham and Isaac are either brothers, or the Laws given by the Father have been displaced by the natural instincts of a mother—as in the scene from *Portnoy's Complaint* when Sophie exclaims: "My Alex is suddenly such a bad eater, I have to stand over him with a knife."

For Roth, in fact, the original crime against the father seems similar to the one that Freud claimed was at the root of primitive rebellion: the sons eating the father in a cannibalistic and sexually charged ritual. Eating and promiscuity are closely linked in Roth's texts, usually as signs of rebellion and indications of the erosion of civilized behavior. They are crimes against the father, and crimes that weaken the power of language itself, the power of words, the power of giving shape to the natural environment through the naming process. As Neil Klugman bemoans the modern situation in *Goodbye, Columbus*: "The sentences lost in the passing of food, the words gurgled into mouthfuls, the syntax chopped and forgotten in heapings, spillings and gorgings."

It is just this dilemma that has sent Roth back to the texts of Eastern Europe, back to Yiddish roots, back in his own stories to Prague. There is something there that Roth wants to find. It is a futile search for patriarchal authority, a bad Jewish joke. But it gives us a clear context for understanding Roth and the dilemma of the Jewish son besieged by the excesses of the modern predicament. If we are Jewish men, it is our life that Roth holds up for examination.

•

"Great men were once capable of great miracles." That is the opening line of one of the great Yiddish short stories by I.B. Peretz, "The Golem." In Peretz's version of the legend, Rabbi Loeb is the great man, capable of great miracles. With the ghetto of Prague under attack, the rabbi goes into the street, halts in front of a mound of clay, and from this bit of nature, molds an image. It is not the clay image that is important, however, but the breath and the word of the rabbi himself. For next, the rabbi blows his breath into the nose of the clay image, and then whispers the sacred Name into its ear. Through the authority of the breath and the power of the Name, the golem is transformed, able then to stop the brute force of the outside world, that irrational force of natural instinct responsible for raping the Jewish women, roasting the children, and slaughtering the inhabitants of the shtetl. For Peretz, the Name brings justice through its power, and then that power ignited by the Name is subdued by the mercy of "the song of the sabbath" sung again by the rabbi who calls a halt to the action of the clay image, the golem itself.

The effective power of the golem here is primarily the power of the ancient law of the fathers, controlled by the knowledge of the Name and the mercy of the sabbath song. The story seems to imply that the rabbi is a great man, capable of great miracles, precisely because he knows the Name and can articulate it. In a sense, he is invested with the paternal authority of the Name. The golem itself is simply clay, and at the end of Peretz's story it lies hidden in the attic of the Prague synagogue, covered with cobwebs. The clay remains, but the Name is forgotten, the patriarchal authority that guided the clay into action. In the end, we are left only with the clay itself, and the difficult, but very modern question, "What are we to do?" It is Roth's question, a question signifying a profound sense of loss.

Peretz's story suggests that the spiritual authority of the Father vanishes in the Yiddish context, though the memory of that absence is maintained. Roth's texts become, in this perspective, commentaries and extensions of this Yiddish dilemma. It is as if memory creates desire, and into that place where spiritual authority once presided eventually leaps the modern will, Portnoy's appetite, for example, Portnoy's craving to eat whatever he sees. But yet, for the modern commentator Philip Roth, there is a lingering suspicion that that assertion of the will, that act of cannibalism only pulls us farther from that which we long for. Our modern appetite creates a trap, another Jewish joke. To attempt to gain such freedom simply leads to a repetition of the original crime against the father, another violation of his law. For Roth, it leads to stories about orgies, bizzarre sexual exploits, men being transformed into beasts.

The typical Yiddish story is not usually like Peretz's "The Golem," but more like his "Bontsha the Silent." It is a story of the schlemiel, the saintly-fool, a story not of "great men who do great miracles," but of "the little man" lacking appetite. "Bontsha was a human being," Peretz tells us, "but he lived unknown , in silence, and in silence he died. He passed through our world like a shadow . . . his feet left no mark along the dust of the street." Bontsha is a man without language, a man of the ironic shrug. He is tried before the Heavenly Tribunal and found by the judge to be "a child of our hearts," a man deserving whatever he desires. But offered the world, Bontsha at heaven's gates responds typically: his simple request—"Every morning for breakfast, a hot roll with fresh butter."

For the epigram to his first book *Goodbye, Columbus*, Roth wrote: "The heart is only half a prophet," and this describes Bontsha's dilemma perfectly. Bontsha's humble endurance makes him a saint of sorts, but it seems also, especially after the Holocaust, to make him a man incapable of becoming a determined self. Like his spiritual brother Gimpel the Fool, Bontsha can never become a father. He will remain at best a perpetual Jewish son. For Roth, the heart can be unremitting in its indiscriminate acceptance of the world, but it cannot then make fatherly choices. But to make fatherly choices without knowing the roots of the spiritual authority that make our willful acts those of the community of the Law is to live in the constant fear that Bontsha continually experiences, a fear that we are treading on others, committing criminal acts motivated only by our individual desires.

Bontsha helps us understand Roth's dilemma. Without the religious and moral underpinning of patriarchal authority found in Talmudic Judaism, we are trapped in the absurdly difficult position of not being able to make a genuinely ethical choice that we are certain is not a crime. In this context, our guilt is not to be doubted. We have a crime, but no gods to disobey. We sense the absence of an authoritative father, but have no idea about how to achieve a realistic embodiment of father—like values within the modern world.

It is in this context that Roth gives us a new sense of the Yiddish hero's "little man." In the late twentieth century, the Jewish-American male, Roth himself, is dogged by the oppressiveness of the absence of the patriarchal tradition. Even with his fame and fortune secure, he simply remains "a little man," a modern schlemiel who has no clear sense of right or wrong, but an overwhelming sense of guilt, brought on not by a Jewish mother, but by the pain of moral impotency.

Roth has said that man is "clay with aspirations," a golem, not with the Name embodied within him, but with the modern will to soar beyond the boundaries of his own body and the Yiddish shtetl mentality, the ghetto of exile. That is Portnoy's problem precisely: a man with a huge appetite, a man who Roth has said is a criminal in the line of Bugsy Siegel and Meyer Lansky. The image of the lost father is Portnoy's problem as it is Roth's: an image of the near impossibility of recovering the source of the Law, the normative tradition of Jewish morality, the articulation of the Name that preserves culture and civilization.

Author's note: I am indebted to the following works of criticism on Roth. They have had an important influence on my interpretation of, and my thinking about, Roth's writing: Judith P. Jones, *Philip Roth*; Hermione Lee, *Philip Roth*; Sanford Pinsker (ed.), *Critical Essays on Philip Roth*; and the texts of Harold Bloom.

Mayn Yingele (My Little One)

Morris Rosenfeld

Ikh hob a kley-nem yin- ge-le a zu-ne- le gor fayn. Ven

ikh der- ze im dakht zikh mir di gan-tse velt iz meyn. Nor

zel-tn, zel-tn ze ikh im mayn shey-nem, ven er vakht ikh

tref im i-mer shlo-fn- dik ikh ze im nor bay nakht.

Ikh hob a kleynem yingele,	I have a son, a little son,
A zunele gor fayn.	A boy completely fine.
Ven ikh derze im, dakht zikh mir,	When I see him it seems to me
Di gantse velt iz mayn.	That all the world is mine.
Nor zeltn, zeltn ze ikh im,	But seldom, seldom do I see
Mayn sheynem, ven er vakht,	My child awake and bright;
Ikh tref im imer shlofndik,	I only see him when he sleeps:
Ikh ze im nor bay nakht.	I'm only home at night.

Di arbet traybt mikh fri aroys,
Un lozt mikh shpet tsurik.
O, fremd iz mir mayn eygn layb,
O, fremd mayn kinds a blik.

It's early when I leave for work;
When I return, it's late.
Unknown to me is my own flesh,
Unknown is my child's face.

Ikh kum tseklemterheyt aheym,
In fintsternish gehilt;
Mayn bleykhe froy
Dertseylt mir bald,
Vi fayn dos kind zekh shpilt.

When I come home so wearily
In the darkness after day,
My pale wife exclaims to me:
"You should have seen our child play.

Vi zis es redt, vi klug es fregt:
O, mame, gute ma,
Ven kumt un brengt a "penny" mir
Mayn guter, guter pa?

"He sweetly spoke, he smartly asked,
'Oh, mama, answer me;
When will Papa come and bring
A penny, just for me?' "

Ikh her es tsu, un yo es muz,
Yo, yo, en muz geshen.
Di foter-libe flakert oyf,
Es muz mayn kind mikh zen!

I hear her speak, I rush within,
Oh, yes, yes, it must be:
My father love is flaring up,
My child must look at me.

Ikh shtey bay zayn gelegerl
Un ze, un her, un sha.
A troym bayegt di lipelkeh:
O, vu iz, vu iz pa?

I stand beside his little bed,
I look and try to hear.
In his dream he moves his lips:
"Why isn't Papa here?"

Ikh kush di bloye eygelekh;
Zey efenen zikh, O kind!
Zey zeen mikh, zey seen mikh
Un shlisn zikh geshvind.

I bend and kiss his pale blue eyes
I see them open then;
They look at me; they look at me!
Then they quickly close again.

Ikh blayb tseveytogt un tseklemt
Farbitert un ikh kler:
Ven du dervakhst amol mayn kind,
Gefinstu mikh nit mer.

Your papa's standing very close,
With a penny for my dear.
In his dream he moves his lips:
"Why isn't Papa here?"

I stand depressed, and all my thoughts
Are bitter and heart-sore:
"One day, when you awake, my child,
You'll not see me anymore."

Morris Rosenfeld (1862-1923) left his native Poland to avoid military service, saying, "I would like to serve my country if there had been any freedom for the Jew." In 1886, he left his new home in London because he heard a rumor: tailors in New York had won a strike, gaining a ten-hour work day. No more twelve hour shifts! But when he arrived in New York, he found that his hopes were without basis.

He took a job in a lower-east-side "sweat shop." At night, he wrote poems in his native Yiddish. They were published in Yiddish-language papers, set to music and sung by thousands of Jews, and then translated into other languages. For a time, he achieved celebrity in the non-Jewish world. But that hope, too, faded, and he died in poverty.

"Mayn Yingele," or "My Little Boy"—written in 1887—stands out as one of the few products of a traditional culture to lament the loss by working men of participation in their children's lives.

"Mayn Yingele" can be heard in the original Yiddish on these hard-to-find recordings: Ruth Rubin Sings Yiddish Folksongs (Prestige International INT 13019), Leon Lishner, Out of the Ghetto, (Vanguard VRS-9068). Doug Lipman sings this English translation on his cassette tape, Milk from the Bull's Horn: Tales of Nurturing Men (Yellow Moon Press, P.O. Box 1316, Cambridge, MA 02238).

—Doug Lipman

III.
ANTI-SEMITISM, SEXISM, AND HETEROSEXISM: COMING OUT OF THE SHADOWS

Moving from a Hasidic tale to an analysis of one of Freud's own dreams, and on through more contemporary pyschoanalytic theory to an analysis she conducted with a client as a therapist, Barbara Breitman, in "Lifting up the Shadow of Anti-Semitism: Jewish Masculinity in a New Light," explores the damage done to Jewish psyches by the internalization of anti-Semitism. The emasculation, one might say psychological castration, of Jewish men by an anti-Semitic culture precludes the positive identification with one's ancestors needed for one's own psychological development. Anti-Semitism in many ways has the effect of reversing masculine and feminine archetypes, as the "blond beast" comes to exercise power over "feminized" men. Breitman documents the devastating personal effects of these conflicting imperatives, and argues that they have also distorted Jewish theology, as the rabbis first developed a prescription for the appropriate Jewish male personality type which internalized many of the submissive values oppressed groups are to display and then, in compensation for this powerlessness, elevated themselves to the status of almost omniscient authorities.

Andrea Dworkin's "The Sexual Mythology of Anti-Semitism" insists on moving beyond mythology to fact. In the face of our accustomed way of thinking of Jewish men as symbolically desexualized, she reminds the reader that in Nazi propaganda the Jewish male was a rapist, and that in the reality of Nazi Germany the Jewish man's castration was also real, not merely symbolic. She articulates the impact of sexualized anti-Semitism on attitudes toward Jewish men and women, Jews and money, and racism.

In "The Jewish View of Homosexuality," Barry Dov Schwartz provides a detailed exegesis of the classic Jewish sacred texts and their accompanying commentaries on the subject. Those unfamiliar with the modes and methods of traditional Jewish scholarship will find themselves introduced to it here. Beginning with a general discussion of Jewish sexual ethics, Schwartz then reveals that in many texts commonly taken to be directed against homosexuality per se, the tradition is really concerned with what it took to be related sins, such as idolatry, prostitution, or the blurring of sex roles and sexual boundaries. The discussion is brought up to date with sections on a variety of current Jewish reactions to the gay community, and the fortunes of the gay Jewish community. [1]

Helen Leneman's "Reclaiming Jewish History: Homo-erotic Poetry of the Middle Ages" exposes the suppression of part of the richness of the Jewish literary tradition. Citing the poems themselves and examples of subsequent censored history, Leneman shows that early and influential Hebrew poets of Muslim Spain, such as Samuel Ha-Nagid, Ibn Gabirol, and Yehuda Halevi wrote stirring erotic verse to other men, poems which have been ignored or misinterpreted by subsequent commentators and scholars.

Note

1. For a survey of recent discussions, see Ellen M. Umansky, "Jewish Attitudes Towards Homosexuality: A Review of Contemporary Sources," *Reconstructionist* vol. 51, no. 2 (October-November 1985/Heshvan-Kislev 5746), pp. 9-15. (This entire issue is devoted to the theme "Judaism and Homosexuality.")

Lifting up the Shadow of Anti-Semitism: Jewish Masculinity in a New Light

Barbara Breitman

There is a Hasidic tale about Yakov, the poor tailor, who was barely able to eke out a living, but who as a young man had been blessed, for a brief interlude, to be a traveling companion of the Baal Shem Tov. One day a friend of Yakov's tells him there is a rich man, so enthralled by tales of the Besht's life, he rewards anyone who tells him a story about the Hasidic master. On his friend's advice, Yakov travels to a nearby town and makes the acquaintance of Moshe, the rich man. Moshe prepares a sumptuous feast for his guest, the likes of which the poor tailor has never seen. At the end of the meal, Moshe waits expectantly for Yakov to tell a story; but to his extreme embarrassment, the tailor cannot remember a single one.

"Don't worry," the kindly Moshe says. "There is always another day." But on the second, the third and the fourth day, until the end of the week, the same thing happens. Mortified by his loss of memory, Yakov finally prepares to leave. Just as he opens the door to be on his way, he remembers this tale.

"One day, as I was traveling with the Besht, we entered the central square in St. Petersburg and found a priest, renowned for his vilification and anti-Semitic hatred of the Jews, inciting a crowd to violence with anti-Semitic rhetoric. The Besht said to me: 'Yakov, go to that priest and tell him I want to talk with him.' Trembling, I approached the priest in the center of the crowd and conveyed my Rebbe's message. 'Go away,' said the priest, 'Tell your rabbi I don't talk to swine.' I repeated these harsh words to the Besht, but he sent me back to demand the priest's acquiescence. 'The Rebbe wants to speak with you now,' I demanded. To my amazement, the priest came down from his rostrum and accompanied me to where the Besht was waiting. The two men went off to a tavern and did not reappear for many hours. When they finally reemerged, they parted company without a word, and we went in our separate directions. The Besht never told me what happened between them."

As Yakov finished this sentence, he looked up and saw that Moshe's face was streaming with tears. "Why do you cry?" the tailor asked. "Because," replied Moshe, "I was that priest. In our talk at the tavern, the Besht reminded me I had been born to Jewish parents who relinquished me as a child to a Russian family who taught me to hate Jews. The Besht told me: 'One day a man will come to recount this story about yourself. Then, and only then, will you know your time for repentance has reached an end, that your t'shuva is complete."

This tale belongs to the genre of legends which recount the healing powers of the Besht, his power to quicken the soul and restore it to life. What is remarkable about this particular tale is the evidence it provides that in the days of the Hasidim, there existed an awareness that anti-Semitism was not only a threat from without, but that it could be taken in to become a disease of the Jewish soul, a disease the Rebbe was called upon to heal, just as he exorcised dybbuks and restored the sick to health.

As a psychotherapist, I have had the privilege of accompanying a sizable number of Jewish men and women on journeys through their unconscious. In that process, I have been impressed not only by how Jewish identity evolves as the true self emerges, but also by the disturbing tenacity and embeddedness of internalized anti-Semitism. The perception Jewish men and women have of themselves and of each other has been radically distorted by anti-Semitism; even our tradition, what we consider halacha and sacred lore, has as parts of It-self, aspects which are actually alien and derivative of anti-Semitism. To come into the fullness of our being, the fullness of our masculinity and femininity, we must cleanse ourselves of the Shadow.

FREUD AND ANTI-SEMITISM

No less a student of the psyche than Freud exposes the inner workings of anti-Semitism as he analyzes one of his own dreams in the monumental *The Interpretation of Dreams*. The dream analysis which reveals the impact of anti-Semitism on the Jewish male psyche and its interference in the process of identification between Jewish father and son is all the more poignant because it was not Freud's intention to elucidate this process. Only his unflagging commitment to the illumination of unconscious process has left us heir to an extraordinary analysis of internalized anti-Semitism.

The incident which triggers the troublesome dream is recorded in the chapter "Distortion in Dreams." In the spring of 1897, Freud learns he had been recommended for an appointment to the position of "professor extra-ordinarius." Knowing that two more senior professors had been denied such an appointment due to "denominational considerations," Freud warns himself about getting his hopes too high. When one of the colleagues visits, recounting how he was denied his promotion because of anti-Semitism, Freud's fears of suffering a similar fate are exacerbated. The morning after his friend's visit, he records this cryptic dream: " . . . I. My friend R was my uncle. I had a great feeling of affection for him. II. I saw before me his face, somewhat changed. It was as though it had been drawn out lengthways. A yellow beard that surrounded it stood out especially clearly."[2]

Freud's initial response is to call the "dream nonsense." But the image continues to haunt him. Knowing he is up against his own resistance, he presses for an interpretation. "My uncle Yosef (who Freud explains earlier he greatly disliked and thought of as a simpleton) represents my two colleagues who had not been appointed to professorships . . . If the appointment of my friends . . . had been postponed for denominational reasons, my own appointment was also open to doubt; if, however, I could attribute the rejection of my two friends to other reasons, which did not apply to me, my hopes would remain untouched. This was the procedure adopted by my dream; it made one of them . . . into a simpleton and the other . . . into a criminal, whereas I was neither one nor the other; *thus we no longer had anything in common* (underlining mine); I could rejoice at my appointment to a professorship and I could avoid drawing the distressing conclusion that (my friend's) report . . . must apply equally to me."[2] Freud exposes the dilemma faced by Jewish men as anti-Semitism seemingly poses two untenable choices: either dissociate from other Jewish men to protect one's chances for survival and success, or continue to identify as a Jew and be subjected to humiliation or denied access to power and prestige in the world of men.

Freud is troubled by his unconscious dissociation from his Jewish colleagues: "I was . . . uneasy over the lightheartedness with which I had degraded two of my respected colleagues in order to keep open my own path to a professorship . . . [3] Bringing the wish for dissociation to consciousness, Freud then blames himself for having this thought, inadvertently multiplying the oppression against the self.

The dream continues to haunt him. He returns to it in the section "Infantile Material," linking it directly to painful childhood memories. Recalling his childhood wish to become a cabinet minister, as this was one of the few positions of political power open to Jews at that time, Freud writes: "Every industrious Jewish schoolboy carried a Cabinet Minister's portfolio in his satchel."[4] "It began to dawn on me that my dream had carried me back from the dreary present to the cheerful hopes of the days of the 'Burger' Ministry, and that the wish it had done its best to fulfill was one dating back to those times. In mishandling my two learned and eminent colleagues because they were Jews . . . I was behaving as though I were the Minister, I had put myself in the Minister's place. Turning the tables on His excellency with a vengeance! He had refused to appoint me professor extraordinarius and I had retaliated in the dream by slipping into his shoes."[5]

Here, Freud acknowledges his unconscious choice to identify with the aggressor to preserve an experience of himself as powerful. What he does not fully grasp is that he has become the perpetrator of anti-Semitism in his own psyche, turning with a vengeance not on His Excellency, but on his own Jewish self who he "mishandles" as if harming someone else because "they are Jews." To maintain an inner experience of the self as powerful, to avoid the pain of experiencing the self as helpless victim, the unconscious choice is made to identify the self with the non-Jewish aggressor, and to dissociate the self from fellow Jews, the victims. This intrapsychic process can be observed in a range of overt behaviors depending on the degree of identification with the aggressor: complete denial of being a Jew, disaffiliation from any form of Jewish community, association mainly with non-Jews and/or maintaining a secret, inner sense of self as superior to other Jews even while in relationship with fellow Jews; but, most painfully, being unable to fully love members of one's own Jewish family—one's fathers, sons and brothers.

Following his associations further, Freud arrives at the painful child-hood memories which illustrate how anti-Semitism can interfere in relation-ships between Jewish fathers and sons, preventing a critically important identification between the generations of men. Freud analyzes a series of dreams based upon his longing to visit Rome. He traces this longing to his childhood identification with Hannibal, the Carthiginian general who fought in the Punic Wars but was fated never to see Rome. Freud attributes his iden-tification with the non-Jewish Hannibal to his boyhood need to find a masculine hero with whom to identify as he began to confront anti-Semitism amongst his schoolmates: "And when in the higher classes I began to understand . . . what it meant to belong to an alien race, and anti-Semitic feelings among the other boys warned me that I must take up a definite position, the figure of the Semitic general rose still higher in my esteem."[6] "And the increasing importance of the effects of the anti-Semitic movement upon our emotional life helped to fix the thoughts and feelings of my youth whose power was still being shown in all these emotions and dreams. I may have been ten or twelve years old, when my father began to take me with him on his walks and reveal to me in his talk, his views upon things in the world we live in. Thus it was, on one such occasion, that he told me a story to show me how much better things are now than they had been in his days. 'When I was a young man', he said, 'I went for a walk one Saturday in the streets of your birthplace; I was well dressed and had a new fur cap on my head. A Christian came up to me and with a single blow knocked off my cap into the mud and shouted: "Jew! Get off the pavement!" 'And what did you do?' I asked. 'I went into the roadway and picked up my cap,' was his quiet reply. This struck me as unheroic conduct on the part of the big, strong man who was holding the little boy by the hand. I contrasted this situation with another which fitted my feelings better: the scene in which Hannibal's father . . . made his boy swear before the household altar to take vengeance on the Romans. Ever since that time, Hannibal had had a place in my fantasies."[7]

The core of the conflict is revealed. To identify with his Jewish father is to identify with the victim, to feel humiliated and emasculated at the hands of non-Jewish men who present an everpresent threat to one's prowess. To be a hero, to be "a man," the son feels he must model himself after a non-Jew, albeit a Semitic general, forsaking not only his Jewish identification, but his own identification with his own father. In Freud's mind there are only two untenable choices: to feel like a man and not identify with his father and with other Jewish men, or to identify with Jewish men and not feel like a man.

Not once does Freud express rage directly at his persecutors or at the anti-Semitic oppression to which he, his father, and his colleagues have been subjected. Nor is he able to acknowledge the courage and the strength necessary to survive as a Jewish man in an anti-Semitic world. When he identifies with the aggressor, he feels powerful; but he has not only become the perpetrator of anti-Semitism in his own psyche, he suffers the guilt of denying his flesh and blood.

THE "AFFECTIVE PROGRAM" OF THE RABBIS

How the elder Freud responded to the anti-Semitic Christian, the response the young Freud saw as "unheroic," was precisely in keeping with what the rabbinic tradition taught as ideal behavior for the righteous man. Having been raised as an Orthodox Jew, it is likely Jacob Freud believed he was instructing his son, not in cowardice, but in righteousness and humility. But Sigmund, like ourselves, was growing up in a different world. Outside the shtetl, his struggle was to survive as a Jew in Christian society. The young boy is thrown into confusion, trying to live in two worlds with conflicting ideals of manhood, and threatened with anti-Semitism.

For centuries, Jewish men have been faced with the dilemma of how to survive physically and psychologically under conditions of oppression. Living in largely self-contained communities, as social intercourse with the outside was severely restricted, Jewish men evolved an ideal of manhood quite different than the masculine ideal of the majority culture. In an essay entitled "The Virtues of the Inner Life in Formative Judaism," Jacob Neusner, noted rabbinic scholar, describes what he calls the sages' "affective program," their prescription for an emotional life based on virtue. He demonstrates the constancy of that program through centuries of otherwise profound change in the theology and doctrines of Rabbinic Judaism, and he attributes that constancy to the unchanging nature of the oppression to which Jews were subjected.

Of what did the program consist? "A simple catalogue of permissible feelings comprises humility, generosity, self-abnegation, love, a spirit of conciliation to the other, and eagerness to please. A list of impermissible emotions is made up of envy, ambition, jealousy, arrogance, sticking to one's opinion, self-centeredness, a grudging spirit, vengefulness . . . . aiming at the cultivation of the humble and malleable person, one who accepts everything and resents nothing . . . Temper marks the ignorant person, restraint and serenity, the learned one . . . A mark of humility is the humble acceptance of suffering . . . Submit, accept, conciliate, stay cool in emotion as much as in attitude, inside and outside . . ."[8] Faced with overwhelming odds and helpless to change the external conditions of their oppression, Jewish men evolved an ideal of Jewish masculinity to function as a strategy for survival: "The human condition of Israel therefore defined a different heroism, one filled with patience, humiliation, self-abnegation. To turn survival into endurance, pariah-status into an exercise in Godly-living, the sages' affective program served full well. Israel's hero saw power in submission . . . ultimate degradation was made to stand for ultimate power."[9]

As the affective program is constant, doctrinal and theological changes are profound. Over time, Neusner notes, the rabbis come to elevate themselves from the status of mere mortals to the status of Torah, come to see the "sage as Torah incarnate." From a purely rational perspective, such an elevation of self would seem to stand in direct contradiction to the rabbinic injunctions about self-abnegation and humility. However, the logic of the unconscious is more circuitous.

Feeling totally debased and helpless to change conditions of external oppresssion, the self compensates for the pain and humiliation suffered on the outside by elevating itself to almost God-like status in the inner world. Psychotherapists see this daily: people who have suffered severe emotional and/or physical abuse at the hands of a stronger person, usually a parent, forced to repress their anger, come to have a deep experience of the self as evil, experience extreme fluctuations in feelings of self-esteem, as grandiose fantasies of supreme power and goodness are created to compensate for and defend against deep feelings of self-loathing and powerlessness.

The sages have dealt with the debasement of anti-Semitic oppression by creating a theology, an ideal of Jewish masculinity, indeed a Judaism, based on their own near divinity as "Torah incarnate." As Jewish men repressed their rage to survive, raised up submission to suffering as an ideal, they compensated by creating a belief system which elevated their own words and thoughts to as near-divine status as possible, without declaring the unspeakable, that they themselves were God.

The ideal of Jewish masculinity and the theological tradition in which it is embodied are in need of transformation. We must be able to distinguish those aspects that are derivative of oppression from what is genuinely inspired. But as feminists working to transform Judaism, male God-language and liturgy, we need to understand we are tampering with a belief and symbol system that embodies the grandiose fantasy of self that has enabled Jewish men to survive psychologically when they could not defend themselves physically against their oppressors. We are up against one of the powerful forms of resistance the psyche, individual or collective, can muster: those defenses created for the preservation of the self in the face of annihilation.

As Jewish men transform and develop new ideals of Jewish masculinity, they have different terrain to traverse than men of the dominant culture. Not the only, but perhaps a crucial difference may be the need to reclaim their rage, even to own their capacity* to do violence. As is true of other oppressed groups, the repression of rage not only perpetuates the sense of self as victim, it cuts people off from a source of vital psychic energy. With the repression of aggression often goes the repression of life force. If libido is the energic glue of connection, aggression is the energic propellent to freedom and independence. It fuels the psychic separation from mother, propels forward movement and growth, and provides the life surge necessary to be active in the world. When the healthy aggression of growth is fused with rage, and therefore repressed as "bad," vital life energy is lost.

Robert Bly has written poetically about the need for contemporary young men to connect with the energy of the "deep masculine," "the instinctive one who's underwater and has been there we don't know how long."[10] Bly is careful to distinguish between "machismo" and the energy of the "deep masculine," which is nourishing and life-serving. For Jewish men, the vital instinctive energy for survival became mixed with rage, was repressed and channeled into the intellect, into the mind. To liberate the energy is to reconnect the mind with the body, restore the Jewish body to full potency.

---

* Owning the capacity to do violence must not be misconstrued as *being* violent. In Israel's excesses, we can see the consequences of Jewish male rage being acted-out, the *capacity* for violence denied while the sense of self as victim is maintained.

The connection between liberation struggles, whether individual or collective, and the reclaiming of anger is not a new one. What is perhaps new, is to name the ways in which the repression of rage, derivative of anti-Semitism, has polluted our Jewish psyches, bodies, relationships and tradition. Neusner acknowledges, "if a person cannot express anger one way, he or she will find some other." The unconscious has a complex repertoire. One way for the psyche to deal with repressed rage is to disown it by projecting it on to another, then experiencing the other as the bearer of the hated emotion, while the self remains the pure, suffering victim. On a broad scale, within Jewish culture, the unconscious rage generated in Jewish men by anti-Semitism has been projected onto Jewish women. Sustaining an image of themselves through the generations as humble, submissive, holy servants of God, devoid of such negative emotions as anger and revenge, Jewish men have unconsciously projected their rage onto Jewish women, experiencing Jewish women as the dominating emasculating persecutor. Christian men, the actual persecutors (when anti-Semitic) seem less to represent the enemy; but rather, an alternative ideal of masculinity offerred by the dominant culture. Caught between two worlds, in search of a hero and desperate to find an alternative to the rabbinic model, contemporary Jewish men may well seek that hero in the non-Jewish man. The Jewish woman becomes the bearer of the Shadow.

Jewish women have, to a disturbing extent, taken in the projection, internalized the Shadow. The characterization of the Jewish man as the long-suffering, passive wimp at the mercy of a larger-than-life, castrating Jewish woman is not merely the "comic" stuff of a Philip Roth or Bruce Jay Friedman novel. Daily, I see Jewish women who hate themselves because they feel, deep down, they are dangerous, murderous bitches undeserving of love; I see Jewish men who suffer enormous guilt about their anger, cut off from their energy, self-controlled to the point of emotional paralysis, and who also believe, deep down, they are evil creatures undeserving of love. To be fully human Jewish men and women, capable of loving our-selves and each other, we need to lift the Shadow of anti-Semitism from our faces.

Writing in the late sixties, a generation after Freud and twenty years after the Holocaust, Eric Erikson observed, "Historical prototypes reappear in the transferences and resistances encountered in the treatment of adult patients." In his analysis of both Jewish and non-Jewish patients, Erikson found an "unruly pair of historical prototypes—an ideal prototype (German, tall, phallic) and an evil prototype (Jewish, dwarfish, castrated) . . . Analysis of this kind permits us, I think, to generalize that the unconscious image of the evil identity, that which the ego is most afraid to resemble, is often composed of the images of the violated (castrated) body, the ethnic out-group, and the exploited minority. Although it manifests itself in a great variety of syndromes, this association is all pervasive, in men and women, in majorities and minorities, in all classes of a given national or cultural unit. For the ego, in the course of its synthesizing efforts, attempts to subsume the most powerful ideal and evil prototypes . . . and with them the whole existing imagery of superior and inferior, good and bad, masculine and feminine, free and slave, potent and impotent, beautiful and ugly, white and black, tall and small . . . in order to make one battle and one strategy out of a bewildering number of skirmishes."[11] Erikson concluded: "Therapeutic as well as reformist efforts verify the sad truth that in any system based on suppression, exclusion, and exploitation, the suppressed, excluded, and exploited unconsciously accept the evil image they are made to represent by those who are dominant."[12]

Looking carefully at Erikson's list of negatives that adhere to the evil historic prototype, one finds both "feminine" and "Jew." "Jew" (meaning Jewish man) and "feminine" are not only associated together, they are associated with "slave, impotent, ugly, small, inferior." To label Erikson a sexist or anti-Semite is, of course, to miss the point. He has, reading the psyches of his patients, accurately documented the unconscious archetypes known and retained in the mythology of Western culture, a mythology which reflects the collective unconscious of white, Christian men. It is a cultural mythology that has repressed the feminine, and attached to it other images the white, Christian, male "ego is most afraid to resemble"—"the castrated body," the Jew and the black. Within the broader culture, it is the Jew (and the black) who have carried the Shadow for white men. From the more powerful to the less powerful, the Shadow is passed down. Christian men to Jewish men, Jewish men to Jewish women. The archetypal association of the Jewish man with the "feminine" has deeply impacted Jewish masculinity. But the true depth of its effect can best be understood after an excursis into current theories of gender identity development.

FAMILIES WITHOUT FATHERS

Feminist theorists have, for years, focused their attention on the devastation wrought by skewed gender roles which assign primary responsibility for child care to women, leaving men emotionally peripheral, but financially powerful. More recently, feminists have taken a closer look at the differential impact this form of child rearing has had on boy and girl children. Nancy Chodorow, author of *The Reproduction of Mothering: Psychoanalysis and the Sociology of Gender*, asserts that as long as the cultural pattern of assigning almost total responsibility for the care and nurturance of children to women persists, leaving men emotionally uninvolved with children, we will continue to perpetuate "asymmetries in the relational experiences of girls and boys as they grow up, which account for the crucial differences in feminine and masculine personality, and relational modes which they entail."[13] More recently, Irene Fast, author of *Gender Identity: A Differentiation Model*, goes even further. Fast asserts that because the initial bonding experience for both boys and girls occurs when the infant's consciousness is too primitive to be able to distinguish self from other and occurs with a woman, all children, regardless of gender, have at the deepest strata of their psyches, a self-experience (identification, self-representation) in which "mother" is most extensively represented. At this early stage, the infant cannot identify that self-representation as "feminine" or "masculine." However, as the child differentiates psychologically from mother, acquiring a mind of its own and the cognitive skills necessary to discriminate male and female, "boys are likely to react intensely to their early perception that they must renounce all their self experience derived from their mothers as alien to themselves as masculine."[14] When there is an emotionally nourishing male parent with whom to bond and identify, the boy can take the image of the "masculine" deeply into himself as well, easing the separation from mother. However, a society whose family configurations and social institutions deny young boys the opportunity of bonding with fathers, prevents the formation of healthy masculinity, and leads instead to the need to repress, repudiate and hold in contempt the "feminine."

When boys grow up in families with emotionally absent men, boys can only arrive at a sense of masculinity negatively—by repressing their identification with mother, by denial and opposition to women, by repudiation of "feminine" qualities. Boys are unable to develop an inner experience of what it means to be masculine, positively, by loving and being loved by a man. Unable to take deeply into themselves an image, a subjective experience of the nourishing male, boys become dependent on external, plastic signs of masculinity. They have difficulty loving other men. In fact, the depth of the actual need may be so great, it creates homophobic terror.

In relationships with women in later life, men raised this way will be terrified of intimacy because they are fearful of a merger with a woman which will draw them back into that primal psychic territory. They need to maintain emotional distance in order to preserve a sense of identity, an inner sense of "maleness." The absence of an emotionally nurturant alternative to mother has not only interfered in the process of gender identification, it has prevented a healthy separation from her. Therefore, men remain deeply but unconsciously dependent on mother, on women; but are simultaneously fearful of intimacy with women, because if their unconscious yearning draws them in too deeply, they can no longer experience themselves as "masculine." Instead, they avoid intimacy to ward off the nameless, dread anxiety attendant upon the experience of losing a sense of self. Emotional detachment, sexual promiscuity, devaluation of or inability to commit to relationship, are possible "solutions."

The "masculine" personality of our time comes to be characterized by deep, albeit unconscious, dependence on women, emotional detachment, reliance on plastic symbols of power and masculinity, difficulty loving other men and nurturing women and children. This characterization is really a caricature of full human manliness. A fully human man, a fully masculine human is a being as capable of love as of work, able to nourish men, women and children, with a sense of self deeply rooted in his being rather than derived from money, power, or notoriety, and with a spiritual connection to the Sources of Life.

Looking at the differential impact on girls growing up in families without emotionally nourishing fathers, we see not only the incompleteness of the feminine personality that results, but the asymmetry of the modes of being in relationships that develop. When girls grow up in families able to form their only significant relationship with mother, a person of the same gender, girls may have the opportunity of bonding with, identifying with a person who is like them-selves. However, the woman with whom they identify is likely to be a person with little independent sense of self, a person who identifies herself primarily as a "being in relationship." Without the built-in distinction of gender, girls have to struggle enormously to create a distinct, separate sense of self. The self-feeling has been bound up with and predicated on being in relationship. Being out of relationship often threatens women with the loss of identity—women may tend to fear they won't know who they are out of relationship. Because many mothers defined themselves primarily as care-givers, either prevented from performing social roles outside the family or having the significance of the roles they did perform devalued, girls are hard pressed to identify with their mother's work.

As adults, when women are in intimate relationships with men or with other women, they are often pressing for a kind of closeness, a feeling of merger that avoids intimacy not by emotional detachment, but rather by denying the different-ness of the Other. Unable to bond with father, a parent of the opposite gender, women come to expect all later relationships, even with men, to feel like the less differentiated relationship possible between two women. The unavailability of father to provide an emotionally nourishing alternative to mother prevents a healthy separation from her for the girl, as it did for the boy. However, the girl does not have to repress her identification with mother as her brother did by creating rigid impermeable boundaries around the self. To the contrary, the girl may confuse "being in relationship" with "having a sense of self." She may never develop a separate, distinct identity as an individual in her own right, outside of relationship.

Super-valuation of caregiving to the exclusion of other forms of creative self-expression, difficulty in functioning independently, willingness to subsume the self in order to preserve the possibility of staying in relationship, and difficulty developing an identity based on creative work, come to characterize the "feminine" personality of our time. Again, this is a caricature. A fully human woman, a fully feminine human, is a being as capable of creative work as of love, able to stand on her own as well as nurture others, with a sense of self rooted deeply in her own being rather than derived as a function of her role in relationship with others, with a spiritual connection to the Sources of Power in the universe.

THE JEWISH FAMILY

Compounding the psychological problems created by skewed gender roles in the family, cultural anti-Semitism magnifies the dilemma of gender identity formation and differentiation. Because of the fusion of the archetype of the "Jew" with the "castrated body" and the "feminine," the Jewish father is significantly devalued. Cultural anti-Semitism robs Jewish fatherhood of psychic potency, just as it bestows that potency on Christian men. In a parallel fashion, cultural anti-Semitism robs Jewish women of their femininity. If cultural anti-Semitism has emasculated Jewish men, it has cast Jewish women in the role of the powerful, castrating persecutor. When your mother is a Jewish mother, her presence looms even larger than life, her psychic size and power greatly magnified by the dynamics of anti-Semitism, just as your Jewish father is diminished in stature. This interferes in both the identification process for Jewish sons, and in the process of separation-from-mother for both sons and daughters. It is no mere coincidence that the Jewish mother has become a paramount symbol for all of American culture of that too much, too much, too much mother; while the culture lifts up as the ideal of femininity the "shiksa goddess," as Lenny Bruce has so affectionately christened her. *For Jews, the masculine and feminine archetypes in the collective unconscious have been reversed by the anti-Semitism of the dominant, white, male Christian culture.* Jewish men may well experience themselves, and be experienced by Jewish women as somehow less masculine than men of the dominant culture; Jewish women may well experience themselves and be experienced by Jewish men as somehow less feminine than women of the dominant culture. Although Jewish men and women may blame each other for this phenomenon, the insidious process has its roots in anti-Semitism.

THE STORY OF MORDECAI

Working as a therapist, there are times when encountering the struggles of an individual, one knows oneself to be in the presence of something larger, of a phase of history as that history has left its imprint on consciousness and been manifest in the life of a single person. " . . . neurosis, seen not just as one man's case history, but within the context of a wider light, is that dial of the instrument that records the effects of a particular stage of civilization upon a civilized individual . . . The most sensitive individual, although not the most normal, may provide the most representative expression of a breakdown which affects other people on a level at which they may be scarcely conscious."[15] Mordecai is such an individual. What I have learned about how the Shadow of anti-Semitism from the collective unconscious interpenetrates the personal unconscious, I have learned from our journey together.

When I met Mordecai, he was twenty-nine years old. Despite his above average intelligence, his emotional and somatic difficulties were so severe, it had taken him ten years to graduate from the ivy league university he attended, with time out for illness and psychiatric treatment. He was suicidally depressed after being asked to leave the graduate program in science where he had spent the last year; he had no money; he refused to work just to earn a living as his father had; he had no male friends; he desperately wanted a relationship with a woman, though he had not had a sexual relationship in years; he had recurring difficulties with sexual impotency.

Mordecai was born the older and only male of two children from a working class, second-generation American Jewish family. His mother was the dominant parent, psychologically more powerful and intrusive than his father, who was the passive, emotionally detached man, submissive to his wife and all other authority figures. Initially, Mordecai saw his mother as the "all Good" one and his father as "all Bad" parent. He identified with the perceived strength in the family, with his mother, and with her ideal for him. His terror of being like his father, who he saw as the passive, weak, victim, was so intense he totally denied bearing any resemblance to him at all.

At first, Mordecai would not even discuss his relationship with his parents because the very act of doing so felt like acknowledging he was a "Jewish mama's boy," an image he found degrading to the extreme. Though he could recount experiences of how mother had prevented him from separating through her extremely harsh, critical and punitive responses to any attempts he made at independent functioning, Mordecai could feel no anger at mother. He totally repressed his rage and projected it onto various establishments he experienced as blocking his efforts at progress.

Mordecai experienced a paranoid fear of being attacked, of being conspiratorily undermined in his efforts at career growth. The unconscious guilt he felt about his rage, compounded by the Oedipal guilt of having been preferred by mother to father, caused him to experience himself as subject to severe punishment at every turn. He often referred to himself as a "sexual eunuch," a castrated, worthless, non-human being. Grandiose visions of becoming a great scientist helped him stay alive when he wanted to commit suicide; feeling like a helpless, powerless victim of the Shadow that pursued him relentlessly.

Mordecai identified his negative, victim self with being Jewish. Though he acknowledged Jews have a reputation for being intellectual, he experienced his interest in being a scientist, that which was powerful and good in him, as a non-Jewish characteristic. Scientifically minded Jewish boys, he asserted, became doctors.

For Mordecai to heal, he had to transform the image of himself as victim. He needed to reconnect with the rage he had once felt but had long since buried. He needed to connect that rage with the people who had abused him. In the process, he might free up energy in his body, break the psychological fusion with mother, and regain his potency. I knew that when the rage broke, it was going to come at me. I was his therapist, of course. I was also a Jewish woman. I had no idea what unconscious symbolism would pour forth with the rage.

Once his sense of connection to me was firmly established, I began to let Mordecai know that if he ever felt angry at me, it would be good for him to get it off his chest. After almost two years, the rage began to break through. Though his own family had had no direct experience with the war in Europe, the imagery associated with the aggression was filled with allusions to the Holocaust. His rage at me as a Jewish woman was intertwined with images of the archetypal oppressor of the Jewish people—Hitler. Though the process unfurled over a number of months, it is possible to see how the imagery emerged following a brief sequence along the journey.

A brief separation in our relationship occurred when I cancelled a regularly scheduled appointment to attend a professional conference. Mordecai tried to call me because he was upset, and though I attempted to return the call, I had been unable to reach him. He was furious at me for not being there, and at himself for needing me. My absence had put him in touch with a dependency he could not acknowledge.

On my return, Mordecai burst into the office screaming that he was furious at the Jewish people. He had had a series of encounters with Jewish women over the weekend who were all dominating, castrating bitches. Jewish women were little Hitlers, he bellowed. Hitler should have killed us all. When he stopped the tirade, which was peppered with other allusions to the Gestapo and Nazis, I suggested he was angry at me, perhaps for not returning his call. Then he attacked me for thinking everything had to do with me, acting just like a Jewish woman. He never expected me to return the call, because I was just a part of the Jewish establishment who didn't care about him. I reminded him I have always returned his calls in the past, and didn't know why he wouldn't have expected me to do so this time.

Still feeling the pain and anger of his frustrated dependence, he launched into a diatribe about a synagogue service he had attended over the weekend. He was furious at the rabbi for saying how wonderful it was Jewish children in Philadelphia remained in the city even after they were grown up. He found it disgusting Philadelphia Jews never left the city, still tied to their parents. The rabbi reminded him of the rabbis during World War II who read Talmud instead of inspiring Jews to fight the Nazis. There were not more Warsaw uprisings, he railed, because the rabbis encouraged passivity. Experiencing his own struggle for independence like the desperate struggle of youths under Nazi domination, Mordecai blamed the rabbis, who he identified with his father, the passive Jewish man who did not teach him how to fight free of his mother, who as dominant parent had become fused in his mind with Hitler and the Nazis.

Over the next weeks, Mordecai's rage continued to spill forth, often filled with attacks on me as a Jewish woman, a Hitler, a Nazi. The image of the "terrible mother" was infused with images of the archetypal oppressors of the Jews. As he began to express more anger, he became more depressed. The emergence of the rage broke the connection with the "good mother," interfered in his connection to me, and left him feeling alone and abandoned. When Mordecai saw a psychiatrist for a medication evaluation to help with the depression, the doctor suggested hospitalization. Mordecai, terrified, ran out of the office, into the streets. For days, he lived in a heightened state of fear and anxiety, convinced I was going to have him locked up, paranoid the police would be waiting for him, like the Gestapo, at his door. At the peak of his rage and fear, attacking me as a member of the "hurting profession," I challenged Mordecai to get in touch with the true source of his rage. "Who yelled at you as brutally as you are yelling at me? If you are treating me this way, this was done to you." Trembling and crying, Mordecai collapsed to the floor, as memories of the "terrible mother's" brutal attacks flooded back into consciousness.

Reclaiming the rage and pain connected with his experiences of being the helpless victim at the mercy of the dominant, "terrible mother" freed Mordecai of the need to project his aggression onto others, which therefore freed him of the paranoid fear of being attacked. In the next few weeks, able now to risk getting overtly angry without fearing annihilation, Mordecai began getting into more arguments. In a crucial sequence of events, he confronted his self-image as a passive, Jewish victim vis-à-vis non-Jewish men, and took action to liberate himself from that role.

Mordecai had entered into an informal business arrangement with a non-Jewish man at school for the sale of his stereo equipment. This man was apparently accustomed to taking advantage of Mordecai, and would not pay the agreed-upon sum at the time of delivery. Mordecai secretly removed the cartridge from the turntable, but then berated himself for acting like a coward, not demanding full payment directly. When, the following day, his fellow student demanded the cartridge and bullied Mordecai by blocking the doorway, trapping him in the room with the weight of his body, Mordecai pushed his way free and let rip with a torrent of verbal abuse. Recounting the moment, he said, "It was as if decades of rage came pouring out of me, rage at my mother, at Hitler, at the non-Jewish boys who made fun of me for being intellectual and not knowing how to fight." He knew his rage far exceeded the incident that had triggered it. But he had walked through the gates of the forest.

A few weeks later, Mordecai made love with a Jewish woman for the first time in ten years.

In a patriarchal culture which, paradoxically, has robbed its boys (and girls) of their natural fathers, tied men to unconscious dependence on women, cut men off from the love of other men, it is Jewish men who became the bearers of the Shadow, made to represent that Man other men were terrified of becoming. Through the mythology of anti-Semitism, Jewish men were cast as the "feminine man," "the castrated man," "the man dominated by a woman," "the man without a land" in a world of warring nations, warring men. To survive, Jewish men buried their rage, and built a sacred theology which raises up their own Image to the status of near-divinity in the inner world of Judaism. Jewish women have become the bearers of the Shadow, the Other within Judaism. Healing requires of all of us that we face the light.

Notes

1. Sigmund Frued, *The Interpretation of Dreams*, trans. James Strachey (New York: Avon Books, 1965). p. 171.
2. *Ibid.*, p. 173.
3. *Ibid.*
4. *Ibid.*, p. 226.
5. *Ibid.*

6. *Ibid.*, p. 229.
7. *Ibid.*, p. 230.
8. Jacob Neusner, "Emotions in the Talmud," in *Tikkun* vol. 1, no. 1 (1986), pp. 74–80.
9. *Ibid.*, p. 81.
10. Robert Bly, *The Pillow and the Key* (St. Paul: Ally Press, 1987), p. 7.
11. Erik Erikson, *Identity, Youth and Crisis* (New York: Norton, 1968), p. 58.
12. *Ibid.*, p. 59.
13. Nancy Chodorow, *The Reproduction of Mothering: Psychoanalysis and the Sociology of Gender* (New York: University of California Press, 1978), p. 169.
14. Irene Fast, *Gender Identity: A Differentiation Model* (New York: The Analytic Press, 1984), p. 104.
15. Stephen Spender, "Introduction," in Malcom Lowry, *Under the Volcano* (New York: New American Library, 1965), p. ix.

THE SEXUAL MYTHOLOGY OF ANTI-SEMITISM

Andrea Dworkin

My family is from Russia and Eastern Europe. Those who did not leave lived in various parts of Eastern Europe and most of them were exterminated by the Nazis. I am one of those compulsive Jews who goes through periods in her life when she can't stop reading about the concentration camps because it happened to the few survivors that I know who are in my family. I grew up, I went to Hebrew school, I was taught largely by survivors; and because my family was just full of empty holes where numbers of people were exterminated, it is all very real to me.

I'm going to talk in general about my feminist understanding of the sexual roots of racism. But in particular I'm going to talk about how anti-Semitism sexualizes both the Jewish male and the Jewish female.

THE JEWISH MALE

Hitler's characterization of the Jewish male was that he was a rapist. This seems very hard for contemporary Americans to grasp because I think we have a concept of the Jewish male that is, in a sense, a reaction to what happened during the Nazi period. Jewish men in this country are seen as being entirely of the head, intellectual rather than sexual (although certainly there are Jewish male novelists who are trying to redress grievances in that area). The reasons, I think, have mostly to do with male supremacy but also with one very specific fact of recent Jewish life: that numbers of Jewish men were castrated in the concentration camps. It is possible to speculate that among Jews who survived the concentration camps is the largest living population of castrated men. Therefore castration among living Jews is not symbolic—it is actual. The state of Israel, for example, was founded in part and very largely influenced in its formation by men who came from a population some of which had been castrated by the Nazis.

The characterization of Jewish men that Hitler made vivid to the masses in *Mein Kampf* is not unique to anti-Semitism but is rather a kind of paradigm for racism everywhere. Making the racially despised male into a rapist makes him into a kind of animal. It animalizes him and makes him into the kind of animal that logically has to be caged and castrated. Castration is a logical answer to this evocation of a rapist frenzy. And remember that the concern is not that he rapes women of his own kind; it's that he rapes the women of the group that is supposed to be racially superior.

Another part of the anti-Semitic portrait of the Jewish male has to do with money. As you know, Jews are supposed to have the money, own the money, control the money, use the money, manipulate the money—and we very often forget that money has a very real sexual dimension to it. If we see all the propaganda about the Jew and money as just having to do with economics, we will miss the whole sexual meaning of the power of the Jew controlling the money. In my book *Pornography* I described how the sexual meaning of money is a characteristic male-supremacist value:

> The sexual meaning of money is acted out by men on a wide scale, but it is also internalized, applied to the interior functioning of male sexual processes. Men are supposed to hoard sperm as they are supposed to hoard money. A central religious imperative (in both Western and Eastern religions) discourages expenditures of sperm not instrumental in effecting impregnation, because wealth wasted instead of invested is wealth lost. The phrase "spermatic economy" expressed this same idea in the secular realm, particularly in the nineteenth century. The idea that when a man spends sperm he uses up his most significant natural resource—that he spills his sons into nonexistence—both precedes and survives specific religious dogma and quasi-scientific theorizing. One meaning of the verb *to spend* is "to ejaculate." One meaning of the verb *to husband* is "to conserve or save"; its archaic meaning is "to plow for the purpose of growing crops." A husband, in this sense, is one who conserves or saves his sperm except to fuck for the purpose of impregnating. In the male system, control of money means sexual maturity, as does the ability to control ejaculation. The valuing and conserving of money, using money to make wealth—like the valuing and conserving of sperm, using sperm to make wealth—demonstrates a conformity to adult male values, both sexual and economic. A boy spends his sperm and his money on women. A man uses his sperm and his women to produce wealth. A boy spends; a man produces . . . The owning and impregnating of a woman in marriage or in some form of concubinage (however informal) are seen as mastery of spending without purpose, the first clear proof that masculinity is established as an irrefutable fact, adult, impervious to the ambivalences of youth still contaminated by female eroticism in which the penis has no intrinsic significance. A commitment to money as such follows as an obvious and public commitment to the display of masculinity as an aggressive and aggrandizing drive.[1]

So when people say that Jews control the money, they are talking about a kind of male sexual power, and on that level too, the Jewish male is supposed to be dangerous to the male who defines himself as racially superior.

THE JEWISH FEMALE

The Jewish woman is traditionally called some version (depending on the language) of "the Jewess"—which is both an extremely condescending term and an eroticized term. The Jewess exists not as a human being but as a sexual being.

Just as the Jewish male is seen as a rapist—animalized, bestial—the Jewess is seen as a harlot. Hitler characterized Jewish women as sexual provocateurs really, or as whores, as sluts, but as very aggressive whores and sluts. This valuation of the Jewish woman did not originate in Nazi Germany. It is very old; it goes back very far in anti-Semitic mythology. It was especially popular in czarist Russia, and it still is very popular in Russia. The Jewess is the seductress.

A very important part of anti-Semitic sexual mythology is that this very provocative, very aggressive slut is going to snare the sperm of the Aryan man—or whoever the superior man may be—and breed half-breed Jewish children. This is a contamination of the superior race, and therefore it is not surprising to find that in the concentration camps there were massive programs to sterilize Jewish women.

THE SEXUAL MEANING OF THE CONCENTRATION CAMP

There were sexual roots at the core of the concentration camp system. Sadistic abuse was sexual—not just the specific sexual acts but all the acts of sadism. All the acts of torture were sexual acts. They were construed to be not only necessary but also pleasurable—and to bring fun to at least some who did them, who did them to the Jews. The first time I ever heard the word "rape" was from an aunt of mine who had been in Birkenau, which was the women's auxiliary of Auschwitz. She had a breakdown one day before I was even ten and told me everything that had happened to her. I'm sure she didn't tell me everything but she told me a great deal. No one else was there; she was very sick, and she was vomiting, and she was extremely upset, and I called my mother, and my mother rushed over. When the crisis was taken care of and we were home, my mother said to me: what did she say to you? what did she tell you? And I said: what is rape? And she said, what did she *tell* you? And I said, well I understand everything she said, but what is rape? And my mother said: it's something that happened to *her*. Later on I found out what rape is; but until the feminist movement what I heard about rape—no matter who had been raped—was that it was something that happened to *her*.

This is the worst thing that happened to my aunt, and I don't know how to talk about it: her sister's infant—fathered by a Nazi guard through rape—was killed in front of both of them. My aunt told me the guards had fun.

And so forth and so on. My point is that all of this is sexual. These are sexual acts committed for sexual reasons; and what happens in an anti-Semitic social system is that the Jewish woman becomes the most eroticized woman because of what is construed to be her race. She is the most purely animalized, characterized especially by smell. She is also considered to be dirt—or, to use the language of Robert Stoller (who is not necessarily opposed to considering people this way), "fecal."[2] When Stoller writes about the eroticization of the fecal, he means Jews, prostitutes, blacks, illiterates, and so on—anyone who has been sufficiently degraded to be really reeking of shame.

It is my opinion—having studied pornography for the last several years —that the concentration camp woman sets the standard for the mass sadism we are living with today. I believe that she is a secret sexual memory. I believe that for men who are acculturated to sadistic expressions of sexuality, there is a great deal of pleasure involved in remembering her—pleasure in thinking of her, knowing who she was. I'm not just talking about the symbolic meaning of the concentration camps; I'm talking about the real effect of what really happened and its ongoing influence in our society, especially in terms of sexual values.

The sexual paradigm of anti-Semitism is lived out even among Jews when Jewish men take their revenge on Jewish women through rape, through prostitution, through forced pregnancy, through literature, and also through pornography. And I ask myself: has he been hurt? And I answer yes. And I say: has she been hurt? And I answer yes. And I say: does he use his hurt to justify hurting her? And I say yes—he tells us that's his reason and that he has a right. And does she accept this reason as appropriate justification? And I say that Jewish women for the most part do—and this is male supremacy, not anti-Semitism.

UNDERSTANDING THE SEXUAL MODEL OF RACISM

I've been talking about anti-Semitism and the sexual model for anti-Semitism, but it is a model that also applies to many other manifestations of racism. I believe racism is always sexualized. One has to get to the sexual roots of racism in order to begin to understand it and to deal with it. What has become clear to me in my study of pornography is that one of its major purposes as a genre is to sexualize racial hatreds.

A long time ago James Baldwin—in some of the best essays that were ever written about what it means to have an identity[3]—said something that nobody very much understood: he said that white people in this country didn't understand that none of them were white until they got here, and I think that's true. I think that what this means for Jews—and I speak as a Jewish woman—is extremely difficult and complex.

I come out of a family in which extermination was part of everyday life—not just in the great absences but in the memories of survivors. My immediate family was very ardently antiracist, very conscientiously antiracist; but my extended family was not, and I grew up trying to resolve, trying to understand, how these people—many of whom were European refugees—could hate blacks so much. They could believe the same things about blacks that I knew had been said about them—and I knew that those things had been said about them because I read those things in books. So—at the age of twelve or so—I would confront them. I would say: but I read *you* smelled like that. I couldn't understand how people who had witnessed and been subject to such devastation could carry the same attitudes toward other people. Of course some did and some didn't; but I found for myself an explanation, even though it isn't a very comforting one. In my family I was able to observe that there were Jews, especially those who had come directly from Europe, who were damn glad that somebody else was going to be killed first. That's something that was very hard to face, but I can tell you that in parts of my family it was a fact. Other parts of my family, though, took their experience and their suffering and they made an identification. They said: there go I. And it seems to me that this is what a Jewish person in this country deals with when dealing with racial hatred against blacks. Within the Jewish community one is always in the situation of making a choice that involves one's real history, not denying it, and one's real place in this country. It's true that one's place in this country is constantly misrepresented, and therefore one is always trying to correct the misrepresentation of it, but one has to get to the next part, which is how racial hatred also operates among Jews toward others.

Notes

1. Andrea Dworkin, *Pornography: Men Possessing Women* (New York: Perigee, 1981), pp. 21-22.

2.   Robert J. Stoller, *Sexual Excitement: Dynamics of Erotic Life* (New York: Pantheon Books, 1979), p. 8.

3.   See especially, *Notes of a Native Son* and *Nobody Knows My Name*, in James Baldwin, *The Price of the Ticket* (New York: St. Martin's Marek, 1985).

The Jewish View of Homosexuality

Barry Dov Schwartz

Jewish sexual ethics can be summed up as being equally concerned with both man and woman. Recognizing libidos, weaknesses, and mental health conditions, Judaism sets out a code of discipline with the goal not of senseless denial with repressions, but an enhancement of relationships. It is the transformation of the human animal to the human person, and therefore, proper sex is not an act, but a process of humanization and personalization. It is the fulfillment of the divine commandment to enjoy the pleasures of sensuality; the body is holy. Although corruptible, the sex impulse is a potential blessing in that it leads to the propagation of the species and the family of mankind. In this way we become partners with God, who brought man and woman into being for partnership and perpetuation. Jewish sexuality is ordered, disciplined behavior without detracting from the pleasure principle. By mastering one's actions, one can use the gifts of nature for the refinement of the universe. Sex and marriage constitute a social relationship as well as an individual one. They are not purely private matters. Sex in the human is never a merely physical concern, nor is it a purely private matter; it has social implications. What goes on between the partners is a concern of society as a whole. Humanization demands that the total union of two persons be made public and protected by marriage as an institution.[1]

Moreover, Jewish sexuality is not concerned with the sexual organs alone. Jewish sex represents a totality of mind, body, personality, feelings and needs—the greatest need of which is to lift people from the biological level to the spiritual one, thus bringing them closer to the Divine Being.[2]

And this is what we learn about sexuality from the Bible. In the first place, sexuality is not presented as being evil, or even earthy. The sexual impulse is not to be construed as an inexorable and terrible necessity, a passionate talent which were better off buried. It is neither something to hide or deny, but rather is a gift of God. It is a spiritual function and has great potentiality for growth in the spiritual dimension. The biblical view of sex is that of full, free, and responsible sexuality within the circumstances of the relationship of marriage.[3]

The conjugal right to know one's spouse not only includes intergenital sexual activity, but also romantic sex play. The Song of Solomon reveals an explicit account of sexual expression between the Shulamite and her faithful shepherd spouse.[4] His rapturous admiration of her body in intimate nakedness is described with approval.[5] Their caressings are detailed with no hint of prudery or shame. Within the marital privilege, carnal, or physical knowledge of the spouse is a divinely blessed prerogative.[6]

Sexual expression is presented in the Bible as an approved, responsible relationship through which the ultimate in human delight is experienced. In addition, this somehow enables one to know God in a full, free way that one might not otherwise be able to attain.[7]

Rabbinic tradition, likewise, denied that the flesh was evil and insisted that sex was good and celibacy the evil and curse, for indeed a celibate is "one who has committed murder . . . and detracted from the image of God."[8] Sex is not sin; sexlessness is sin. Sex is natural and the ideal. Judaism stresses that although God created humankind bisexually, they were purportedly divided into two sexes—"male and female He created them,"—thus making it clear that human sexuality was designed by God. The "maleness" of man and "femaleness" of woman originated in the mind of God. "In His image," male and female, are alike yet different, with neither sex being inferior nor superior. This bearing of the image of God distinguishes human life from all other forms of life. A serious contemplation of all that this means cannot help but have an effect on sexual attitudes and conduct both before and after marriage as well as on all other aspects of man-woman relationships. When one is conscious that the partner is made in the image of God, and that one must consider that person in relation to God, self-centered exploitation, manipulation, or domination of a woman or man becomes mockery against God. Marriage, sex and love are holy dimensions within Jewish tradition.

Although many precautions were instituted, the rabbis were of the opinion that homosexuality was an activity for the heathen and not for the Jew: "Israel is suspected of neither pederasty nor bestiality."[9] Nonetheless, precautions were ever present, undoubtedly to preserve this reputation held by the Jews. It is interesting to note here the debate which centered around Rabbi Judah's statement that two unrelated men may not sleep together under the same blanket.[10] He was overruled, based on the premise that Jews would never even consider an act of homosexuality.[11] Maimonides codified this into law: "A Jew is not suspected of sodomy or buggery. Therefore one is allowed to be alone with them. But if one takes care not to be alone with a male or an animal it is praiseworthy."[12] Rabbi Joseph Karo later repeated and added: "In our century [sixteenth] when there are many loose men around [*pritzim*], one should refrain from being alone with another male."[13] A contemporary, Rabbi Solomon

Luria, disagreed even with this prohibition, and declared that a male is even permitted to share the same bed and blanket with another man since homosexuality is so rare among Jews. One who refrains from doing so as a special act of piety is guilty of self-righteous pride.[14] A century later, Rabbi Joel Sirkes suspended Rabbi Karo's prohibition because such acts were nonexistent among Polish Jewry.[15]

This fascinating debate which lasted many hundreds of years certainly is indicative of the rabbinic attitude toward homosexuality as well as the temptations of homosexuality.

Homosexuality, the condition of physical acts of love with others of the same sex (the prefix *homo* is from the Greek meaning *same* and not from the Latin meaning *man*), is a term that refers to both male and female. Jewish law, however, distinguishes between male and female homosexuality, and therefore, when referring to female homosexuality, we shall specifically indicate lesbianism. In contrast to male homosexuality, lesbianism is not even mentioned in the Bible. There is no direct prohibition, either because it was relatively unknown, or because of the later rabbinic view that the male was responsible for the *mitzvah* of procreation. Whatever the biblical thinking was, Jewish law treats the female homosexual more leniently than the male, and refers to lesbianism only indirectly. Commenting on "the doing of the Canaanites,"[16] the rabbis warn against female homosexuality as well as male homosexuality. What was the nature of these "doings"? "You might think the verse refers to a prohibition against erecting buildings and planting vineyards in the same manner as the Canaanites. But the verse specifically states *chukim*; namely, the Jews should not follow the laws of these people nor in the 'doings' of their ancestors. And what were they wont to do? A man would marry a man and woman should marry a woman."[17] So, this was considered legal behavior. Therefore, Jews are prohibited in following these "doings" and the statutes of the Canaanites.

In the Talmud,[18] Rav Huna viewed lesbianism on the same level as harlotry. Although technically there was no intercourse, the lesbian was not a complete virgin, and this made her unfit to marry a priest.[19] The final law differs with Huna's stringent decision, and legislates that the act is immoral, condemnable and prohibited, but not punishable. The Talmud does not equate lesbianism with premarital intercourse or prostitution, and Maimonides even rules that a man need not dismiss a wife guilty of this act (as he would be required to do if she were proven guilty of adultery).[20] Maimonides does, however, recommend flogging as a sign of our disapproval of this act, and he cautions her husband to watch her carefully so as to prevent her associating with other women known to be promiscuous lesbians.[21] Undoubtedly, the rabbis considered lesbianism as an obscene practice. Although there are no records to validate the sentiment that Jewesses did not practice lesbianism, we can be certain that the rabbis did not consider sexual activities between females as of any consequence. True, Samuel's father did not permit his daughters to sleep together, but even here it was probably for the purpose of not having them become accustomed to another's body in bed so as to arouse them sexually (*i.e.*, heterosexually).[22]

Although the specific injunctions regarding homosexuality are to be found in the book of Leviticus,[23] we can begin our excursion on this topic by studying a few episodic narratives in the book of Genesis, as elucidated in the Talmud.

Upon disembarking from the ark, Noah's three sons are involved in some strange activities with their inebriated father. Genesis 9:22 indicates that Ham saw his father's nakedness and rushed to tell his brothers, Shem and Japheth, who immediately proceeded to cover the nakedness, making certain not to even glance at this embarrassment. When he awoke in a sober state, Noah realized what Ham did and in Gensis 9:25, pronounced a curse on Ham's son, Canaan, while at the same time blessing Shem and Japheth. Ham's guilt was not only that of seeing and being a witness, but of being personally involved in some definitive illicit act. According to Nachmanides, the sin committed was that Ham saw the nakedness of his father and did not act respectfully. He should have covered his nakedness and not told even his brothers. But Ham told them about the incident in the presence of many people in order to deride Noah. Noah's embarrassment was that the disgrace was known to many.[24]

One observation may here be in order. Whatever the exact nature of the sin inflicted upon Noah, one thing is stated categorically: it happened while Noah was drunk. The immorality (castration or homosexuality) was accomplished while one of the partners was under the influence of alcohol. It is impossible to believe that Noah slept through either procedure. He was a passive partner weakened morally by drunkenness.[25] If homosexuality did take place, it was (a) not due to any sexual dysfunction or abnormalities, (b) engaged in by men who were normally and nominally heterosexual, and (c) an act of folly not punished by death. Later in this paper, the implication of these items will become clearer. One may suggest, although not conclusively, that, on the basis of some rabbinic commentaries and linguistic analyses, Noah and Ham were involved in a specific illicit sexual relationship; namely, sodomy.

Noah's punishment is not mentioned, but Ham's is very clear: he is to be an *eved*, a slave, or perhaps (homiletically) to remain a slave since he evidenced such weakness already, as being a slave to his passions—even without regard to his father's honor.[26]

In rabbinic literature, Sodom was generally synonymous with inhospitality, niggardliness, heartlessness, and oppression of the poor.[27] Every prophetic reference to Sodom includes a litany of sins, none of which refer to sexual licentiousness. The Talmud enumerates the sins of the people of Sodom: envy of the wealthy, meanness to orphans, thievery, murder, perversion of justice. "Men of Sodom have no place in the world to come." The *Midrash Hagadol* of the fourteenth century states about Genesis 19:5 that "Scriptures inform us that they were steeped in incest, pederasty and bestiality," much the same as the men of Gibeah.[28]

Moreover, the total destruction of the land of Sodom as well as its population points to an interesting correlation between sexual immorality and the condition of the earth. It is an ancient theory that the fertility of women is intrinsically bound up with the fertility of the earth. Any factor which might impede the normal flow of fertility, reproduction, and growth among humans has a negative effect on nature paralleling it with barrenness, famine, and drought. In other words, morality and nature have a linkage: "What nature abhors, the law prohibits."[29] As long as Jews obeyed the laws of morality, Israel's land and people flourished and grew. On the other hand, adultery, as well as any other immorality mentioned in the Bible, leads to sterility of the earth and even worse calamities. Normal, healthy relations and unions cause proper rainfall and change of seasons; illicit relationships cause the plagues, storms, floods, famine. In fact, there are numerous Midrashim to this effect. The flood, for example, was caused by illicit sexual relations such as pederasty and intercourse with animals.[30] Fornication was regarded as the cause of the destruction of Sodom and Gomorra,[31] and, according to Rabbi Simlai, it inevitably brings in its train great calamities in which the good and the wicked perish alike.[32] Likewise, homosexuality was against the laws of nature, and therefore forbidden by penalty of national disasters such as the flood, the destruction of Sodom, and the "vomiting of the land" as mentioned in Leviticus in context with sexual violations.

Commenting on Leviticus 18:25, Nachmanides in his commentary ad locum asserts: "Scripture was very strict in forbidding these sexual relationships on account of the land which becomes defiled by them, and which in turn will vomit out the people that do these abominations ... Thus the Land which is the inheritance of the Glorious Name, will vomit out all those who defile it and will not tolerate worshippers of idols, nor those who practice immorality."

This idea is further developed by Raphael Patai[33] who brings to light the following citations:

> Rabbi Yase ben Durmasqith said: They (the generation of the deluge) sinned

with their eyes which are like unto water (by looking at strange women and inviting them to immorality), even so the Holy One blessed be He did not punish them but with water. Rabbi Levi said: They spoiled their seed (by having adulterous and unnatural connections), even so the Holy One blessed be He upset unto them the order of the world.[34]

Rab Hisda said: "They sinned with a hot thing (namely, the heat of fornication), and with a hot thing were they punished"; namely, as Rabbi Johanan put it, "every drop of water that the Holy One blessed be He let fall on them, He boiled in hell, then brought it up and let it fall upon them." So it happened that the hot waters of the Deep "scalded their flesh and flayed them . . ." Moreover, "the waters of deluge were thick like the male *semen*."[35]

If one concludes (as we did with reference to Noah) that homosexuality was practiced in these two cities, here again it is clear that the perpetrators were men who were normally and nominally heterosexual and not exclusively homosexuals (even though homosexuality was common), such acts were the result of moral depravity, and not due to any sexual abnormalities; and finally, homosexuality is not the sole cause of the destruction of these cities, and thus, those involved in acts of sodomy were not punished by death solely because of homosexuality. The only condemnation is for their inhospitality and maltreatment of guests (including rape of male and females).[36]

Our survey of Genesis and other biblical references highlights that nowhere is there a clear reference to acts of homosexuality definitely taking place. We can assume they did with Noah and in Sodom, and we may speculate about Joseph, David and Jonathan. Only when we study Leviticus do we have categorical verses condemning male homosexuality.

The direct biblical prohibition of homosexuality is found twice in the book of Leviticus. In Leviticus 18:22 it is written: "You shall not lie with a man as with a woman, it is an abomination (*toevah*)." In Leviticus 20:13 it further states: "And if a man lie with a man as with a woman, both have done an abomination (*toevah*); they surely be put to death, their blood is upon them." There exist two other references to a homosexual union. Leviticus 18:7 speaks of a man lying carnally with his father, who is liable to two penalties (one for lying with any male, the other for his father).[37] The second reference is to Leviticus 18:14, where a man is forbidden to lie carnally with his father's brother.

These Levitical verses cannot be studied without immediately citing one further reference, Deuteronomy 23:18: "There shall not be a *kadish* from the daughters of Israel and there shall be no *kadesha* of the sons of Israel." *Kadesha* or *kadesh* is most frequently translated as "sodomite," female or male. Rashi ad locum comments that the *kadesha* is one who is devoted and always prepared for illicit intercourse, and the *kadesh* is one who is always prepared for pederasty. Thus, it would appear that we have here an additional verse stressing that homosexuality is abominable, punishable, and unfitting behavior for "the sons of Israel."

Nachmanides makes some interesting observations about the verses prohibiting homosexuality. Now, the reason for the prohibitions against lying carnally with a male or an animal is well known, as it is an abominable act and is not for the preservation of the human species, because the copulation of male and male or of man and animal will not beget offspring.[38] As to the verse in Deuteronomy 23:18, the Ramban makes the suggestion that it refers to a prohibition directed to courts against allowing the existence of houses of ill-fame:

> It appears to me concerning this prohibition that it constitutes an admonition addressed to the members of the court that they should not permit one of the daughters of Israel to sit in public view at the crossroads for the purpose of illicit intercourse, or prepare herself a tent of prostitution as is customary in foreign lands where they sit at the door with timbrels and harps, similar to what is written (Isaiah 23:16). And similarly Scripture warns the court concerning a *kadesh*. And in line with the plain meaning of Scripture, even if he should lie with women in a tent which he prepared himself for such illicit relations or that he should sit in public view at the crossroads (on the lookout for such women), he warned the court (against permitting such activities).[39]

Punishments are varied and detailed. With reference to age, we find that both the active and passive partners of a homosexual liaison are culpable and are stoned, if they have reached their years of majority. But, if either one is under the age of nine years and one day, both are exempt from the Torah, but the older one receives lashes according to legislation.[40] And if one of the partners was between the age of nine and a day and under thirteen and a day, the older is stoned (whether he was the active or the passive), and the younger one is absolved from the Torah, but receives lashes.[41] Moreover, the Talmud elaborates that if the sexual activity was with an *adrogynos* (hermaphrodite), one is liable only if he had intercourse with the male side; but if he indulged with the hermaphrodite's femininity, then he is excused and receives lashes.[42]

The punishment of stoning is warranted only if there were witnesses to the act.[43] This punishment is derived from a similarity of phrases used in Leviticus 20:13 and 20:27: "Their blood shall be upon them."[44] Moreover, if one has accidental homosexual relations with his father or paternal uncle he must offer two atonement sacrifices.[45] And if one partner is asleep and the other awake, or if one is forced by a second, the former is guiltless and the later is punished.[46] The act need not be a complete one. As long as there is the slightest penetration, the act is considered punishable. Maimonides[47] comments:

> An initiator is one who inserts the entire glans penis, whereas a consummator is one who inserts the entire penis. The insertion of only part of the glans is equivalent to one who has carnal contact of sexual organs (without actual penetration). The emission of semen has no relationship at all to the matter of the punishment. Therefore, as soon as he inserts his organ, he incurs the punishment, even if he withdrew immediately . . . And if a man had sexual intercourse with any one of the forbidden unions without having an erection, he does not incur punishment, even if he emitted semen, because there is difference of opinion on this question, and the Talmud does not provide the final ruling; and one does not inflict punishment save in a matter which is clear, and about which there is no doubt. However, such an act is (still strictly) forbidden and this is what the Sages have called having intercourse with a dead organ,[48] meaning his organ is flaccid like a corpse.

Heathens, perhaps because they are suspected of homosexuality, are to be punished more severely for this crime than Jews, who are not suspected of such action. The prohibition of homosexuality for heathens is derived from Genesis 2:24: "Therefore shall a man leave his father and his mother and he shall cleave to his wife and they shall be as one flesh." The derivation from this verse presents an excellent example of the analytical methods of the rabbis. "Leave his father," this includes his father's wife, "his mother" literally, "and he shall cleave," but not to a male since only the opposite sexes can cleave to each other; "to his wife," but not to his neighbor's wife; "and they shall be as one flesh," this excludes relations with animals, who cannot become one flesh with man.[49] This prohibition also includes a heathen slave, who is executed for homosexuality.[50] A heathen is executed for homosexual relations with a child as well as with an adult.[51] A gentile who commits a homosexual act intentionally is executed by the sword, although one sage insisted that the execution was by strangulation. This punishment applies even if there was no previous warning by witnesses. The testimony of one witness as to the commission of the crime is sufficient as in one-judged court. Either can be a relative but not a woman, who is disqualified from being either witness or judge.[52] A gentile is allowed to incriminate himself and is judged on his confession.[53] Accidental homosexuality is not punished, but if done intentionally, yet in ignorance of the law, the heathen offender is nevertheless executed.[54] He is not considered guilty until the court rules to that effect.[55] If he was forced to commit a homosexual act, he is innocent.[56] In addition, a minor, deaf person, or an imbecile is not punished because he is not considered legally responsible for his actions.

Returning to our discussion on kadesha, it is interesting to note that Louis M. Epstein[57] theorizes that although sacred prostitution and sodomy were always considered highly immoral acts worthy of heathens alone, there is, nonetheless, no direct prohibition either in the Covenant Code or in Deuteronomy. He develops his thesis that sodomy was not common among the Hebrews, but crept in under the guise of religious service performed by *kadishim*, and became part of the temple cult. This was totally pagan practice stemming from the Canaanites and still persisted during the reign of Rehoboam, as explicitly stated in 1 Kings 14:24. Kings Asa and Jehasofot attempted to clean up this idolatry, but it was not eradicated until Josiah,[58] which lead to the prohibition in Deuteronomy 23:18. *Kadesh* takes on the meaning of a male votary attached to the temple as a priest who sexually serviced male and female worshippers. The proceeds from this "sacred prostitution" would go in to the Temple coffers. This vocation was common also among the women, and the female is known as *kadesha*.[59] 1 Samuel 2:22 makes mention of Eli being very upset with this practice. The Talmud[60] views the *kadesh* as purely a homosexual prostitute, but most indications lead to the conclusion that what is meant here are heterosexual prostitutes consecrated to serving God in the precincts of the temple, and which lasted through the reform of Josiah.

Raphael Patai[61] asserts that the *kadesh* was a male prostitute connected with the fertility cult centering around the mother figure Ashera. These male prostitutes were visited by childless women in order to become impregnated. Patai points out that such pilgrimages to holy places for the purpose of removing the curse of barrenness is still in vogue today in all parts of the Middle East. The *kadeshim* may also have functioned in magic rites in the fertility cult to insure fruitfulness in nature, the autumn rains, crops, increase in domestic animals, etc.

Also common among the pagans, and often associated with the cult, was transvestism—deriving sexual pleasure from wearing garments of the opposite sex. This would explain the prohibition of Deuteronomy 22:5: "A woman shall not wear that which pertaineth to a man, neither shall a man put on a woman's garment; for all that do so are an abomination unto the Lord thy God." Epstein[62] identifies this verse with homosexuality, and the urge for people to imagine themselves as the opposite sex. The Bible treats this behavior "not as a pathology but a moral depravity."[63] Commenting on Deuteronomy 22:5, Rashi explains that a man dressed as a woman will be drawn to groups of women and women dressed as men will be attracted to men's circles. In both cases, such intermingling would lead to lewdness and illicit relations.

Targum Yonatan, the Aramaic Bible commentary, interprets "clothing of a man" to mean the Tallit and Tefillin, and therefore forbade women to wear them. Philo and Josephus[64] interpret this verse as a prohibition against men disguising themselves as women in warfare—a sign of cowardice:

> They . . . indulged themselves in feminine wantonness till they were satisfied therewith; while they decked their hair and put on women's garments and were besmeared with ointments; and that they might appear very comely, they had paints under their eyes and imitated not only the ornaments but also the lusts of women, and were guilty of such intolerable uncleanness that they invented unlawful pleasures of that sort. And thus did they roll themselves up and down the city as in a brothel-house and defiled it entirely with their impure actions; nay, while their faces looked like the faces of women, they killed with their right hand; and when their gait was effeminate, they presently attacked men and became warriors, and drew their swords from under their finely dyed cloaks and pierced through everybody whom they lighted on.[65]

Maimonides believes that the Bible had in mind to discourage masquerading in the garments of the opposite sex during ritual worship and in orgies. For this reason Maimonides places this law in his code in the section on idolatry.[66] The Halacha stresses the sexual immorality involved in wearing the garments of the opposite sex, for it leads to all kinds of immoralities, including homosexuality. Epstein writes:

> Perhaps the biblical author knew of the psychosis of males desiring and imagining themselves to be females, and of females delighting in imagining themselves males, and creating the illusion by donning the garments of the opposite sex . . . At first blush the prohibition should apply only to full disguise of man for woman or woman for man, but not to wearing an article of dress or ornament belonging to the other sex. According to the halakic interpretation, if this injunction is to preserve the distinction in dress between male and female, even minor changes of dress of one sex for the other's is prohibited.[67]

It becomes obvious that homosexuality in the Bible is not dealt with in isolation. It seems to be connected with idolatry in general, and idolatrous cultic ritual in particular. This is not to say that regular, secular sodomy was not to be found, but rather to indicate the general overall biblical context of the practice of homosexuality.

Of all the denominations within Judaism, the Orthodox has been most vituperative and vitriolic against homosexuality. Beginning in 1978, a campaign was begun in order to block the passage of the gay rights bill in New York City. Dr. Bernard Fryshman, Chairman of the Commission on Legislation of Agudath Israel of America, declared that a gay rights bill is an infringement upon the religious rights of Americans and a severe blow to fundamentals in education. He announced that the Orthodox Jewish community will mobilize to defeat any measures which would compel schools to hire homosexual teachers or require that a family rent to an avowed homosexual couple:

> Jewish law prohibits parents from allowing their children to be taught or

counseled by people who are sexually perverted, such as homosexuals. Loyalty to ethical Jewish teachings, as well as our concern for public morality in society at large, moves us to launch an all-out, city-wide effort to defeat the proposed gay rights bill.[68]

The Rabbinic Council of America also issued a statement against homosexuality. The president, Rabbi Walter S. Wurzberger, warned against permissiveness which will:

corrode the value structure that alone can provide the foundations for a healthy family life. Religious leaders dare not succumb to the temptation of surrendering to the blandishments of a hedonistic culture that frowns upon any interference with the pursuit of pleasure ... Homosexuals are entitled to a sympathetic understanding of their plight and are deserving of every possible help. But we dare not place the mantle of respectability upon a practice which flouts all biblical precepts of morality. It is inconceivable that a deviation which is explicitly denounced in the Bible should be legitimatized as an alternative life style.

A similar statement was issued by Rabbi Abraham B. Hecht, President of the Rabbinic Alliance of America. He declared that America's Torah leadership is not against . . .

the personal rights of individuals to practice perversion in privacy, but we cannot stand by quietly as society legitimizes homosexuality as a viable and acceptable social norm. The rabbinical position on homosexuality has been unchanged since the dawn of Judaism—it is an abomination that recognizes no extenuating circumstances and is in the same class as pederasty.

The most erudite and perspicacious article written on the subject of homosexuality was penned by a leading Orthodox rabbi, presently the president of Yeshiva University. In an article in *Jewish Life*, (Jan.-Feb. 1968) as well as in the 1974 *Encyclopedia Judaica Yearbook*, Rabbi Norman Lamm outlines the Halachic issues and concludes:

Homosexuality, whether male or female, is thus considered abominable, and can never be legitimized in the eyes of Judaism. This by no means implies that Jews who live by Judaism are lacking in compassion for the man or woman trapped in this dreadful disease, suffering the loneliness, the humiliation, and the social ostracism to which such individuals are condemned by their unfortunate tendencies. Certainly the homosexual who genuinely desires to emerge from his situation ought to be helped by all the means at our disposal whether of medicine or psychotherapy or counselling. But the compassion and help extended by society should in no way diminish the judgment that *mishkav zachar* is repungnant.[69]

Subsequent issues of the above-quoted magazine shared with the reader letters to the editor strongly criticizing Rabbi Lamm's point of view, which was considered too liberal.[70]

However stringent Lamm may appear to be, and however strongly he feels that severe laws against homosexuality must remain on the books, nonetheless, "there is nothing in the Jewish law's letter or spirit that should incline us toward advocacy of imprisonment for homosexuals . . . we must be no less generous to the homosexual than to the drug addict to whom the government extends various forms of therapy upon request . . . jail sentences must be abolished for all homosexuals, save those who are guilty of violence, seduction of the young, or public solicitation."[71]

Lamm also opposes separate homosexual congregations, and encourages existing congregations to extend hospitality and membership: "Homosexuals are no less in violation of Jewish norms than Sabbath desecrators or those who disregard the laws of Kashrut."[72]

In the same issue, another article describes the founding of a gay synagogue in Los Angeles and its subsequent affiliation with the Pacific Southwest Council of the Union of American Hebrew Congregations.[73] Rabbi Sanford Regins also relates his association with the homosexual synagogue.[74] Another gay synagogue, Congregation Etz Chaim of Miami, has also applied for membership in the Union of American Hebrew Congregations.[75]

At the 1977 Convention of the Central Conference of American Rabbis, a resolution was introduced defending the rights of homosexuals. The following is a text of that resolution:

> *Whereas* the UAHC has consistently supported civil rights and civil liberties for all persons, and,
>
> *Whereas* the Constitution guarantees civil rights to all individuals,
>
> *Be It Therefore Resolved* that homosexual persons are entitled to equal protection under the law. We oppose discrimination against homosexuals in areas of opportunity, including employment and housing. We call upon our society to see that such protection is provided in actuality.
>
> *Be It Further Resolved* that we urge congregations to conduct appropriate educational programming for youth and adults so as to provide greater understanding of the relation of Jewish values to the range of human sexuality.[76]

Rabbis in the Conservative Movement have also expressed themselves clearly on this subject. Rabbi David M. Feldman, who has written extensively about every phase of Jewish sexual attitudes, made a definitive statement which appeared in *Sh'ma* magazine. He not only presents the traditional material but introduces one existing responsum written by Rabbi A. I. Kuk in 1912. In the case of a man who was a *shochet* (ritual slaughterer) who was suspected of being involved in homosexual acts, Rabbi Kuk rules "that the *shochet* can be returned to his post simply because the evidence against him was heresay. Moreover the man may have already repented."[77] Like Rabbis Solomon Freehof and Norman Lamm, Feldman concludes: "Judaism does declare homosexual indulgence a sin . . . Having said so, we can temper our judgment of the act with compassion for the actor . . . the prohibition is absolute . . . it is akin to Onanism, and as such is repugnant to the Halachic tradition."[78] Feldman differentiates between homosexuality, homosexuals and homosexual fantasies, and cites the various Halachic principles guiding these various principles. The same issue of *Sh'ma* contains an article "To Be A Jew And A Homosexual," to which the reader is referred. Asher Bar Zev similarly writes emphasizing the abominable aspects of homosexuality, but with the feeling that homosexuals should not be penalized: " . . . it is clear that whether we think of homosexual behavior merely as a personal preference or as a pathological state, in either case it can be accepted as licit behavior within Jewish tradition."[79]

Making headlines in the American Jewish press was the article by Barry Dov Schwartz in which he defended the existence of gay synagogues.[80] Schwartz begins his article with a historical review—Pagan, Jewish, Christian —followed by a detailed Halachic examination of the topic. He urged the acceptance of homosexuals "as human beings without their homosexuality being sanctioned or condemned."[81] He emphasized that accepting is not tantamount "to condoning or encouraging homosexuals."[82] In accepting homosexuals openly we need not sacrifice our traditional standards and the Jewish ideal of heterosexuality. Because homosexuals have traditionally felt unwelcomed in existing religious institutions, they have formed their own synagogues, which "perform a vital religious function at the present time."[83] Schwartz concluded with the plea that Jewish religious and communal agencies be more concerned and receptive to the problems of homosexuals. "Homosexual men and women need support . . . with our help they can enter a House of God where they can find understanding, sympathetic rabbinic guidance and spiritual and emotional support from the congregation of Israel."[84] The following issue of the United Synagogue Review (Fall 1977) contains letters to the editor which range from supportive to abusive of Rabbi Schwartz's point of view. Unprinted letters which the author received are even more extreme than those appearing in the magazine.

In response to a query posed to the Rabbinical Assembly Committee on Jewish Law and Standards: "Can a gay synagogue be accepted into membership by the United Synagogue," the law committee, under the chairmanship of Professor Seymour Siegel, responded: "No. Separate synagogues should not be established."[85] Addressing himself to this issue, Rabbi Schwartz addressed the Seventy-eighth Rabbinical Assembly Convention, April 1978.

> Separate gay synagogues have been formed precisely because the homosexual has not been comfortable in existing religious institutions. We should strive to remedy this situation and thus make gay synagogues obsolete. Until that time, if any gay Jew is striving for happiness and trying to integrate his entire life with a love of Judaism, then I personally feel that compassion and logic dictate that we should encourage Jewish homosexuals to maintain their religious tie—even if it unfortunately means separately, in their own synagogues . . .

> Homosexuals should not be denied housing and employment because of their homosexuality . . .

> We need not subscribe to the new morality, the so-called "great orgy" to the twentieth century.

> We need not yield to the madness that seizes society at many times and in many forms. We need not acquiesce to the standards of the age of nihilism and we need not mimic Christian denominations who have taken a totally liberal point of view.

> What we can do is assist the committed Jew who happens to be a constitutionally confirmed homosexual to continue his relationship with Judaism.[86]

Perhaps the most liberal point of view ever expressed was by Rabbi Hershel J. Matt, who suggested that homosexuals be accepted as rabbis. As for the Jewish community, it has an obligation, Rabbi Matt says, to:

> . . . demonstrate such feelings of compassion by willingly associating with homosexuals and engaging in acts of kindness and friendship—so that the particular individuals we meet will not feel grudgingly tolerated but will see that they are included within the circle of our love.

> Even the role of rabbi should be open to a homosexual if he or she honestly holds the conviction—and would conscientiously seek to convey it to others—that, in spite of his or her homosexuality, the Jewish ideal for man and woman is heterosexuality.[87]

One of the most prominent members of the Rabbinical Assembly, Rabbi Robert Gordis, has a chapter on homosexuality in his 1978 book.[88] Like those who wrote on this topic before him, he too feels that homosexuality is not normal, but should be decriminalized:

> Homosexuality is an abnormality, an illness which, like any other, varies in intensity with different individuals. Until more efficacious means are discovered for dealing with their problem, homosexuals deserve the same inalienable rights as do all their fellow human beings—freedom from harassment and discrimination before the law and in society.

> There can be no question that homosexuals are entitled to more than justice before the law. It is not enough merely to remove the various kinds of legal disability and overt hostility to which they have long been subjected. Whatever evaluation is placed upon their condition, be it moral, medical, or psychological, they are human beings, our brothers and sisters, who deserve compassion and love from their fellow men and, above all, from their brothers in kinship and in faith.[89]

The gay Jewish community has come out of the proverbial closet. There are scores of gay synagogues throughout the United States, Canada and Israel. There are gay "rabbis" who have remained anonymous.[90] An interview with a gay rabbi appeared in *Gaysweek*.[91] The introduction of the article offers the following synopsis:

> David Rothenberg has met and talked with several gay rabbis. They range in age from late-20s to mid-60s. Some are single and as many are married. They represent reformed, conservative and orthodox Jewry. They share one common feeling as gay rabbis: they perceive that their professional contribution would be terminated if they were to come out. Rothenberg learned from the gay rabbis that they meet at various conferences and attempt to sensitize their brethren. One of the rabbis agreed to a question and answer interview with the guarantee that he remain anonymous. This religious leader has his own congregation, which is located in an area outside a large Eastern city.[92]

Letters to the editor by gay Jews appear frequently in American Jewish journals.[93] The oldest gay synagogue in this country is Beth Chayim Chadashim in Los Angeles, California, which was founded in 1971. The most active gay synagogue is Congregation Beth Simhat Torah in Greenwich Village, New York, founded in 1973. One can ascertain an overview of its program and philosophy by reading its monthly bulletin, *Gay Synagogue News*. It is apparent that the synagogue is a traditional one, and there are members who have a deep familiarity with Jewish law and customs. There is a great feeling toward Israel, and there are annual appeals for a U.S.A. and Israel Tree.[94] There is a gay grove, and a plaque honoring Congregation Beth Simhat Torah stands in the American Bi-Centennial National Park in Israel with the words: "In honor of all the gay men and women who worked and fought to create and maintain a Jewish homeland in Eretz Israel."[95] The synagogue sponsors a weekly *oneg-Shabbat*, and in June 1976, a Bar Mitzvah was celebrated. There was also a wedding. I quote in full the article describing this event:

> Under the velvet canopy the rebbe presided, as the two chasonim, both dressed in light tan suits, with matching brown ties, exchanged vows of love in the presence of their closest friends. The several male attendants wore light blue turtleneck sweaters and hand-knitted blue and white yarmulkes. The ceremony was concluded with the mutual breaking of wine glasses as those who had gathered together burst into song—Siman Tov and Mazal Tov. Dancing and salads were enjoyed by all. The couple will continue to reside in their Brooklyn apartment.[96]

A highlight for gay Jews is its international conference. In 1977, 201 participants including 83 members of the New York gay synagogue, 73 members of 10 other gay Jewish groups in the United States, Canada and Israel, and 52 non-affiliated people from 14 cities in the United States and Canada were represented:[97]

> For many out-of-towners, the services were the most moving and instructive part of the conference. One member of the Miami synagogue said, "For years I have been praying each day, but never have I felt such a oneness with so many people and with God."
>
> Of course, given the variety of the participants, not everyone could respond to our style of workshop with the same enthusiasm. But everyone was touched in some spiritual way, and by the time we sang our last farewell song, swaying arm-in-arm, there was scarcely a dry eye in the house.
>
> The workshops, covering a wide variety of topics of gay, Jewish, and gay Jewish interest, were mostly successful, with an exchange of ideas and experiences on a consistently serious and enthusiastic level.
>
> Among the workshops that led to post-conference follow-up were the ones on Aliyah . . ., Social Action Projects . . ., and Parshe of the Week. A compilation of the "Hidden Treasures" column which appears in most issues of this newsletter, discussing the weekly Torah readings, will be mailed to participants in that last named workshop. Copies will be available to others who are interested in learning relevant ways of explaining and interpreting the Torah.[98]

It is hoped that a future international conference will soon take place in Israel. Ironically, the gay organization, headquartered in Tel Aviv, is called the Agudah. There is also a gay beach (Hof Hanachim) in Tel Aviv.[99] On the subject of names, the gay Jewish group in Montreal also has a fascinating one. It is known as Naches.[100] In each bulletin there is a review of all the activities from Boston, Chicago, Texas, Philadelphia, Toronto, Washington, Minneapolis, New Jersey, Iowa, Paris, Australia, and San Francisco. There is no doubt, at least to this writer, that those involved in the gay synagogue in New York have great Jewish pride, and a desperate need to be associated with the Jewish community. Whether the Jewish community will help them meet their needs remains to be seen.

Notes

1. Eugene Barowits, *Choosing a Sex Ethic* (New York: Schocken Books, 1969), pp. 53-83.

2. *Ibid.*, p. 63-83.

3. David M. Feldman, *Birth Control in Jewish Law* (New York: New York University Press, 1968), chap. 1, 2, 3, 4.

4. Song of Songs 7:7, 11. See also Midrash Shir Hashirm Rabbah 1:1. All biblical passages are from New York: Pandes Publishing Co., 1951.

5. Robert Gordis, *Love and Sex* (New York: McGraw-Hill, 1978), pp. 102-104.

6. Raphael Patai, *Family, Love and the Bible*, (London: Macgibbon and Kee, 1960), p. 149.

7. *Ibid.* See also Seymour Siegel, *Some Aspects of the Jewish Tradition's View of Sex* (mimeographed material), passim; and *The Holy Letter*, trans. Seymour Cohen (New York: Ktav Publishing House, 1976), pp. 42, 175, passim.

8. Yevamot 62b; 63b. All Talmudic Sources are from the Babylonian Talmud, (Vilna: Romm, 1895).

9. Kiddushin 82a. See also Maimonides (New York: Pandes Publishing Co., 1963), *Issurei Biah* 22:2.

10. Mishnah Kiddushin 82a.

11. *Ibid. The sages note that the law prohibiting an unmarried man to be a teacher for boys, was not because of fear of homosexuality, but because of the visits of the mothers to the schoolhouse.*

12. *Maimonides Mishna Torah (Vilna: Rosencrntz, 1900), Issurei Biah* 22:2

13. Joseph Karo, *Schulchan Aruch*, Even HaEzer:24 (Vilna: Romm, 1911). Note that there is no direct legislation against homosexuality in the *Schulchan Aruch*.

14. Yam Shel Shlomo, Kiddushin chap. 4, Law 23, see also *Otzar Haposkim*, chap. 9, pp. 236-238.

15. *Bayit Chadash* to Tur, Even HaEzer 24 (Vilna: Romm, 1921).

16. Lev. 18:3.

17. *Sifra Dvei Rav*, (Jerusalem: Om Publishing Co., 1946), chap. 12:9, 8.

18. Talmud, Shabbat 65a and b.

19. Rashi ad locum qaualifies the reference to meaning only the high priest based on Lev. 21:14. But Tosfot ad locum suggests that it also refers to a *kohen hedyot* because the lesbian is guilty of *znut*. The prohibition for any priest to marry such a woman is found in Lev. 21:7.

20. Maimonides, Mishnah Torah (Vilna: Rosencrantz, 1911), *Issurei Biah* 21:8.

21. *Ibid.*

22. Louis Epstein, *Sex Laws and Customs in Judaism* (New York: Ktav Publishing House, 1948), p. 138, note 33.

23. Lev. 18:22; 20:13. See also 18:7, 18:14.

24. *Perush Haramban* Al Hatorah, vol. 1 (Jerusalem: Masad Horav Kook, 1944), p. 65. See also English translation by Charles B. Chavel, vol. 1, (Shiloh Publishing House, 1971), p. 140.

25. See *Gen. Rabah*, 36; *Lev. Rabah*, 12; *Midrash Hagadol*, 9:21.

26. See Hirsch, 9:25: "They are slaves of their own sensuality, and they sink lower and lower to finally become 'slaves of slaves.' " Also note proximity of verses in Deut. 23:16 and 17.

27. Sanhedrin 109 a, b.

28. Judges 19.

29. Epstein, *Sex Laws and Customs in Judaism*, p. 132.

30. *Lev. Rabah* 23:9; *Gen. Rabah* 32:7, 28:9.

31. *Lev. Rabah* 23:9; *Num. Rabah* 9:33.

32. *Gen. Rabah* 26:5.

33. Raphael Patai *Man and Temple in Ancient Jewish Myth and Ritual*, (New York and London: Thomas Nelson & Sons Ltd., 1947), p. 140.

34. *Gen. Rabah* 32:7; cf. Sanhedrin 108a.

35. Sanhedrin 108b; cf. Rosh Hashanah 12a; Zebahim 113b.

36. See Patai, *Family, Love & the Bible*, p. 153, where he concludes that the mob in Sodom and in Gibeah (Judges 19:22-25) was addicted to homosexuality, and "there is no reason to suppose that the mores of these two localities were greatly different from those of the other Canaanite and Israelite towns and villages..." And never is there "a word of condemnation for homosexuality per se."

37. In Sanhedrin 54a, Rav Judah ascribes this sin to 'heathens', but the sages realize that he was using a euphemism for a Jew (who should be—but not always is—above being involved in such immoral activities).

38. *Perushei Hatorah - Ramban* (Jerusalem: Mosad Horav Kook, 1962)(Hebrew). *Ramban Commentary on the Torah*, trans. Charles B. Chavel (New York: Shiloh Publishing House, 1974). Lev. 18:22.

39. Ramban ad locum points out that the terms *kadesh* and *kadesha* are an expression of readiness. Thus, the woman who guards herself from forbidden relations and lewdness is called *k'doshah* (holy), while she who separates herself from holiness and becomes defiled with illicit sexual relations is called *k'deshah*. This name (k'deshah) applies to her only becuase she is always ready for this abomination, for she has no moment for propriety and holiness at all.

40. Maimonides, *Mishna Torah - Yad Chazokah* (Vilna edition, 1900), *Hilchot Issurei Biah 1:14*. Note Sanhedrin 54b, where it is suggested that since a female is adjudged capable of intercourse from the age of three years old, the same should apply to a male.

41. This latter view is studied in *Sefer Ha-Chinnuch* commandment 209 but differs from every existing view where there is never punishment for anyone under the legal age of maturity.

42. Avodah Zarah 15b. See also Yevamont 83b. See also Maimonides Issurei Biah 115 and his *Commentary on Mishnan*, Sanhedrin, chap. 7, Mishnah 4.

43. *Issurei Biah* 14.

44. Sanhedrin 54a; Keritot 5a.

45. Sanhedrin 54a.

46. Maimonides, *Hilchot Issurei Biah* 1:18.

47. Maimonides, *Commentary on Mishnah*, Sanhedrin, chap. 7, Mishnah 4. See also *Issurei Biah* 110.

48. Sanhedrin 55a; Yebamoth 95b; Shebuoth 18a.

49. Sanhedrin 58a.

50. *Hilchot Issurei Biah* 14:18.

51. Hilchot Melachim 9:6.

52. Hilchot Melachim 9:14.

53. *Sefer Ha-Chinnuch* commandment 192. The *Sefer Ha-Chinnuch* was written in the thirteenth century, possibly by Rabbi Aaron Ha-Levi of Barcelona. On the authorship of *Sefer Ha-Chinnuch*, see G. Appel, *A Philosophy of Mizvot: The Religious-Ethical Concepts of Judaism, Their Roots In Biblical Law and Oral Tradition* (1975), pp. 191-93.

54. Hilchot Melachim 10:1.

55. Rashi on Yavamoth 47b, quoted in Mellier, *Rape and Other Sexual Offences in the Hebrew Law and in the English Law 94*, 1960 (unpublished dissertation in Hebrew University Library).

56. *Hilchot Melachim* 10:2.

57. Epstein, *Sex Laws and Customs in Judaism*, p. 135.

58. 1 Kings 15:12, 22:47; 2 Kings 23:7.

59. In addition, the verse in Hosea 4:14, "For they associate themselves with Zonot (harlots) and sacrifice with Qedesot" would seem to indicate that the Qedesa, as distinct from the Zona, had a temple function. In this case, a Qodes would be a male sacred prostitute relating to the fertility cult,

a cult which, by definition, had no use for homosexual relations.

60. Sanhedrin 24b.
61. Raphael Patai, *The Hebrew Goddess* (London: MacGibbon and Ree, 1960), p. 45. See also p. 295, note 56.
62. Epstein, *Sex, Laws and Customs in Judaism*, p. 64.
63. *Ibid.*
64. Philo, *On Courage*, ed. Cohn, 2 (Loch Library), p. 324; Josephus, *Wars* (Boston: Whiston, 1811), pp. 5, 9, 10.
65. Josephus, *ibid.*
66. *Sefer Hamitzvot*, Negative Commandment 40.
67. Epstein, *Sex, Law and Customs in Judaism*, p. 64-65. See also p. 66 for examples of practical application of this prohibition.
68. *Jewish Press*, (20 January 1978), front page. See appendix of *Jewish Press* article, 14 July 1978. Also issue of November 25, 1977, where there is an exchange of letters of homosexuals to the editor.
69. Norman Lamm, *Jewish Life* (Jan.-Feb. 1968), p. 14.
70. See especially *Jewish Life* (May-June 1968).
71. Lamm, *op. cit.*, p. 204.
72. Lamm, *op. cit.* p. 205.
73. Lamm, *op. cit.*, pp. 33-40.
74. Lamm, *op. cit.*, pp. 41-49.
75. *Jewish Post and Opinion* (28 March 1978).
76. *The Jewish Post* (10 February 1978).
77. David Feldman, "Homosexuality and The Halacha" *Sh'ma* (19 May 1972).
78. *Ibid.*, pp. 100-102.
79. Asher Bar-Zev, "Homosexuality and The Jewish Tradition," *Reconstructionist* (May 1976).
80. Barry Dov Schwartz, "Judaism and Homosexuality," *United Synagogue Review* (Summer 1977).
81. *Ibid.*
82. *Ibid.*
83. *Ibid.*
84. *Ibid.*
85. Minutes of Rabbinical Assemly Committee on Jewish Law and Standards, May 27, 1976.
86. Quoted in *Jewish Week/American Examiner* (9 April 1978).
87. Hershel J. Matt, "Sin, Crime, Sickness or Alternative Life Style?: A Jewish Approach to Homosexuality," reprint from *Judaism: A Quarterly Journal of Jewish Life and Thought*, vol. 27, no. 1 (Winter 1978).
88. Robert Gordis, *Love and Sex: A Modern Jewish Perspective* (New York: Farrar, Straus and Giroux, 1978), chap. 10.
89. *Ibid.*, p. 160.
90. *Jewish Post & Opinion* (10 Feb. 1978; 3 March 1978).
91. *Gaysweek* (24 Oct. 1977).
92. *Ibid.*
93. See especially the *Jewish Floridian*, the local Jewish weekly, on the issues relating to the Miami homosexual bill in the summer of 1977; *Jewish Press* (5 Jan. 1979).
94. *Gay Synagogue News* (October 1976).
95. *Ibid.* (January 1978).
96. *Ibid.* (December 1976).
97. *Ibid.* (June 1977).
98. *Ibid.*
99. *Ibid.* (February 1977).
100. *Ibid.* (January 1978).

Reclaiming Jewish History:
Homo-Erotic Poetry of the Middle Ages

Helen Leneman

Historians must guard against a tendency to read the value system of their own time into a period of history far removed from that value system. This can be especially true in the history of literature. The homo-erotic poetry of Jewish writers in eleventh century Muslim Spain has been largely ignored until recent times. Indeed, there are even twentieth-century Jewish historians who still choose to deny the existence of such poetry. This poetry developed in a very specific period of Jewish history, that of the so-called Spanish Golden Age, because of the freedom and tolerance of that society. No less a contributing factor was the apparent Arab predilection for homosexuality in their society as well as their literature. However, these influences have been used by some historians as excuses to deny its authenticity, rather than explanations for its genesis, indicating their personal prejudice. My premise is that this cover-up has denied several generations an acquaintance with some exquisite love and erotic poetry.

About two hundred years after the rise of Islam, in the tenth century C.E., the entire Jewish population of the Middle East, and most of Spain, spoke Arabic. The Jewish and Arabic cultures influenced each other. Though Arabic never became the first language of the Jewish community, the flowering of Arabic literature in Spain, particularly poetry, motivated and inspired Jewish writers to elevate Hebrew by creating secular poetry in that language.[1]

The Hebrew poetry created in Muslim Spain, considered by S.D. Goitein to be the most perfect expression of Jewish-Arab symbiosis, is an example of a borrowed style that took on a poetic life of its own. There had been popular secular poetry among Jews in the centuries preceding Islam, verifiable in Talmudic literature, but it was not preserved; we will never know how much has been lost to us. Only religious subjects were considered worthy of being transmitted in that culture. Though Jewish poets had scruples about using their holy tongue for love poems, they saw devout Muslims writing such poetry in their own holy tongue. These poets took over certain themes of Arab poetry, their aim being to express ideas in Hebrew that were regarded by the existing society as proper for poetical expression.[2]

In seeking the origins of erotic Arab poetry, some writers have cited the influence of Islamic Sufism in which the "unbearded young man" was taken as an image of divine beauty. This became an impetus for increased expressions of homosexuality, which subsequently became more acceptable in Jewish society as well.[3] Mediterranean society also had had a relevant Hellenistic model.

Samuel Ha-Levi ben Joseph Ha-Nagid or Ibn Naghrela was one of the fathers of secular poetry among the Jews of the Middle Ages. He was born in Cordova in 993 and died in Granada in 1055. He was educated in a Talmudic academy that had been only recently established in Spain. He was thus the first Jewish scholar to grow up on Spanish soil. In 1027 he was appointed Chief Rabbi, the spiritual head of Granada Jewry. He was not only a professional scholar, but also a statesman, politician and general. For many years he was in fact the head of the government of Granada.[4]

Sameul Ha-Nagid is credited with introducing poetry of war and battle into Hebrew literature. The three works of poetry he is noted for are Ben Tehillim, Ben Mishlei, and Ben Kohelet.[5] He was one of the first to be influenced by Arabic literary modalities, which opened up new possibilities of form and content. This Arabic influence has been used by some writers to explain the homo-erotic component of many of Samuel's love poems.[6]

Samuel Ha-Nagid was a pioneer in the development of secular themes. Love and drinking poems were a large part of his total output. These poems were recited in the salons of the Andalusion aristocracy, accompanied on instruments by attractive young men and women. These were referred to in poems as zvi and ofer (gazelle and deer), in the masculine or feminine gender. They are frequently the love object in Samuel's poems. In his brief introductory biography, Leon Weinberger states: "Although the love of young boys was not unusual in Europe in the High Middle Ages, it is not likely that Samuel is to be taken literally."[7] It is strange that Weinberger does not mention the surrounding Arab culture. His rationalizations for the above statement are firstly, that Samuel observed Jewish law precisely; and secondly, that these poems follow a stylized pattern of contemporary Arab poetry.[8] To the first of these I would respond, who can vouch for Samuel's precise observance of Jewish Law? This can easily become a circular argument: he was an observant Jew; hence, his homo-erotic poetry was not what it appears to be; he did not write homo-erotic poetry, therefore, he was an observant Jew. As for the second argument, it boils down to confusing form and content: simply because in form his poetry imitated Arab form, this does not diminish the personal element of Samuel's sexuality present in these poems.

In Samuel's love poems, it is not always clear whether the object is male or female; the beloved features tend to follow a set pattern. The relationship of the poet to his love object was also standardized, be the object male or female.[9] Actually, it is fairly common practice to disguise homo-erotic poetry by changing the genders; Michelangelo's grand-nephew is said to have done so with all his great-uncle's sonnets.[10] Samuel's so called "friendship poems" also followed patterns: a faithful covenant bound the friends, separation pained them.[11] Weinberger, in his remarks, uses the pronouns "their" and "her" when citing examples of the possessive in Samuel's poetry, as though unable to use the pronoun "his," in spite of the equal representation of males and females in the poems. For instance, in giving examples of descriptions of the gazelle, he says, "Their faces radiate light . . . their eyes are dark . . . they stand tall like the palm tree." And of the object of the poet's desire, Weinberger writes of "the suffering he endures from the fierce arrows which the beloved emits from her eyes."[12]

Although Weinberger does include a number of Samuel's homo-erotic poems in his book, the very subtle moral censorship present in his introduction is disturbing. The issue here is whether poetry is mere empty form, or rather a vessel containing the true emotions of the poet. Weinberger seems to accept Samuel's poetry as the latter only when the emotions expressed are acceptable in his own value system; in other cases, he claims poetry is mere form. "Samuel is deeply devoted to the Biblical-Rabbinic tradition, even as he is capable of writing odes to handsome young men that border on the erotic," writes Weinberger. In his next sentence, almost a disclaimer, he says that perhaps we should not take the poet too seriously, since in one of Samuel's poems the poet wrote, "Neither are all the words of the poet veritable!"[13] This form of censorship is so subtle that it is quite possible the writer is not even aware of it. This makes it nonetheless insidious, presenting as it does a false, or at least incomplete, picture of Samuel Ha-Nagid and his poetry. At least, though, Weinberger does provide some of the controversial texts.

There is an interesting reference in Samuel's poem "A Place for Festivities" to "young men who fear the Lord and are beautiful to look at, even for the boys among them," which seems a casual reference to the cultural milieu in which Samuel lived and wrote. To cite an example of what Weinberger considers "bordering on the erotic," in the poem "A Ransom," Samuel says that a young lad, seeing a cup in Samuel's hands, said, "Drink the wine from between my lips!" In the poem "Captured Without a Net," Samuel writes of the eyes of the young lad ("zvi") who have ravished his heart: "My desire for you is yet like a flame within me." This poem imparts a sense of ravishing joy after a night of love, sharply contrasting a poem to a young maid, "Her Translucent Glass," which is devoid of sensuality, and in which "the tips of her fingers are red from the blood of her victims."

The poem "You are Angry with Me" crosses the border into the erotic: writing of the young boy ("gazelle" or "fawn" in different translations) who said, "Bring me down honey from your swarm of bees (or hive)," to which Samuel responded, "Give me some back from your tongue." The boy in this poem became angry and yelled, "Shall we sin before the living God?" to which Samuel responded, "Let your sin be with me." Obviously, Samuel knew of biblical and rabbinic strictures regarding homosexuality, yet he apparently considered himself beyond reproach. Voluptuaries can make their own laws. In a similar exchange, in "The Gazelle that Stutters," his lover wants to say "evil" (ra), but it comes out as "touch" (ga); when he tries to say "stop" (sura), it comes out as "belly" (suga); and the poet "hastened to it, fenced about with lillies"—an erotic image taken from Song of Songs. Another reference to sin can be found in the poem "All Young Lovers," in which Samuel prays to God to change the heart of the boy who has betrayed him. But, since all young lovers are unfaithful, Samuel prays to God to " . . . forgive him his sins, or failing that, punish me instead."[14]

Though Samuel Ha-Nagid's homo-erotic poetry is probably the best known such Hebrew poetry of his age, other Jewish poets were known to have written similar verse. The most famous of these succeeded Samuel. Ibn Gabirol was born in Malaga around 1021. His poetic talent matured early; he was famous in distant lands by the age of sixteen. He was very melancholy from a young age, but his life was brightened by a deep friendship with the distinguished astronomer Jekutiel. He called Jekutiel a "luminous star . . . all the other stars in heaven pale before him"; and, addressing the goddess of song, he wrote, "sing your song of praise, sing of the beloved, the chosen, the best of all lords and nobles, sing of Jekutiel, the light of the world . . ." Elsewhere he wrote that there was not enough water in the world to extinguish the flame of his love for Jekutiel. These verses have been classified as "friendship" rather than "love" poetry. One writer categorically stated that there are no love poems in Ibn Gabirol's legacy.[15] This is an example of a historian imposing his value system onto a figure who was not restricted by these same values. The friendship between Ibn Gabirol and Jekutiel had a tragic ending, when in 1039 Jekutiel was slandered and punished by death. Ibn Gabirol wrote a poem of 200 verses mourning his friend's death.[16] It is not known if the slander involved Jekutiel's relationship with the young poet.

Later in life, Ibn Gabirol wrote a group of poems in the classic style of Song of Songs. In these poems, the flaming speech of earthly love is transformed into mystical religious fervor; they are considered to celebrate the bond of love between the beautiful bride, Israel, and her loyal beloved: "Why, my beloved, gazelle, have you left my garden to feed in the garden of Jaksha . . .

Come, return to the garden, and there we shall eat choice fruits . . ."[17] This poetry can be construed as mystical, but it can also be interpreted sexually. After all, Song of Songs is also erotic poetry that has been interpreted at different times as mystical.

Yehuda Halevi, another poet of this era, was born in 1080 and died around 1142. He studied Talmud and medicine as well as Greek-Arabic philosophy. He began writing poetry at the age of thirteen or fourteen. He wrote a series of poems of friendship (Shirei Yedidut) adorned with beautiful portrayals of nature.[18] His love poems are often outspoken. He wrote poetry and epigrams to beautiful boys. At least twenty-one of his poems are addressed to the "gracious gazelle," though, in S.W. Baron's words, he never "transcended the bounds of propriety." This noted historian, too, is applying his own values to a culture that held totally different ones. Baron further surmises that some of Halevi's poems probably shocked his contemporaries, and that they were allegedly cause for regret later in his lifetime.[19] Other contemporaries of Samuel Ha-Nagid who also wrote love poetry to young boys were Ibn Sahl, Ibn Ghayyath, Ibn Sheshet, and Ibn Barzel.[20]

An illustrative example of censored history can be found in the large collection *A Treasury of Jewish Poetry*, edited by Nathan and Maryann Ausubel. In the lengthy introduction, there is no mention whatever of erotic poetry, let alone homo-erotic poetry. Yet in the section titled "Love—Man and Woman," on a page devoted to love poems of Yehuda Halevi, two of the three poems are addressed to men—and these are not "friendship poems": "Into my eyes he loving looked, My arms about his neck were twined . . . Upon my dark-hued eyes he pressed His lips with breath of passion rare . . ." Or the other poem, " . . . O happy that night, when sunk on your breast, your kisses fast falling, and drunken with love." The title of this poem? "He Comes."[21] There has obviously been a cover-up of sorts on the part of Jewish historians, who choose to either ignore these homo-erotic poems, or treat them as an insignificant part of the total output of certain Jewish poets.[22]

In dealing with homosexuality in the Middle East, it is important to make a distinction between the legal position and folk mores. Both the Torah (Leviticus 18:22, 20:13) and the Koran (26:165-66) forbid it. However, homosexuality was clearly present in biblical times, and folk mores have not generally disapproved. The story of David and Jonathan has been held up as an example of homosexual love,[23] though this story, of course, is never explicitly sexual. In I Samuel 18:1 we find, "Jonathan's soul became bound up with the soul of David; Jonathan loved David as himself." And in II Samuel 1:26, "I grieve for you, my brother Jonathan, you were most dear to me, your love was wonderful to me, more than the love of women." Those who would call this love nonsexual are the same that would call Platonic love nonsexual. It is my belief, however, that sexual love need not be explicitly described to be understood for what it is. Arab culture, however, did tend to be more explicit:*Arabian Nights* is casual throughout about homosexual love.

Partly due to the attitudes of Islamic culture, homosexuals flourished in cities throughout Spain after the Muslim invasion. Some scholars consider it an upper-class phenomenon, since it was the artists of the upper class, in any age, who left a record of their society for history to examine. But there is no way of determining the presence or absence of homosexual activity among the lower classes, since no records exist. The Koran does have mildly negative attitudes toward homosexuality, but Islamic society in general has ignored this, and their culture has treated homosexuality with either indifference or admiration. The Arab language has a huge vocabulary of homo-erotic terminology. These tendencies were exaggerated in early medieval Spain, when erotic verse about homosexual relations made up the bulk of published Hispano-Arab poetry. Many authors of homo-erotic poetry were teachers of the Koran, religious leaders or judges, and many wrote liturgical poems as well.[24] This multifaceted quality was also seen in Jewish poets of the same era.

Jewish historians are quite willing to accept the fact of homosexual activity and literature in Arab culture. In writing of Hebrew poetry under the Arabic influence, S.W. Baron says, "At times Platonic love was transferred to the poet's male friends, but without smacking of quite the outright homosexuality that characterized much of contemporary Arabic poetry."[25] Baron even questions the reliability of poetic evidence for Arabic homosexuality, when he says that it is not known if the homo-erotic element is a reflection of the author's personal sentiment, or rather of a conscious or unconscious imitation of accepted literary fashions.[26] Naturally, if he can question the poetic evidence in the case of Arabs, he is convinced that erotic Hebrew poems to male friends are "clearly the reflection of poetic fashion taken over from the Arab environment, for there is no evidence that Jewish society countenanced homosexual love, even in spiritualized forms." Baron mentions a reconstructed case in which a poet/cantor's attachment led to blackmail and disgrace.[27] It is not clear what sort of evidence Baron would need in order to be convinced of the presence of homosexuality among Jews.

To ignore, deny or denigrate the beautiful love poetry written to men by poets such as Samuel Ha-Nagid, Ibn Gabirol and Yehuda Halevi because of its homo-erotic element is to cheat history of a rich literary legacy. Prejudice must be laid aside if we are to have a true, uncensored history of Jewish literature available to subsequent generations.

Notes

1. Israel Zinberg, *A History of Jewish Literature*, vol. 1 (Philadelphia: Ktav 1972), p. 14.
2. S.D. Goitein, *Jews and Arabs* (New York: Schocken, 1955), p. 159.
3. *Ibid.*, p. 153.
4. Zinberg, *op. cit.*, p. 25.
5. *Encyclopedia Judaica*, (Jerusalem: Keter, 1972), p. 815.
6. Jerome Rothenberg, ed., *A Big Jewish Book* (New York: Crown, 1978), p. 626.
7. Leon Weinberger, *Jewish Prince in Moslem Spain* (University of Alabama, 1973), p. 14.
8. *Ibid.*, p. 14ff.
9. *Ibid.*, p. 14ff.
10. Boswell, *op. cit.*, p. 18.
11. Weinberger, *op. cit.*, p. 15.
12. *Ibid.*, p. 15.
13. *Ibid.*, p. 17.
14. All translations are from Weinberger, *op. cit.*, pp. 101ff.
15. Zinberg, *op. cit.*, p. 38.
16. *Ibid.*, p. 38.
17. *Ibid.*, p. 52.
18. *Ibid.*, p. 83.
19. S.W. Baron, *A Social and Religious History of the Jews*, vol. 7 (New York: Jewish Publication Society, 1952), p. 296.
20. John Boswell, *Christianity, Social Tolerance and Homosexuality* (Chicago: University of Chicago Press, 1980), p. 233.
21. One notable exception to this is the Israeli scholar Chaim Schirmann, who was apparently the first to point out the significant homo-erotic element, not only in Samuel Ha-Nagid's poetry, but in several of his contemporaries. In addition to Schirmann, Eddy Zemach and Tova Rosen-Miked have just written *A Sophisticated Work* (Jerusalem: 1983), treating the erotic poetry of Samuel Ha-Nagid. All of these works are in Hebrew. Time and space limitations prevented me from making use of these sources for this paper.
22. Nathan and Marynn Ausubel, eds., *A Treasury of Jewish Poetry* (New York: Crown, 1957), p. 45.
23. Raphael Patai, *Sex and Faith in the Bible and the Middle East* (New York: Doubleday, 1959), p. 168.
24. Boswell, *op. cit.*, pp. 196-7.
25. Baron, *op. cit.*, p. 158.
26. *Ibid.*, p. 308.
27. *Ibid.*, p. 297.

IV.
MEN OF THE WORLD: MEN'S MOVEMENTS AND SOCIAL ACTIVISM

In "Judaism, Masculinity and Feminism," Michael Kimmel turns the badge of shame which others wish to attach to commonalities between political, sexual, and religious/ethnic deviations into a badge of honor. He writes of how his Jewish heritage forms and informs his commitments to justice in various arenas. To maintain this stance he must fight against the anti-intellectualism of American culture, which views intellectual Jewish men as "less than men."

"A Jewish Men's Movement" is Robert Rosenberg's call to enact a specific political agenda for Jewish feminist men, ranging from transforming traditional Jewish men's groups, whether in sports or study, to involvement in child care, to the creation of new rituals.

The staff of Gay Community News in Boston departed from their usual policy of letting readers "speak out" to make a strong statement in their own name that "Our Movement Is No Place for Jew-hating." Our enemies see our common ground even when we don't, they note, adhering to principles of unity of coalition politics, and citing parallels between anti-Semitism and the oppression of gays and lesbians, including stereotypes about wealth.[1]

"Jewish Men and Violence in the Home—Unlikely Companions" breaks a silence about Jewish men's violence.[2] Bob Gluck uncovers the Jewish Prince's hidden rage, in which men who victimize women actually feel themselves to be the victims. While a fear of airing one's dirty linen in public, common to all oppressed groups, has kept the problem under wraps in the Jewish community, Gluck shows that the tradition has indeed discussed the issue, citing authorities like Maimonides and other oft-cited rabbis, and urges that the problem be placed high on the community's public agenda.

Those familiar with feminist theory may find themselves feeling that

Arthur Waskow speaks the feminist critique of patriarchy without naming it as such. "Adorning the Mystery: A Vision of Social Activism" instead speaks in another idiom, using values present in the Jewish tradition but not sufficiently taken into its mainstream to critique both that mainstream and the non-Jewish world. In Waskow's hands, the Sabbath rest from work becomes a form of essential political activism.

My own essay, "Toward a Male Jewish Feminism," attempts by way of conclusion to articulate some of the theoretical and political framework implicit throughout this book. It argues the male stake in a Jewish feminism and a transformed feminist Judaism, dealing with a wide range of issues, including family life, social equity, economic and political justice, and spirituality.

Notes

1. See Richard Plant, *The Pink Triangle: The Nazi War Against Homosexuals* (Henry Holt and Company, 1986).
2. The slogan "Break the Silence to End Men's Violence" is taken from the annual BrotherPeace demonstrations and activities sponsored by the Ending Men's Violence Task Group of the National Organization for Changing Men.

Judaism, Masculinity and Feminism[1]

Michael S. Kimmel

In the late 1960s, I organized and participated in several large demonstrations against the war in Vietnam. Early on—it must have been 1967 or so—over 10,000 of us were marching down Fifth Avenue in New York urging the withdrawal of all U.S. troops. As we approached one corner, I noticed a small but vocal group of counter-demonstrators waving American flags and shouting patriotic slogans. "Go back to Russia!" one yelled. Never being particularly shy, I tried to engage him. "It's my duty as an American to oppose policies I disagree with. This is patriotism!" I answered. "Drop dead, you commie Jew fag!" was his reply.

Although I tried not to show it, I was shaken by his accusation, perplexed and disturbed by the glib association of communism, Judaism, and homosexuality. "Only one out of three," I can say to myself now, "is not especially perceptive." But yet something disturbing remains about that linking of political, religious, and sexual orientations. What links them, I think, is a popular perception that each is not quite a man, that each is less than a man. And while recent developments may belie this simplistic formulation, there is, I believe, a kernel of truth to the epithet, a small piece I want to claim, not as vicious smear, but proudly. Because I believe that my Judaism did directly contribute to my activism against that terrible war, just as it currently provides the foundation for my participation in the struggle against sexism.

What I want to explore here are some of the ways in which my Jewishness has contributed to becoming an anti-sexist man, working to make this world a safe environment for women (and men) to fully express their humanness. Let me be clear that I speak from a cultural heritage of Eastern European Jewry, transmuted by three generations of life in the United States. I speak of the culture of Judaism's effect on me as an American Jew, not from either doctrinal considerations—we all know the theological contradictions of a biblical reverence for women, and prayers that thank God for not being born one—nor from an analysis of the politics of nation states. My perspective says nothing of Middle-Eastern machismo; I speak of Jewish culture in the diaspora, not of Israeli politics.

The historical experience of Jews has three elements that I believe have contributed to this participation in feminist politics. First, historically, the Jew is an *outsider*. Wherever the Jew has gone, he or she has been outside the seat of power, excluded from privilege. The Jew is the symbolic "other," not unlike the symbolic "otherness" of women, gays, racial and ethnic minorities, the elderly and the physically challenged. To be marginalized allows one to see the center more clearly than those who are in it, and presents grounds for alliances among marginal groups.

But the American Jew, the former immigrant, is "other" in another way, one common to many ethnic immigrants to the United States. Jewish culture is, after all, seen as an ethnic culture, which allows it to be more expressive and emotionally rich than the bland norm. Like other ethnic sub-groups, Jews have been characterized as emotional, nurturing, caring. Jewish men hug and kiss, cry and laugh. A little too much. A little too loudly. Like ethnics.

Historically, the Jewish man has been seen as less than masculine, often as a direct outgrowth of this emotional "respond-ability." The historical consequences of centuries of laws against Jews, of anti-Semitic oppression, are a cultural identity and even a self-perception as 'less than men," who are too weak, too fragile, too frightened to care for our own. The cruel irony of ethnic oppression is that our rich heritage is stolen from us, and then we are blamed for having none. In this, again, the Jew shares this self-perception with other oppressed groups who, rendered virtually helpless by an infantalizing op-pression, are further victimized by the accusation that they are, in fact, infants and require the benificence of the oppressor. One example of this cultural self-hatred can be found in the comments of Freud's colleague and friend Weininger (a Jew) who argued that "the Jew is saturated with femininity. The most feminine Aryan is more masculine than the most manly Jew. The Jew lacks the good breeding that is based upon respect for one's own individuality as well as the individuality of others."

But, again, Jews are also "less than men" for a specific reason as well. The traditional emphasis on literacy in Jewish culture contributes in a very special way. In my family, at least, to be learned, literate, a rabbi, was the highest aspiration one could possibly have. Now, in a culture characterized by love of learning, literacy may be a mark of dignity. But in the United States, whose profound anti-intellectualism has marked its uniqueness to Richard Hofstadter, one of our greatest historians, literacy is a cultural liability. Americans contrast egghead intellectuals, divorced from the real world, with men of action—instinctual, passionate, fierce, and masculine. Senator Albert Beveridge of Indiana counseled in his 1906 volume *Young Man and the World* (a turn-of-the-century version of *Real Men Don't Eat Quiche*) to "avoid books, in fact, avoid all artificial learning, for the forefathers put America on the right path by learning from completely natural experience." Family, church and synagogue, and schoolroom were cast as the ennervating domains of women, sapping masculine vigor. In fact, recent historical research suggests that the Boy Scouts of America was founded in 1910 deliberately to stem the tide of this feminization of American culture, which had, in the words of Chief Scout Ernest Thompson-Seton, turned "robust, manly, self-reliant boyhood into a lot of flat-chested cigarette smokers with shaky nerves and doubtful vitality."

Now don't get me wrong. The Jewish emphasis on literacy, on mind over body, does not exempt Jewish men from sexist behavior. Far from it. While many Jewish men avoid the Scylla of a boisterous and physically harassing misogyny, we can often dash ourselves against the Charybdis of a male intellectual intimidation of others. "Men with the properly sanctioned educational credentials in our society," writes Harry Brod, "are trained to impose our opinions on others, whether asked for or not, with an air of supreme self-confidence and aggressive self-assurance." It's as if the world were only waiting for our word. In fact, Brod notes, "many of us have developed mannerisms that function to intimidate those customarily denied access to high educational institutions, especially women."[2] And yet, despite this, the Jewish emphasis on literacy has branded us, in the eyes of the world, less than "real" men.

Finally, the historical experience of Jews centers around, hinges upon our sense of morality, our ethical imperatives. The preservation of a moral code, the commandment to live ethically, is the primary responsibility of each Jew, male or female. Here, let me relate another personal story. Like many other Jews, I grew up with the words "Never Again" ringing in my ears, branded indelibly in my consciousness. For me they implied a certain moral responsibility to bear witness, to remember—to place my body, visibly, on the side of justice. This moral responsibility inspired my participation in the anti-war movement, and my active resistance of the draft *as a Jew*. I remember family dinners in front of the CBS Evening News, watching Walter Cronkite recite the daily tragedy of the war in Vietnam. "Never again," I said to myself, crying myself to sleep after watching napalm fall on Vietnamese villagers. Isn't this the brutal terror we have sworn ourselves to preventing when we utter those two words? When I allowed myself to feel the pain of those people, there was no longer a choice; there was, instead, a moral imperative to speak out, to attempt to end that war as quickly as possible.

In the past few years, I've become aware of another war. I met and spoke with women who had been raped—raped by their lovers, husbands, and fathers, women who had been beaten by those husbands and lovers. Some were even Jewish women. And those same words—"Never Again"—flashed across my mind like a neon meteor lighting up the darkened consciousness. Hearing that pain and that anger prompted the same moral imperative. We Jews say "Never Again" to the systematic horror of the Holocaust, to the cruel war against the Vietnamese, to Central American death squads. And we must say it against this war waged in our society, against rape and battery.

So in a sense, I see my Judaism as a reminding me every day of that moral responsibility, the *special* ethical imperative that my life, as a Jew, gives to me. Our history indicates how we have been excluded from power, but also, as men, we have been privileged by another power. Our Judaism impels us to stand against any power that is illegitimately constituted because we know only too well the consequences of that power. Our ethical vision demands equality and justice, and its achievement is our historical mission.

Notes

1. This essay was originally prepared as a lecture on "Changing Roles for the American Man" at the Ninety-second Street Y in November, 1983. I am grateful to Bob Brannon and Harry Brod for comments and criticisms of an earlier draft.
2. Harry Brod, "Justice and a Male Feminist," in *The Jewish Newspaper* (6 June 1985), p.6.

A Jewish Men's Movement

Robert Rosenberg

What does Jewish feminism mean for Jewish men? It feels like a Chinese box sort of question leading backwards and forwards to other more inclusive and more specific questions. Is there a Jewish feminism to begin with? What is the specific relationship of Jewish men to sexism within the Jewish community? What does feminism mean for men in general, anyhow?

Let's assume for a moment that everyone reading this article agrees that feminism generally includes the recognition of sexism and patriarchy as social and political evils to be struggled against, and the idea that the reordering and re-visioning of our world from a long suppressed female perspective will be a very positive and liberating thing. Let's also assume that we agree that "Jewish feminism" means both applying these insights to our lives, personally and communally, as Jews, and bringing our unique perspective as Jews to the wider feminist movement. And last, let's assume that we all think it's a great thing for men to apply feminist insights to their individual lives and behavior, and at the same time get involved with any and all movements to end the oppression of women and to dismantle patriarchy.

This still leaves us grappling with the issue of Jewish men, and the issue of what Jewish men with a progressive and feminist perspective should be up to politically. Is there a possibility of a specifically Jewish men's movement?

Jewish men bring opposing traditions to the whole issue. We are often viewed as weak, not sexual; in fact, emasculated. Jewish women are often seen as strong, powerful, and in some mysterious way "outside of sexism." On the other hand, Jewish men are trained to be argumentative, rational thinkers, something which is in some sense very male. Yet we are often considered the most sensitive and least sexist of men. Some people might think Jewish men need feminism least of all, while others might think we need it the most. The truth, of course, lies somewhere in between. And part of what is exciting about Jewish men and feminism is opening up our whole understanding of the strengths and weaknesses of Jewish culture in relationship to sexism and masculinity.

What would a Jewish men's group look like that based itself on traditional ways that Jewish men associate—the minyan, the political study group, the basketball court—and turned it around, went beyond it, transformed it? Why do Jewish men have to sit on the sidelines and watch as Jewish women create new liturgies and rituals, or delve into their history and their individual pasts to tell new stories and find new insights? We men can and should be doing the same. The reality of male supremacy within Jewish (and most) cultures only hides the fact that it is just as much of a struggle for Jewish men to refashion our lives in the light of feminism, with new myths, ideals, and traditions, as it is for Jewish women.

As activists, Jewish men need to speak up and become involved *as Jewish men*. Jewish men for choice, Jewish men against homophobia, Jewish men as non-sexist childrearers, are all heartening and progressive images, for men and for women. And we need to find the issues that are specifically ours to tackle. For instance, circumcision, or homophobia among Jewish men.

Progressive, feminist-minded Jewish men can begin to really think deeply about the issues just touched upon here. We can actively shape a new perspective for Jewish men that can be brought into the Jewish community as a model of feminist change and activism. We can work as allies with a wider feminist movement. Working from the grassroots up, from the heart of our many communities, we can reshape our lives as Jewish men and really begin a "Jewish men's movement."

The Gay Movement Is No Place for Jew-hating

The Staff of Gay Community News

An article we published in late December about the experience of being Jewish in the U.S. at Christmastime and the responses to it raised some important issues and strong emotions among members of the staff; these issues and feelings relate to the specific experience of Jews in the U.S. and in the gay and lesbian movement and the specific ways "anti-Semitism," or institutionalized anti-Jewishness, is manifested. (We're choosing to use "anti-Jewishness" in recognition of the separate experiences and different oppressions of other peoples who also claim the name of "Semite.")

As we discussed our reactions, we realized that despite the large contribution of Jews to this newspaper over the years and the large number of us currently on staff, we have not been vocal on the subject of Jewish oppression. In fact, that very silence—as though the issue is either not important enough or too controversial to touch—seems in itself to be the kind of expression of anti-Jewishness that is all too common in our movement.

Therefore, we've decided to take this opportunity to "speak out" ourselves. We do so for a number of reasons. In part we want to support Jewish members of our staff and of our community. We want to acknowledge the deep-rooted fear many Jews feel, fear that making themselves visible as Jews will elicit hatred or scapegoating of the sort Jews have had to cope with for centuries; we want to reassure them that such bigotry will not go ignored or unchallenged in the progressive gay and lesbian community. And equally important, we want to remind ourselves and each other of the first rule of coalition politics: "an attack on one must be answered by all." Scapegoating, blaming one group and pitting others against it, runs counter to our vision of liberation.

Whether anti-Jewishness appears in subtle or overt form, it cannot be divorced from the history that most Jews carry always in the back of their minds. Some of us on staff lost relatives in the Holocaust. Some of us are the children of people who fled the pogroms—rape, murder, thievery—of Eastern Europe. And we know that the oppression of Jews did not begin with the Holocaust, or in this century. In the 1100s entire Jewish communities were destroyed in France. Jews were the victims of the Spanish Inquisition in the

1400s. Hundreds of thousands of Jews were killed in massacres in Poland in the 1600s.

Such oppression did not end with the closing of the concentration camps. We—Jew and gentile alike—have grown tired of hearing that Jews somehow brought this oppression on themselves, that oppression directed at Jews is harmless, or as is commonly asserted, that Jewish oppression no longer exists in this country or in this decade. Jews in the U. S. are currently being scapegoated as the financiers of the Midwestern farm crisis. Synagogues are being bombed in France and vandalized in the U.S. Jews in the Soviet Union are denied the freedom to emigrate.

Paramilitary right-wing groups in the U.S., such as Posse Comitatus, use the same rhetoric used in the Holocaust to rationalize the "need" to exterminate the Jews, and the Ku Klux Klan places Jews high up on its hit list, along with blacks, gay people, and other groups. (They see our common ground even when we fail to.)

Anger at Israel has often been used as a smokescreen for anti-Jewish sentiments; as progressives we must continually separate out and clearly articulate that support for the Jews as a people has nothing to do with upholding the policies of the Israeli state. We feel as free, but no freer, to criticize Israel than we do any other state (most especially our own) which supports right-wing causes around the world, including the contras' war on Nicaragua and apartheid in South Africa, or which has racist policies toward groups of people within its own borders. With complete consistency we can support the liberation struggles of Palestinians and oppressed peoples of color within this country, and support Jewish pride and an end to anti-Jewish violence, discrimination, and rhetoric as well.

Given the persistence of old stereotypes about Jews and money, media accounts that portray gay people as a new wealthy, propertied class that is somehow "taking over" in urban areas can give Jewish gay men and lesbians an ironic sense of déjà vu. That can feel particularly absurd to those who, like the majority of people in this country, live on workers' wages—or especially, on women workers' wages—and rent their homes. Such bigoted stereotypes, whether they're applied to Jews, gay people, or any other group, are not only inaccurate, but are dangerous to us all.

We are committed to fighting class exploitation and to forming coalitions against oppression of all kinds. This requires us to be critical of those landlords and merchants who exploit other people, and to criticize any middle- and upper-class people who fail to ally themselves with those less privileged than themselves, whether the people falling into those categories are Christian or Jewish, gay or straight. Of course, the great majority of such people are white, Christian-raised, and straight. No statistics exist about the percentages of Jewish people in the U.S. working classes and middle classes. (Federal law prohibits the U. S. Census from asking questions which categorize Americans by religion, legislation supported by many Jews who fear such information could be used to round them up some day.) But detailed studies of the small, ingrown group that controls our country's largest corporations indicate that there is precious little room "at the top" for Jews, despite the persistence of stereotypes that they "run everything." In fact, there is substantial evidence that their exclusion is very conscious and deliberate. Of course we're not asking for "affirmative action" for Jews into a class we're out to abolish. Rather, we're pointing out that the powers-that-be are actively invested in perpetuating anti-Jewishness.

While the women's movement and some segments of the so-called "straight left" have taken up the issues of Jewish identity and anti-Jewish prejudice as these relate to their own communities, the gay and lesbian movement has produced little on the subject. We expect politically conscious lesbians and gay men to recognize that perpetuating anti-Jewish rhetoric—or remaining silent while others do—promotes the same ideology and system of ranking that bolsters the status quo, providing encouragement to those who would queer-bash us, deny us our rights, or ghettoize any of us on the basis of our sexuality, class, or color. We encourage more dialogue on the subject.

Jewish Men and Violence in the Home— Unlikely Companions?

Bob Gluck

This article is dedicated to Bernadette Powell, unjustly remaining in prison after ten years, a battered woman whose determination and strength have been an inspiration for my work.

CASE HISTORIES

My first impression of "George" was of a quiet, articulate, gentle man, not unlike many of the men I befriend. He told me that he is very sensitive to feeling hurt. This is especially true when he offers his help to others—and feels rebuffed. In his marriage he insists on being the primary "emotional care giver." In fact, when his wife offers her help and caring, "George" quickly feels "overly mothered." "George" soon finds himself in an emotional state he can but poorly handle. At these times, he flies into what he described as an "uncontrollable rage."

"Mark" is similarly quiet, bright and polite. After talking for a while, this seemingly gentle man struck me as unusually unassertive. Mark rarely asks for what he needs, yet he gets furious when his needs aren't met. He generally hides his feelings, supposedly to protect everyone who is close. Like "George," "Mark" is married, yet copes with his wife's expression of her individuality. If she withdraws from "Mark's" anger, it further enrages him and he feels victimized by any display of her own anger.

Unlike "George" and "Mark," who are soft spoken and about thirty, "Brad" is middle aged and vocal. He claims that no one sees him as a "nice guy." He is physically large and places his body in relation to others in a way which is intimidating. Nonetheless, there is something endearing about the twinkle in his eye. There is at times a gentleness to his voice quite in conflict with his manner during moments of impatience or conflict.

Brad works daily with young adults, yet at home feels perpetually frustrated with his family. He feels that they, and especially his wife, never seem to cooperate with his desires, despite the fact that he "tells them what to do." He is constantly yelling and he acknowledges that his voice frightens his family. He is angry about their growing distance from him.

"George," "Mark" and "Brad" have much in common. They all are greatly controlling of their partners, yet each professes he is fundamentally powerless. Each man perceives his partner as angry, untrustworthy and controlling. Their partners are to be blamed for the bulk of the men's problems. For all these men, physical violence is the main instrument of their controlling behavior. Each initially denied he had a problem, and each greatly minimized or denied the violence of their abuse. One thing further: all three of these men are Jewish.

"Violent Jewish Men." Somehow this phrase doesn't sound right. The images we hold of Jewish men don't generally include physical assault. The face on which we picture Jewish men is the one initially presented by "George," "Mark" and "Brad": quiet, unassuming, caring. Few in the Jewish community consider violence an attribute of our fathers, brothers, friends or lovers. When it is exposed, we consider it an aberration, one not to be discussed.

"George," "Mark" and "Brad" are men I have known through my work in a counseling service for men who abuse their partners. Most of my clients are not Jewish. Yet, the percentage of Jews on my caseload equalled that of the Jews on the caseload of all therapists in my family service agency. The domestic violence-free Jewish community is a myth. It is a dangerous myth, for it is its perpetuation which provides a cloak for abuse to continue unabated. This myth is belied by a slowly increasing discussion of the issue among Jews. It is also refuted by the evidence of traditional Jewish texts.

Why Is There Abuse in the Jewish Community?

How might I describe a typical Jewish abusive man I might see as a client? This is difficult, for there is probably not one character type of "abusive man" for any population. The violence of these men isn't reducible to one "cause," and so I will attempt to depict some of the most commonly-shared characteristics.

In many ways the Jewish batterers I've met share major characteristics with the non-Jewish batterer. He comes from no one economic, social class or educational background. Some abuse substances and others do not. As I suggested earlier, the abusive man tends to control others, yet he feels that it is they who control *his* life. His self-esteem is likely to be low, and he easily feels humiliated, frustrated or hurt. At the same time, this man is unlikely to identify or articulate any of these feelings. Such a man will tend to label all uncomfortable emotions "anger," but claim it is really "the other" who is angry, and not he. When not raging, he may feel depressed.

The abusive man, despite his violence, is usually unassertive. He generally has a poor ability to communicate or resolve conflict and will choose to "stuff" feelings, allowing them to build, knowing that catharsis will come through an episode of violence and rage. While not all my clients acknowledge early experiences of child abuse or sexual assault, my growing assumption is that they must have experienced some form of early wound to their sense of self, coupled with role models of men who utilize instrumental violence. Such models are easy to find in modern society. Life with intimates becomes a form of reworking this pain.

The choice of women as major victims is partially a function of their availability. An individual in a relationship is inherently emotionally and physically vulnerable to the abusive partner. The abuser uses this vulnerability as a weapon via threats, manipulation, humiliation, as well as actual physical violence. Few batterers I've met seem able to sustain intimacy, and they often act to sabotage the relationship. He is often a loner, except for his partner, and he is largely dependent upon her.

The abuser chooses women as victims also because, in his perception, they can be dominated in the face of his self-doubt. Society will generally allow a woman to be victimized, denying credence to her cries for help and making her escape from the situation socially and economically difficult. The man will likely experience few impediments to his controlling behavior, and both community and society will respond with few sanctions in punishment.

It is becoming clear that women are not the sole victims of domestic violence. Abuse extends beyond the heterosexual world. Gay male and lesbian violence is currently receiving more attention, and counseling services are becoming available for these populations as well. The hesitancy of the gay and lesbian communities to discuss abuse is founded on one of the concerns of the Jewish world—safety from oppression. Abuse in gay relationships may well share other commonalities with violence amoung Jews due to a shared male history of mistreatment and negative stereotyping from outside groups.

The admittedly small sample of Jewish men I have counseled was comprised of largely professional, well-educated adults in their thirties. These men tended to feel more genuinely embarrassed and humiliated by their behavior than most of my clients. Shame was a theme which repeatedly appeared in sessions. In this, abusive clients experienced many of the issues faced by non-abusive Jewish men I've known and worked with. It is my hypothesis that early role modeling of violence combined with a lower threshold of emotional pain tolerance moves a man into violent behavior.

One such area which often affects many Jewish men is a personal history of assaults on gender identity in adolescence. While this is true to some degree for all boys, for Jews the ingredient of anti-Semitism adds poignancy. This is because societal stereotypes of Jewish men contain a component of denigration of their masculinity ("wimp," "momma's boy," "sissy Jew-boy"). Such emotional (and physical) assaults are not only received from outsiders, but are passed down from generation to generation from fathers who were similarly denigrated in their own youth, and who yet struggle to overcome their own identity confusion and self-hate. The result is a heritage of rage which can rarely be acknowledged or directly expressed. Popular myth states: "Jewish men aren't angry people. They are warm, calm and patient." The experience of many raised in at least the Eastern European Ashkenazic heritage, with which I am most familiar, suggests a more complex reality. Anger and bitterness are part of this reality. Jewish men may even be more emotionally expressive in their anger than those in the societal mainstream.

Another source of difficulty expressed by my abusive clients, but shared with many Jewish men, is gender role conflict. Adolescent Jewish men must ask: "Should I act aggressively as necessary to get by in the wider world of young men, or more like a non-violent, non-aggressive 'mensch' as Jewish society might desire?" "Should I study hard or even take music or art lessons (and be called a sissy in school), or spend my time training for competitive sports teams?" How can these seemingly conflicting demands be balanced? As a young Jewish man who faced such issues, I can recall having received little assistance or clear thinking.

Role conflicts scarcely end with adolescence. The growing Jewish man must ask how to balance the expectation of being a caring husband, sharing in chores and child rearing, with the demand of meeting an unreachably high work and study achievement level. My clients have difficulty coping with the disappointment, shame and rage they feel about the early mistreatment they experienced at home and in the world—and about the ongoing personal role identity conflicts they find little help resolving. They feel misunderstood by women and by non-Jews, who point to what appears to be relatively "princely" treatment they received as children. They want others to know that, while their Jewish families have the appearance of being close and seem to attend especially well to male children, their own experience was material care but a lack of emotional intimacy and support.

A significant reason why male emotional pain sometimes gives way to domestic violence is the underlying sexism and negative attitudes toward women in Jewish tradition and broader society. Jewish abusive men tend to deny negative feelings about self and externalize them onto others. Female partners are convenient targets because of the legion of negative images all Jews learn about Jewish women. Abusive men attempt to muzzle difficult emotions by controlling others and by lashing out in violence.

Jewish tradition speaks about wives with high praise. The Talmud teaches (Baba Metzia 59a):

> R. Helbo said, "Be careful about the honor of your wife because blessing enters the house only because of the wife." And this is what Rava said to the towns people of Majozi: "Honor your wives so that you may be enriched."

Notice that this praise is largely limited to women in their marital role. Tradition teaches as well that women, especially those who are unmarried, are untrustworthy demons who prey on men. One example among many from the Talmud (Yevamot 63b):

> Turn your eyes away from your neighbor's charming wife, lest you be caught in her net. Do not visit with her husband and share wine and strong drink with him. For through the form of a beautiful woman, many were destroyed.

Projection of men's fears and sexual desires has a clear, long-standing tradition.[1] Early evidence of male externalization of negative feelings dates to the imagery of biblical prophets Jeremiah and Hosea. Both represent attempts to help the Israelite people cope with the trauma of national collapse by use of metaphor. These prophets explain the cause of the collapse as the infidelity of Israel, the unfaithful wife of a monogamous God, from whom she "strays" and "whores."[2] God's response is rage and Israel's banishment (divorce) in exile. Jeremiah also presents a vision of hope for the restoration of "Maiden Israel" (Jer. 31:17):

> Yes, cure I'll bring you, of your wounds I'll heal you, "Outcast, that Zion, for whom nobody cares."

Contemporary Jewish men— abusive and not—seem to often harbor modern negative stereotypes of Jewish women. Their assertiveness is often considered threatening, the sign of a "castrating bitch." The Jewish woman is, in appearance and character, contrary to the American Jewish male image of the ideal mate for a man who is successful in American society (blond and quiet). It is interesting to see how many non-Jewish men find these same characteristics appealing. Might it be that the abusive man lashes out at his Jewish partner in part because she is an ever-present reminder that he himself is Jewish?

TEXTUAL TRADITIONS ABOUT DOMESTIC VIOLENCE

Spousal abuse has been an issue in the classical Jewish sources since the early medieval period.[3] Maimonides and the other major promulgators of Jewish legal codes discuss and rule on it, as do commentators on the Talmud. The responsa literature also contains numerous citations of questions about abuse. Most rabbinic authorities (Rabbi Meir of Rothenberg, Rabbi Solomon Luria, The Tur, the Shulhan Aruch and its glossator Rabbi Moseh Isseries) strongly disapprove of such behavior, reflective of a Talmudic concern that husbands honor their wives.[4] Rabbi Meir, for example (Responsa, *Even ha-Ezer*, #297) states, for example:

> A Jew must honor his wife more than he honors himself. If one strikes his wife, he should be punished more severely than he would be for striking another man. For a man is enjoined to honor his wife, but is not enjoined to honor the other man . . . . If this man persists in striking his wife, he should be excommunicated, lashed and suffer the severest punishment, even to the extent of amputating his arm. If his wife is willing to accept a divorce, he must divorce her and pay the ketubbah.

Rabbenu Tam, the commentator Rashi's grandson, simply states:

> Wife beating is unheard of among the children of Israel.

Rabbi Moses ben Maimon, Maimonides, stands nearly alone in condoning physical abuse. In the Mishneh Torah (*Sefer Nashim*, chap. 21, no. 10), he states:

> A wife who refuses to perform any kind of work she is obligated to do may be compelled to perform it, even by scourging her with a rod.

This position is remarkably close to the famous "rule of thumb" of English Common Law, which allows a husband to hit his wife so long as he does so with a stick no thicker than his thumb. While Maimonides's stance is cited to support a favorable opinion of abuse by at least one later authority, his ruling stands outside the norm. Rabbi Abraham ben David Posquieres, one of his major commentators and critics, comments:

> I have never heard of women being scourged with a rod.

Maimonides's stand may be reflective of practice in the Islamic world in which he wrote, or his own stern outlook. Might it reflect more of the reality of Jewish practice than others are willing to admit? This is a question we must ask, for while the rabbis generally condemn spousal abuse, the plethora of discussion about the issue brings the statements of Posquieres and Rabbenu Tam in question. Clearly, there was much abusive behavior the rabbis found necessary to address and condemn. Spousal abuse must have presented a continual and pressing problem for Jewish communities for at least a millenium. This is scarcely surprising since traditional Jewish marriage is a contract between two partners unequal in status and power.

COMMUNAL AWARENESS ABOUT DOMESTIC VIOLENCE

It is clear that violence against women has been a perennial issue for the Jewish community. This is difficult for many Jews to accept because a violent image squares neither with the societal stereotype nor with our peaceful image of Jewish men. Tradition teaches that a husband is to heed the warning of the Talmud (Sota 47b):

> An arrogant man is not accepted even in his own household . . . at first members of the family jump to his every word, after a while they find him repulsive.

Other rabbinic literature offers similar advice; for example, Pirkei d'Rabbi Nathan (chap. 41):

> At all times, let a man be as supple as the reed and not rigid as the cedar.

The Jewish community succeeds at denying abuse in our midst because we project negative aspects of the male experience upon women. Recall that it is the Jewish woman who is stereotyped as bossy, tough and aggressive. She is considered able to handle any challenge, and she (especially when single) is often seen as a dangerous provocateur. Jewish men are the ones traditionally and popularly perceived as the victims in gender relations. Meanwhile, in the morass of these stereotypes, the Jewish home is supposed to be a protected island of peace. Our difficulty acknowledging Jewish domestic violence is compounded by our great fear of anti-Semitism; conditioned, we may naively believe, by how the wider world perceives our character and actions.

I believe that there is an additional obstacle toward a Jewish communal acknowledgment of abuse. Admitting a violation of *"shalom bayit"* is an embarrassing *shanda* (disgrace). In our communities, information perceived as negative travels rapidly. There is a way in which our experience of anti-Semitism has caused us to internalize fault for our national experience into internalized negative self-image. This compounds the effect of our prophetic teachings that sociopolitical failings are rooted in our personal failures. The result is that we are all fighting a battle to prove that we aren't bad people. Publicized abuse flies in the face of this attempt. Unpublicized abuse, however, is the chief means of abuse's unchallenged perpetuation.

There are few reputable statistics about abuse amoung Jews. A Los Angeles study found that 50 percent of the Jews interviewed reported instances of violence—and a hospital emergency room worker was quoted as reporting that 20 percent of Jewish married women were battered, as are all married women.[5] In Israel, it is estimated that 30 percent of Israeli children grow up in homes where their mother was abused.[6]

Jewish communities have been slow to allocate resources to address the problem of domestic violence. I know of but three Jewish-sponsored programs offering services to battered women (in New York, Chicago and Los Angeles). Only one shelter exists in the U.S. which can meet the needs and requirements of traditional Jewish women: Transition Center in Far Rockaway, New York City.[7] I don't know of one Jewish agency with a program for the treatment of batterers. Few Jewish agencies have placed abuse on their counseling training or family life education priorities list.

I am hopeful that this situation will soon change. A path has been cleared by the National Council of Jewish Women which has, in the past six years, published two valuable books: *Domestic Violence: An NCJW Response* (1981), and a guide to establishing and running a program for battered women. Guidance is also to be found from our Israeli sisters who have established several shelters in Israel (the fruit of a long grass roots struggle). Recently, an Israeli counseling project for the male perpetrators of abuse also opened its doors.

COUNSELING APPROACHES FOR ABUSIVE MEN

It comes as a surprise to many that there are men involved in the struggle to end domestic violence. Many of my colleagues over the past seven years of anti-abuse work have, in fact, been Jewish men working in groups and agencies outside the Jewish community. Most of our work has been community education and advocacy in support of women's groups—and direct services, education and counseling for abusive men.

Men's work with batterers is a direct outgrowth of the battered women's movement of the 1970s through today. It began during the mid-seventies as the activity of a small number of men's counseling collectives, such as "Emerge" in Boston, "Raven" in St. Louis and "Men's Work" (which I co-founded) in Ithaca, New York. We urged men to take responsibility for men's violence against women. We wished to educate the wider community with a feminist analysis of the consequences of sexism, which stand as the basis of male violence.[8]

Our initial approach was to verbally educate other men and to support women by providing child care for victims, and help fund and provide advocacy for shelters. While we chose not to talk in place of women, we found that our male voices could speak directly to the male experience. The move into counseling batterers came as we learned that we could speak compassionately, yet decisively, to other men with the knowledge that men as a whole are socialized to build their identities around models drawn from a sexist system. This is a system which allots power and benefits to men, despite its human cost to them. Men thus learn to have a great stake in the maintenance of sexism.

Men, even Jewish men, are taught limited emotional options and are socialized to replace caring and peaceful, self-assertive relations with others with a drive for power over those less powerful. We, who began to counsel batterers, found that we could beneficially use our commonality with violent men to intervene and interrupt the displacement onto women of their rage and desire to control.

Over the past ten years, what was originally a small grass-roots men's movement has spawned a growing interest in the issue of batterer counseling. This has included not only numerous men's groups, but social service agencies as well. By 1986, there were approximately 150 known services providing services to batterers in the United States. Many of these (such as the batterer counseling sub-unit of the family service agency for which I have worked the past two-and-a-half years) remain true to the original feminist analysis and work in tandem with women's groups.

The most effective work I and others have done has been with men in structured psycho-educational groups. These groups meet regularly for several months with a regular membership and mix educational material with opportunities to build therapeutic relationships with peers and counselors. Issues addressed include: identifying and coping with emotions, understanding the nature of abuse, acknowledging that one is an abuser, attitudes toward women, substance abuse, skills for relationships, and conflict resolution. I have never run a group exclusively for Jewish men who are abusive. While there are advantages to having a diverse group, a "Jewish" group might offer the commonality and safety for healing of the psychic hurts borne by Jewish men who act violently.

The major issue to be addressed throughout counseling is denial and minimization of abuse and externalizing all negative feelings onto others. This makes work with batterers challenging and difficult. Nevertheless, initial research done at my agency suggests a high success rate for those clients who commit themselves to counseling.

I am able to hold out hope of change for abusive men because I feel strongly that their behavior is learned. It has become progressively clearer to me that the perpetrator of violence can make the choice to end the violence. Learned behavior can be unlearned. Men who make basic choices about "how" they batter, e.g., hit with which hand, how hard, for how long, etc., can learn to acknowledge the decision-making that goes into their behavior.

Responsibility is an important issue for men who abuse because studies suggest that many episodes of violence are not preceded by any overt behavior on the part of the victim. Episodes of violence have an instrumental place in a wider pattern of power and control of the victim. Once responsibility for the actual violence is assumed, the entire pattern can unravel. This is a challenge for all abusive men. For Jews it is especially difficult because it goes so contrary to Jewish male self-image and is such a humiliating fact to acknowledge.

While I believe that counseling batterers can be effective, I am aware that it can reach only a very small number of abusers. Most men will not consider counseling an option. These men see the woman as responsible for provoking the violence (if it is even acknowledged) or consider the prospect of acknowledging the need for help as too frightening and threatening. It seems clear to me that the most effective tool of interrupting domestic violence is a dramatic legal intervention. Arrest and the threat of arrest is a powerful deterrent to abuse, although the legal system and police have been painfully slow in acknowledging their part in stopping abuse. Often, however, it is facing the consequences of continuing to abuse that moves a man to seek counseling. A combination of legal intervention, counseling, and shelter for victims is an appropriate approach at the present time.

The need for educating the Jewish community about abuse is great. There is an enormous need to advocate getting the issue on the communal agenda—of Jewish social services, synagogues, systems of Jewish (and rabbinic) education—as well as openly discussed in the Jewish press. We need to put our heads together to creatively discuss ways to address the fear and denial which allows it to remain under the covers.

While sexism among Jews is addressed on some levels, it will never be eradicated without directly acknowledging and fighting its most devastatingly violent symptoms. Similarly, domestic violence will never end until the full spectrum of violence against women—rape (including marital rape), sexual abuse and harassment, economic exploitation and political powerlessness—is recognized and stopped. That all these are symptoms of sexism and instruments of its perpetuation is generally denied by our community. It is encouraging to see that some movement has occurred on other issues formerly denied by our community, most notably alcoholism. The task is great, but change is possible.

I see unlocking the secrets of abuse as beneficial not only to women, but critical to men as well. Jewish men who seek counseling can play a pioneering role in speaking about the psychic hurts experienced by Jewish men. Jewish men speaking honestly and courageously about our experience can help remove the blinders which prevent men from looking seriously at the high costs sexism has exacted from men as well as women.

Acknowledgments: I wish to thank the men with whom I worked in Ithaca, New York, from 1979-81, most notably Fred Sack, Randy Wills (who co-founded Men's Work), Erik Bendix (my counseling partner in our first sessions with men who abuse), Jeff Bradley, Bob Love and Allen Rosenthal. I would also like to thank Paul Bukovec, my colleague, supervisor and friend at Project Rap in Philadelphia, with whom I have learned much, including the value of loving struggle.

Notes

1. Recall that the primal "fall" from the Garden of Eden came to pass, according to tradition, because of Eve, whose punishment is "your urge shall be for your husband, and he shall rule over you." (Gen. 3:16).

2. Examples of Jeremiah's language: she is "wicked:" 1:16, 7:12, 23:22, "treatrous": 12:1, 6; "a whore" (z'n'h): 2:20, 3:1, 3:3, 3:6-8, 5:7, etc.

3. For further material and discussion of sources see Rabbi Julie R. Spitzer, "Spousal Abuse in Rabbinic and Contemporary Judaism," Rabbinic Thesis, HUC-JIR, 1985; F. Klagsbrun, *Voices of Wisdom: Jewish Ideals and Ethics for Every Day Life* (New York; Pantheon Books/JPS), 1980.

4. See, for example, Baba Metzia 59a, Yevamot 63a, Sanhedrin 76b. For earlier material, see *Wisdom of Ben Sira*, 25:1. For source material in English, see Montefiore and Loewe, *A Rabbinic Anthology*, (New York: Schocken Books, 1974), and D. Feldman, *Marital Relations, Birth Control and Abortion in Jewish Law* (New York: Schocken Books, 1968, 1974).

5. Giller and Goldsmith, 1980 Master's Thesis, HUC-JIR/USC, quoted in Spitzer, *op. cit.* See also, J. Goldberg, "Beating of spouses: Yes it does happen in Jewish families," *Jewish Exponent* (Philadelphia) (11 July 1986); B. Trainin, "Facing up to the problem of Jewish wife abuse," *The Jewish Week* (25 January 1985), p. 24.

6. Figures from R. Elliott, "Israel's battered women helped by new network," *The Jewish Week*, New York (8 March 1985), an article about Thelma Peskin-Halpern of Save Our Sisters in Israel; also see J. Bat-Ada, "Porn in the Promised Land," *Lilith* no. 11 (Fall/Winter 1983); "Families in

Crisis", *Jerusalem Post* (US edition) (4 July 1986), p. 5.

7.   Transition Center, sponsored by the Associated YM-YWHAs of Greater New York, see B. Trainin *op. cit.*

8.   Feminist theorists who contributed greatly to my understanding of the dynamics of abuse and sexism include: Susan Brownmiller, *Against Our Will: Men, Women and Rape* (New York: Ballantine Books, 1976); M. Daly, *Gyn/Ecology* (Boston: Beacon Press, 1978); A. Dworkin, *Woman Hating* (New York: Dutton, 1974); D. Martin, *Battered Wives* (San Francisco: Glide Publications, 1976); K. Millett, *Sexual Politics* (New York: Avon Books, 1969, 1970); L. Walker, *The Battered Woman* (New York: Harper and Row, 1979). The theoretical perspective of the Emerge counseling collective in Boston was also influential in my initial work.

Adorning the Mystery: A Vision of Social Activism

Arthur Waskow

This article is taken from a speech given in Madison, Wisconsin on March 29, 1987, and transcribed by Alan Cohen.

The concept of *Tikkun Olam* has long provided the traditional spiritual roots of Jewish social activism. The Hebrew words *Tikkun Olam* are usually understood as "Repairing the World," but these words are used in other senses elsewhere in the Torah. *Olam* (the world) can mean "the hidden" or "the mysterious"; thus in some ways *olam* is the mysterious eternity beyond space and time. *Tikkun* is "the adornment," as of the bride in the traditional Cabala. So *Tikkun Olam* can mean "to adorn the mystery." How is adorning the mystery connected to repair of the world?

It seems to me that the most crucial repair the world needs in our generation is this very adornment of mystery. Our most profound sickness is the sense that there is no mystery. This arises from the truth that in the last 500 years the human race has been very good at knowledge: at rolling back ignorance, at learning and doing, and at making and shaping. We are learning the fabric of the material universe, learning the cellular processes of psychology and physiology and history, learning what makes us human, and learning to shape and control.

But the human race has gotten so good at making and learning that we have come to think that rolling back the frontiers of ignorance means that there is no mystery. Mystery is what we don't know, can't know, and can, if we choose, *celebrate* not knowing.

In our generation, we have begun to see that we are moving rapidly to an abyss. We are coming to understand that if we establish total control, what we'll do is "total" the planet (to use an image that comes not accidentally from Detroit).

We have begun to grapple with that danger, recognizing it most clearly in the possibility of a worldwide nuclear holocaust. All this is a recitation that most of us are used to. What has *Tikkun Olam* got to do with it?

MAKING SHABBOS

One way of thinking about our modern world is that it is a world that in 500 years has never "made *Shabbos*"—honored the Sabbath. It has never paused to say: making and doing and learning to control is not "the goal." The goal is to integrate that into celebration, meditation, repose, and pleasure in the world as it is created. The sense of mystery is what is at the heart of *Shabbos*. *Shabbos* may not be all there is to be in the world, but for sure, the six days of work make sense only because of their flowing towards *Shabbos*.

Some scholars claim that in Babylonia there was an institution called *Shapatu* which operated something like the seventh day. It was a day of not working, and it arose from terrible fear. They didn't know what to do next, and it scared them. So they went home, inside, and they avoided doing anything. What the Israelite people did was to take that sense of mystery in the world, of needing to pause, and turn it emotionally and spiritually upside down. They said: "It's all right—there is mystery in the world. We don't know what to do next, and that's wonderful! We'll celebrate, and sing, and we'll dance. We'll study the ultimate teachings, not to control but simply to search."

In ignoring *Shabbos*, we have flattened out time and abolished any sense that there is rhythm and holiness in time. We have turned time instead into a commodity, to be used for production. In that way of thinking, *Shabbos* is a "waste of time," literally. Think what you could be doing, what you could be making, if you didn't make *Shabbos*.

One profound healing that the world needs today is to recover the sense of mystery which is experienced by treating time as having different rhythms— including taking time for not doing and not thinking. If we can do that healing, we open up the possibility of healing the planet before it destroys itself. And from that we can undertake some new doing, some new project.

It's not that the modern world ought to be written off. Rather it can be seen as a completed painting which you don't keep painting on top of anymore. You take it off the easel, and you celebrate the fact you've finished the painting. Then you put a new canvas on the easel and you go about making something different. We are at that point in human history.

RENEWAL, NOT RESTORATION

What evidence is there that this could be done? What would we need to do that? Already there is evidence that larger and larger parts of the human race are groping in this direction. The religious upheavals in Christianity, Judaism,

Islam (to some extent), and Buddhism are attempts—sometimes clearly defined, sometimes inchoate and vague—to recover some sense that there is *wisdom* predating 1492, and before the advent of socialism, liberalism, nationalism, and science. Often these upheavals carry with them the notion that the whole business is sick and dangerous and needs to be gotten rid of. There are elements in the religious resurgence around the globe that turn in that direction. Sometimes they're willing to use the technology—whether it's cassette recordings in Iran or national television in the United States—without letting any of the mentality of modernity in.

But the other response from the religious tradition has been what I would call religious *renewal* rather than religious *restoration*. That is, the attempt to absorb modernity, to accept its truths as divine and to reconnect modernity with what went before. It is an attempt to understand modernity in its context, instead of trying to eliminate it.

To think of modernity as part of a great spiral is an attempt to integrate it into a profoundly religious view of history, rather than to view it as Satanic, as some religious restorationists basically feel. For this process of integration and renewal, the Jewish people have a history that can be made available to ourselves and to the rest of the human race. At least once before we have been confronted with a world in which the leap in human power was very considerable. That historical moment occurred when Hellenism flooded the Middle East. It drowned out militarily our ability to preserve our own kind of society, and it drowned out intellectually our sense of what the world is about.

The Jews absorbed large chunks of Hellenism and created something that appeared totally different from Biblical observance. It was a time of going back to the most ancient texts in order to understand the new ways and to create a framework for absorbing and transforming Hellenism. That's what we accomplished about 2000 years ago.

Now, we and the world stand in a very similar relation to modernity as we then stood to Hellenism. We need to recover the creativity, the radical and the conservative creativity, that the rabbis of the Talmud drew on. If we can pull off that creation, what we come out with will be as different from the last 2000 years as the creation of that period was from biblical times preceding it.

THE TECHNOLOGICAL JUBILEE

What can we draw on? How can we reaffirm the sense of mystery so that our modern world of doing and producing fits into the sense of mystery. To start, let us draw on three passages of ancient Torah which to me seem most clear about that process: *Shabbat*, the Sabbatical Year, and Jubilee, the penultimate sabbath.

The Torah says that every seventh year all debt should be annulled, and the land should stand at rest. It should get to make *Shabbos* just like everybody else, because the earth (adamah) was as deeply God-given as Adam, its cousin. In the fiftieth year, the year following the seven times seventh year when debts had already been annulled, you took the next step toward equality: you shared the land again, family by family; but again, you didn't work the land. Would you believe—the poor who this moment got back the land they had lost—they weren't allowed to work it the year they got it back! No, they had to sit and look at it, rejoice with it, and celebrate with it. That was the legal proof that the land didn't belong to anybody, it belonged to itself and God.

Now what would it mean to draw from this idea? If the problem is that we make no *Shabbos* and speed everything up faster and faster, then one idea is to shut down that part that makes it all go faster.

That part is technological research and development. What if we said, for one year out of every seven we will give you a *real* Sabbatical. Not the Sabbatical year where you go off and do all the research that you haven't had time to do, and work twice as hard as you do usually, but the Sabbatical year where you really rest. You will think about values and goals. And we the society will live that year with you. It's not only the engineers and the scientists who do this; those who make the decisions in society, they will do this, too. All of us will spend some time celebrating and re-evaluating. And out of that, maybe, will come some new direction when the "work week" starts again, and we put a new canvas on the easel.

GOING PUBLIC JEWISHLY

Let's take another example. In the two great eras of Jewish history, Biblical and Talmudic, there were different ways in which the Jewish people thought about how you brought decency and holiness into the world. In the Biblical era, it is clear that the Israelite people had the notion that a decent society included: observing the Jubilee and *Shabbot*, limiting slavery, giving severance pay when slaves left, and, in general, trying to make decent the way society operated. The only way we could bring that into the world during Biblical times was to conquer the land of Canaan, get rid of everybody who didn't agree with doing it that way, and make that society. It was very activist, and it seemed to say that the only way to bring about that result was to use violence when necessary.

The rabbis in the Talmudic Period undertook a very different approach. The rabbis said, "First of all, we can't pull it off. Second, we can imagine other ways of bringing holiness into the world, namely, doing for ourselves in the nooks and crannies of other societies."

Out of that sense of the world comes the *midrash* of the *Tzaddik* (Righteous One) in Sodom and Gomorrah, who is going around ranting and arguing, proclaiming and demanding. Finally he is visited by somebody who says, "Listen, I don't understand what you're doing. You've been here fifteen years doing all these things, and those folks don't change." And the Tzaddik says, "Listen, for the first seven years I was doing it in the hope that they would change, but in the last seven years I was doing it in the hope they wouldn't change me." I think that was the Rabbinic model for what it meant to build Judaism. The bargain was basically that we give up on the hope of transforming the rest of the world except through prayer and divine intervention.

But that period is over, too. First, we began to have more of a sense of our own power to change the world. Second, other parts of the human race got themselves more power and showed that they could shatter our nooks and crannies with pogroms and Nazism.

The question that now stands before us is what it now means to carry our vision of repairing the world into being. What would it mean to draw on both the Biblical and Rabbinic periods? It would mean drawing on the deepest roots of ancient Jewish spirituality, combining them with the non-violent, Rabbinic ways of being in the world, and bringing them into the world to transform it.

Slowly it has already begun to happen. When Soviet Jews went into the streets to dance and celebrate the Torah, they were doing something absolutely extraordinary. They were doing what looks like, on one level, the same thing ghetto Jews did when they took the Torah into the streets, but it's not. It's one thing to take to a ghetto street, in your nook and cranny, to dance to reaffirm your own place. It's another thing to go out into streets which are not ghetto streets, in a top-down, Pharaonic society, to dance with the sense of being Jewish. That dancing is a kind of resistance, and it made extraordinary waves in that and other societies. In the late 60s and early 70s, Jews made Passover *seders* in public spaces in the United States. They were doing that in recognition that racism and war against the people of Vietnam were Pharaonic activities. Jews, through the Passover ritual, could say, "No, you can't do that." Jews stood on the edge of the White House lawn, just outside the fence, in 1970 and poured blood, for the First Plague, on the fence; and released frogs for the Second Plague on the lawn, and so on through the nine Plagues (but not the Tenth). And Jews smashed a Golden Calf, the idol of war, technology and money, outside the White House in 1969.

More recently Jews built *sukkot* (the open-roof booths of the Harvest festival) all over the country. The *sukkah* is the exact opposite of a fallout shelter because it is vulnerable. The *sukkah* says: The only way you get security in the nuclear age is by everybody recognizing that everyone lives in a *sukkah*, totally open. The rain will rain in. If it's nuclear rain, it too will rain in. If you try to make a *sukkah* raintight, you don't have a *sukkah* anymore.

Jews are doing these things in the "public sphere." We are connecting our lives today to these symbols and messages and proofs from our tradition about the limits of power, about what it means to be vulnerable. And we are only in the first stages, the first years, of building a way for Jews to move into public spaces to say these things. There is much more from our tradition to draw on and to envision.

We can even use the little things of Jewish tradition in this process. For example, I have this notion that one meaning of the *tsitsis* (the fringes of the prayer shawl) is that good *tsitsis* make good neighbors—not good *fences*, but good *fringes*. What are fences? Sharp demarcations: this side mine, that side yours. "Good fringes" means that your power dwindles away from the edge of your person and along the edge of you property. In the land of Israel, the corners of the fields were sort of yours and sort of not. You owned them, but you couldn't use the produce from them. The corners, like the corners of the prayer shawl, were for other people, for the community. What made them holy was that they were yours and were *not* yours. Like *tsitsis*, which are cloth fading away to the air, they were and weren't yours.

If we follow that teaching at the political level, we can envision that every country might have demilitarized zones on its borders—areas which are ours, and not ours. Areas we're allowed to have cops in, but not armies. They are our sovereign territory, but there are certain things we can't do with that piece of sovereign territory. They are the *tsitsis* of the post-modern state.

THE TASK REMAINS

What I am describing is what I think is a hinge moment of Jewish and planetary history. We are at the moment when we need to create the next steps. This is the next era of Jewish life, when we need to uncover, revise, and discover aspects of Torah that have been hidden from us.

Finally, in the process of doing this, in the process of doing this discovering, what about God? The first response of modern persons to the new powers of the human race was to say, "I look out there and nothing's happening.

I look in here, and everything's happening. There is no God." I think that was an authentic religious response. It was a reality. But as we have gotten further into that process, we begin to be very nervous about that response. Authentic, but insufficient. Does that mean we go back to the old images of God, one who stands outside the world, outside of history? I would say not. It seems to me that God has chosen to move to a different place, and that the most authentic religious response to that is to see God in another place.

Two hundred years ago one of the great Hassidic teachers of the town of Chernobyl said, "Everything is God." What is the world? The world is God, wrapped in robes of God in such a way as to appear to us—who are ourselves God-wrapped-in-robes-of-God—to be material. And we ourselves? We appear to ourselves to be simply material. And what is our task? To unwrap those robes, and to discover that we are God, that what we do is God.

I have an eerie sense that the nuclear catastrophe—at Chernobyl!—was the result of attempting to climb the ladder of that teaching, but not getting far enough on the ladder. What $E=mc^2$ says is: matter is energy, wrapped in robes of energy, so as to appear to be matter. And you can un-robe the matter and turn it into energy, which is what fusion and fission do. And that's a step up the ladder. But if you stop there, it's a very dangerous place. This unwrapping of the robes of matter to see energy, raw energy, is very different from unwrapping the robes of the material to discover that it is spirit. I think that's the remaining task for us.

This does not mean we have no limits. The very first part of our tradition, about what it means to be God, is that for the ultimate productivity of the creation of the universe, even God had to protect and preserve by *not* doing, by *not* creating, by *not* working on the Sabbath. As in the story I read to children, God asks, "Then what can I make on the seventh day?" The answer is to make *not* making.

I think we, who have become so God-like in our powers, need to say to ourselves: We can make everything, and therefore, we can *end* everything. What we should do, for a moment, is to make nothing.

Toward A Male Jewish Feminism

Harry Brod

My identities as a man, a Jew, and a feminist all lay claim to my full allegiance. They are not isolated roles, to be simply juxtaposed alongside others I assume in my life. Each identity encompasses a view of the whole. My life embodies integrated meaning, rather than fragmentary experience, only if I can unite them into a multifaceted identity. What, then, does it mean to claim an identity as a male Jewish feminist?

I can give only a preliminary answer, since I regard the integration of these standpoints as a goal yet to be achieved. This goal requires, for example, that I not allow much of the feminist critique of mainstream masculinity to bypass my culture, but instead determine how feminism applies to Jewish men. The stereotype of the boisterous, hard-drinking, brawny brawler is not part of my culture. Yet its analogue appears when Jewish men practice their own brand of intellectual muscle-flexing, trying to destroy one another's arguments rather than armaments.

The status of intellectual rather than physical achievement in Jewish culture produces a mode of sexism different from the mainstream, a style in which intellectual is more common than physical male intimidation of women. (To say this is not to succumb to a myth denying physical abuse in Jewish as in all other communities, but to acknowledge cultural differences.) Common male pretensions to omniscience violate both Jewish and feminist ethics. I therefore try to undermine the mystique of male authority by practicing what I call "verbal footnoting," giving credit to the sources of my ideas and information whenever possible.

We need to separate positives from negatives in Jewish traditions. Jewish masculinities offer many positive models. For example, an aspect of the tradition stresses that the man deserving honor as a child's real father is not the biological sire nor the provider of life's material goods, but he who educates the child into moral life and values.[1] But men's distance from family life, another aspect of the tradition, is not only oppressive to women, as it keeps them tied to the home, but a loss to men as well. In all branches other than Reform Judaism (in a very controversial recent change), legal status as a Jew still passes to the child only through the mother. This denies men's abilities to nurture and transmit their heritage.

While some think of feminism as divisive to the Jewish community, I find this view backward. The Jewish community is already divided along gender lines and damaged by sexism. Feminism offers the only hope of uniting on a firm foundation. The Jewish community's sexism is a fundamental way it internalizes and perpetuates anti-Semitism. Stereotypes of the "Jewish American Princess" and "Jewish Mother" scapegoat and shift on to women anti-Semitic criticisms of Jews for striving for economic success and security, and taking care of their families. Furthermore, Jewish men have often tried to compensate for lesser power relative to other men by exerting authority over "their" women. In institutionalized Jewish life, this takes such forms as excluding women from rituals and rabbinic offices, not counting women in the minyan (the prayer quorum of ten Jewish men), inequities in divorce and other laws, inadequate recognition of women's volunteer labor, and many other injustices identified by Jewish feminists. Interpersonally, it appears when men pressure women toward marriage and child rearing, denigrate their skills, intelligence, beauty, and sexuality in unfavorable comparisons to "American" femininity, relegate women to preparing and cleaning up the holiday meals over which they preside, or act in other sexist ways. A Jewish feminism which eliminates this false escape valve for anti-Semitic pressures can only strengthen the Jewish community, bringing it to full strength by fully integrating Jewish women, and empowering Jewish men to face the real obstacles to be overcome.

One of the great tragedies of oppression is its internalization, whereby oppressed peoples turn against themselves and their allies. Marginalized and threatened by WASP norms, efforts by Jews to be "one of the boys," in the vain hope of finding acceptance and safety through conformity to those norms, fuel Jewish collusion with gay and lesbian oppression, to give but one example. Aside from all the other important reasons to oppose such oppression, recent history clearly shows where Jewish solidarity should be. There are essential parallels between anti-Semitism and gay and lesbian oppression. In both cases, while one cannot visually determine a person's identity as readily as in such categories as sex and race, stereotypes insist that one can. Consequently, anti-Semitism and gay and lesbian oppression are uniquely suited to terrorize the population as a whole, rendering everyone suspicious of their neighbors and vigilant over themselves, lest they be taken for one of *them*. Gay and lesbian oppression therefore functions as a rallying point for the forces of repression in the United States and elsewhere in the current period, as anti-Semitism did in Europe of the thirties and forties. Faced with attempts to impose monolithic WASP norms on all of us, the pluralisms espoused by Jewish, women's, and gay and lesbian liberation movements are each necessary for each other's survival.

A strong feminist commitment by Jewish men would be of great help in forging political alliances. Active involvement with feminism by men demonstrates by analogy that "you don't have to be Jewish" to make Jewish issues your priority. One can also demonstrate the interconnections among different forms of oppression. For example, among its other evils, much of the New Right's anti-abortion rights stand is also anti-Semitic in that its abortion-is-murder argument attempts to make a (minority) Christian ethical position the law of the land, not to mention the offensiveness of the abortion-as-Holocaust analogy propagated by some elements.[2] Even when it has in some cases been opposed to abortion, Jewish law has never punished abortion as murder, and has in some cases considered therapeutic abortion not only permissible but mandatory, as for example, to save the mother's life.[3]

A treatment of Judaism such as this must also address spiritual questions. How does feminism affect Jewish spirituality? Recently Rabbi Laura Geller has argued that while first stage Jewish feminism is concerned with questions of gender related to equal access and justice, the new second stage raises further questions about the transformation of the very nature of Judaism.[4] Feminist spirituality has profound implications for men. Whatever one's concept of spirituality, theistic or not, spirituality involves some form of self-transcendence. I would argue that unless one intimately knows one's self, one will only reproduce rather than transcend it in one's spiritual practice. Male barriers to intimacy, self-disclosure, and surrender are therefore likely to inhibit one's prayer or meditation unless one has engaged in conscious feminist struggle to overcome them.

Spirituality, on most conceptions, requires a fine balance between two aspects. As Jonathan Omer-Man recently put it at "Wrestling With the Messenger: A Conference on Jewish Men's Spirituality," spirituality is at the same time the ultimate assertion of one's self, "the path to the optimal version of myself," and the ultimate loss and immersion of one's self in the face of something higher. Many people have found useful the analysis of Carol Gilligan and others suggesting that men experience the world more in categories of separation and independence, constructing moralities of rights which demarcate the self from others, while women's experience revolves more around connectedness and interdependence, constructing moral relations of caring with and for others. Given our different histories, men are more likely to have difficulty experiencing relatedness, and women self-assertion, in following spiritual as well as secular paths. It is in this vein that I conceive of distinctive male and female spiritualities. One need not postulate some ultimate metaphysical or religious dualism, but simply recognize the historical development of male and female cultures, just as my speaking of a male Jewish feminism should not be taken to imply that I thereby postulate two Jewish feminisms, one male and one female. Ultimately there are, or perhaps one should more precisely say there should not be, neither two feminisms nor two Judaisms, for to assert such dualisms would be to reify and validate precisely the dichotomies one is aiming to overcome. Nonetheless, given our historical legacies, it is appropriate at times to highlight the different paths through with different groups may come to shared understandings, and to use differentiated terminology to do so.

A new feminist Judaism's recognition of gender differences, and of the effects of traditional normative Judaism's privileging the male side of the difference, might affect such central notions as the priority of convenantal obligations. This is one of the fundamental principles underlying the entire structure of Jewish law and ethics, according to which, the Jewish people having entered into a covenant to obey divine commandmants, it is more meritorious to do that which God has commanded than that which is simply voluntary. For once contract and duty are seen as male values, rather than ideals intrinsic to or necessarily normative for the structure of relationships, other ethical tenets and principles latent in Judaism might come to the fore. For example, the principle that various laws may, and perhaps must, be broken to save a life has long been recognized in Jewish law, but it has generally been understood as an exception to other rules, an exception built into the rule structure itself, relating the rules to each other in a hierarchical or meta-structural way. Perhaps, however, what is manifest here is not one rule which limits others, but the beginnings of an alternative ethical system in Judaism which places less value on law as law and more on life-affirming relationships.

One might in the light of such considerations also re-examine the central Jewish theological tenet of the ineffability of the name of the deity. Behind this idea that God is unnameable lies a long philosophical tradition, which recognizes that to name something is to define it, and that definition is by its nature delimitation, a setting off of one thing as separate and apart from something else, and hence a specification of the limits of the thing in question. It follows then that the infinite cannot be named. One may further say that to know the true name of something is to know its essence, and hence to have a kind of power over it. For this reason, Adam is called to name the animals, as a sign that they are under his dominion. All of this can be quite reasonably stated in gender neutral terms, and provides ample grounds for accepting God's name as unutterable. Yet, I often become suspicious when an idea, even a quite reasonable one, is so widely and unquestioningly accepted. As often turns out to be the case, might the reasons for its acceptance have to do not with its intrinsic merits, but with its serving some vested interests of those propounding the idea?

Psychologists often speak in neutral terms of men's "low self-disclosure rate." Behind this innocent-sounding phrase lies a disturbing truth. Recognizing that knowledge is power, we often maintain power by not giving others knowledge about us.[5] Is our hidden God really a God men have constructed in their own image, a God who maintains his power by not revealing himself, as men maintain their power by not revealing themselves? Is this a distinctively male theology, which then in self-justifying and circular fashion validates men's power over women, in that male behavior appears to emulate the divine? Whatever one thinks of the merits of this conception of the deity as a hidden god on purely theological or philosophical grounds, there are clear grounds in the Jewish tradition for viewing the use of such a theology as validating of human male behavior as idolatrous. For not only is it to impose a human image on God, thereby delimiting the unlimited, but it is also a kind of hubris or arrogance, in that men thereby attempt to arrogate to themselves the privilege of ineffableness that is God's alone, and through this arrogation to hold semi-divine power. The distinction between the human and the divine should then be understood as a call to men to disclose and reveal themselves, to surrender the power they gain from remaining unknown.

If one's name, then, is understood as a revelation of one's real self, as Jewish and other traditions understand it, the response to the question "what's in a name?" should be "everything." It is not a coincidence that high on the agenda of introducing feminist practices into mainstream Judaism is the addition of naming ceremonies for girls. In light of this we must look again at the significance of men's traditional naming practices. What has it really meant, for example, that we take our father's first name as our last? And how can we measure or regain what we lost through all the assimilationist name changes at Ellis Island and afterwards, as well as the erasure of our matrilineal names? In the famous, or infamous, 1969-70 Chicago Seven riot-conspiracy trial, the following was Abbie Hoffman's response when asked to state his name: "My slave name is Hoffman. My real name is Shaboysnakoff. I can't spell it." The statement about the name's spelling is more than a confession of ignorance. It is an accusation hurled against a society which has robbed him of his identity, an especially pointed accusation when one recalls that the judge's name in the case was also Hoffman—Julius Hoffman, also a Jew, whom Abbie called "Julie" throughout the trial. At one point Abbie told Julie in Yiddish that his behavior was a "Shande fur de Goyim," a common phrase whose literal translation is "disgrace for the Gentiles," but which Abbie later translated for the unknowing as "Front man for the WASP power elite."[6]

The dynamics of Jewish masculinity have impact in other social areas as well. Often, men who come after those who have fought a war feel the lack of a comparable battleground to prove their own masculine prowess. They tend to go "in search of enemies" (this is the apt title of John Stockwell's book about the U.S. government's manufacture of a war in Angola right after the end of direct U.S. military involvement in the war in Vietnam). For Jewish men, the Holocaust left a complex legacy. The charge of having gone "like lambs to the slaughter" hangs particularly heavily on them. One must question how much of the misappropriation of the "Never Again" slogan as a justification for militaristic and aggressive politics and policies stems from a need to rescue one's masculinity from the burden of this calumny perpetrated on Jews by the outside world. Furthermore, one must reconsider how the false male notion of heroism as manifest only in battle has misshaped the debate on the nature of resistance even within the Jewish community. The courage needed to face moral ambiguity, a courage shown by many who made their own and the community's survival their supreme value, even at the risk of the charge of non-resistance or even collaboration, has often been under-valued.

In addition to broad psychological dynamics, specific life-cycle events such as circumcision, puberty, aging, and various transitional points for one's social self all call for new male consciousness. For example, in his seminal book *Godwrestling* Arthur Waskow argues that the concept of Jubilee in the Hebrew Bible should be used as a model for political and economic transformation. Every fiftieth year, one must proclaim liberty throughout the land, return to one's family and ancestral home, redistribute material wealth to reestablish equality, and let the land lie fallow to replenish itself. What would happen if we applied the jubilee model as a solution to male mid-life crisis? This is strikingly similar to what modern developmental psychology tells us: in their fiftieth year men need to leave the work cycle and reconnect to their families. There is an old Yiddish-English pun that "Shabos," the Jewish Sabbath, really means "Sha boss!"—"Be Quiet, boss!" I consider such appropriations of the tradition essential tasks of Jewish male feminism.

All this and much more is part of a Jewish feminism of, by, and for men.

Notes

1. See the essay by Michael Gold in this volume.
2. See *Abortion and the Holocaust: Twisting the Language*, pamphlet published by The Religious Coalition for Abortion Rights, 100 Maryland Avenue, N.E., Washington, D.C. 20002.
3. See David M. Feldman, *Marital Relations, Birth Control, and Abortion in Jewish Law* (New York: Schocken, 1974) and Rachel Biale, *Women and Jewish Law* (New York: Schocken, 1984).

For an Orthodox Jewish feminist pro-reproductive choice statement, see Blu Greenberg, *On Women and Judaism: A View from Tradition* (Philadelphia: Jewish Publication Society of America, 1981).

4.   See Rabbi Laura Geller, statement on "What Kind of *Tikkun*," *Tikkun* 1:1 1986. On Jewish feminism generally, see Susannah Heschel, ed. *On Being a Jewish Feminist: A Reader* (New York: Schocken, 1984); Susan Weidman Schneider, *Jewish and Female* (New York: Simon & Schuster, 1984); and *Lilith* magazine.

5.   See the Introduction to this volume.

6.   From the chapter "A Tale of Two Hoffmans," in John Murray Cuddihy, *The Ordeal of Civility: Freud, Marx, Levi-Strauss and the Jewish Struggle with Modernity* (Boston: Beacon Press, 1987).

CONTRIBUTORS

Barbara Breitman, MSW, is Director of WomenReach at Jewish Family and Children's Service of Philadelphia, a psychotherapist in private practice, and a feminist who is deeply concerned and involved in the women's spirituality movement, a member of Banot Esh and B'nai Or.

Harry Brod, editor of *The Making of Masculinities: The New Men's Studies* (Allen & Unwin, 1987), and author of numerous articles on men's studies, is currently a Liberal Arts Fellow at the Harvard Law School. He was the Founding Editor of the *Men's Studies Review* and Founding Chair of the National Men's Studies Association.

Larry Bush, now writing as Lawrence Bush, is author of *Bessie*, a novel (1983) and *Rooftop Secrets and Other Stories of Anti-Semitism* (1986), a book for kids. He is the father of twins and works at home in Accord, New York.

Andrea Dworkin is one of the leaders of the contemporary women's movement, and the author of several books, including *Pornography, Right-wing Women*, and most recently *Intercourse* and the novel *Ice and Fire*.

Gay Community News is located at 62 Berkeley St., Boston, MA 02116. Half-year subscriptions are $20.

Bob Gluck, MSW, has worked as a therapist and community educator with men who are abusive since 1980. He serves as rabbi of a Philadelphia area synagogue and teaches workshops about creative sacred music-making.

Rabbi Michael Gold is the spiritual leader of Beth El Congregation in Pittsburgh, PA. He is the author of *And Hannah Wept: Infertility, Adoption and the Jewish Couple*, published by the Jewish Publication Society.

Barbara Gottfried is an Assistant Professor of English at the University of Hawaii at Manoa. She has published articles on Chaucer and Dickens, and is co-author of the Philip Roth volume of the University of South Carolina's "Understanding Contemporary American Literature" Series.

Rabbi Gary Greenebaum is the Director of the B'nai B'rith Hillel Foundation of San Francisco.

Joshua J. Hammerman now serves Temple Beth El in Stamford, Connecticut, having left his first pulpit in Peekskill, New York after four years. Ordained in 1983, Rabbi Hammerman's articles have appeared in several periodicals in addition to the *New York Times*, including the *Baltimore Jewish Times* and *New York Daily News*.

Michael S. Kimmel teaches courses on gender, masculinity, and sexuality in the sociology department at S.U.N.Y. at Stony Brook. He is the author or editor of several books, including *Men Confronting Pornography* (Crown, 1988), *Men's Lives* (Macmillan,1988), and *Changing Men: New Directions in Research on Men and Masculinity* (Sage, 1987). He is series co-editor of a book series, "Men and Masculinity" at Beacon Press.

Lori Hope Lefkovitz, Assistant Professor of English at Kenyon College, is author of *The Character of Beauty in the Victorian Novel*.

Helen Leneman worked as a cantor in the Los Angeles area for the past several years, and recently completed her Master's degree in Judaic Studies at Hebrew Union College. Cantor Leneman is currently pursuing a Doctorate in History at the University of Maryland in College Park.

Doug Lipman is a story-teller and singer in the Boston area, whose cassette tape *Milk from the Bull's Horn: Tales of Nurturing Men* is available from Yellow Moon Press, P.O. Box 1316, Cambridge, MA 02238.

Letty Cottin Pogrebin, a founder, editor, and columnist for *Ms.* magazine, is the author of six books, including *Growing Up Free, Family Politics*, and most recently *Among Friends*.

Max Rivers is editor of *The Other Gender*, published by the Male/Female Relationships Task Group of the National Organization for Changing Men.

Robert Rosenberg is a New York City filmmaker, father, and activist with New Jewish Agenda.

Zalman Schachter-Shalomi is the leader of the B'nai Or Religious Fellowship, and author of *Fragments of a Future Scroll* and *The Encounter: (Yehidut), A Study of Counselling in Hasidism*.

Barry Dov Schwartz is Rabbi of Temple B'nai Sholom in Rockville Centre, New York.

Arthur Waskow is a member of the faculty of the Reconstructionist Rabbinical College, director of The Shalom Center, editor of *New Menorah* (the B'nai Or journal of Jewish renewal), and author most recently of *These Holy Sparks*, a history of the movement for Jewish renewal.

Robert P. Waxler is a Professor in the English Department at Southeastern Massachusetts University and co-director of the SMU Center for Jewish Culture. He has published articles on English, American, and Jewish literature.

Chaim Waxman, the author of numerous publications on the sociology of the Jewish community, has taught at Tel Aviv University and in the Sociology Department at University College, Rutgers University.